THE
PASTA
BIBLE

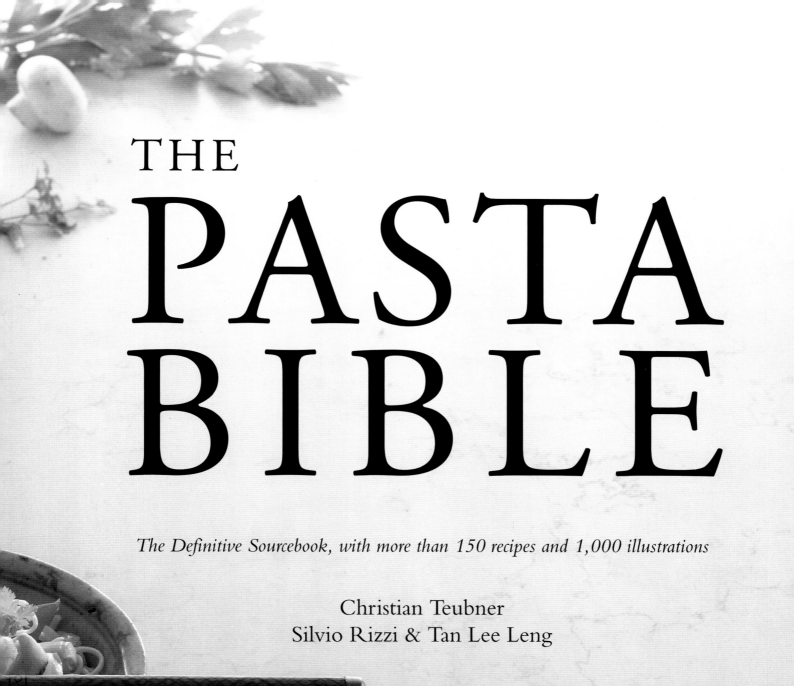

THE
PASTA
BIBLE

The Definitive Sourcebook, with more than 150 recipes and 1,000 illustrations

Christian Teubner
Silvio Rizzi & Tan Lee Leng

WEIDENFELD & NICOLSON
London

First published in Great Britain in 1998 by
George Weidenfeld & Nicolson
The Orion Publishing Group
Orion House
5 Upper St Martin's Lane
London WC2H 9EA

First published in the United States under the title
The Pasta Bible by Tan Lee Leng and Silvio Rizzi.
Original edition published under the title
Das Grosse Buch der Teigwaren – Pasta, Knodel, Gnocchi
Copyright © 1994 by Teubner Edition, Germany
English text copyright © 1996 by Transedition Ltd,
England.
Published by arrangement with Penguin Studio Books,
a division of Penguin Books USA, Inc.

ISBN 0 297 82383 3

Printed by Butler & Tanner, England

Contents

All recipes serve 4 unless stated otherwise.

A tale of pasta

Is the history of pasta at all important? After all, eating and drinking are part of life, and all that really matters after a meal is whether or not it was enjoyable and sustaining. Few classic dishes can be attributed to a creator who might be worthy of a monument; perhaps the only examples are mayonnaise and praline, whose originators are named in the *Larousse Gastronomique*. Even in the case of more recent creations, *cordon bleu* for example, the trail ends somewhere in the grand European hotels of the turn of the century. And from old recipe collections it has been proven that it was not the Tatin sisters who 'invented' the upside-down apple tart, in the sense that Edison invented the light bulb.

There has also been a great deal of bluster about the discovery of pasta, with national pride playing no small part, particularly among the Italians. If dough can be said to be amorphous or unshaped, then pasta becomes a synonym for shaping or designing. There is, in fact, etymological justification for this. The word 'dough' is related to the Sanskrit *dheigh*, which means to knead or to work. Thus the dough is an undefined mass waiting to be shaped into noodles and so on. And the word 'noodle' itself goes back to the Latin *nodus* or *nodellus*, meaning 'node' or 'nodule'. Remarkably, however, this

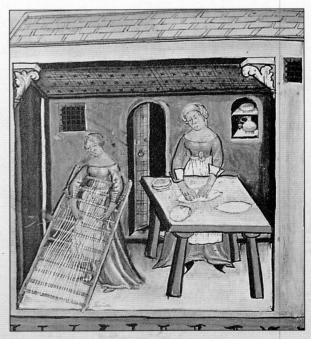

'Pasta needs careful preparation' has been the recommendation since time immemorial. *(From the 14th-century* Domestic manual of the Cerruti family, *Austrian National Library, Vienna.)*

loan-word has survived only in English, French (*nouilles*), and German (*Nudeln*). The German word for knot or node has the same root and gave rise to the name for another kind of food made of dough, the *Knödel*, or dumplings, of southern Germany and Austria.

'Roll it out on a bench' used to be the instruction for rolling out pasta dough. In the course of time, the 'bench' became the kitchen table or the sideboard and, today, a pastry board.

In front of a pasta shop in Apulia, Italy, 1909. As the region developed economically, the spaghetti-maker and -seller played an increasingly important role in the community.

Apicius was one of the first to describe pasta as dough cut into flat strips.

The dim and distant past

The story of the Venetian Marco Polo, who is said to have seen noodles being made in China, and then to have brought some of this new food home with him, is probably just an entertaining anecdote: his account of his journey, dictated in prison in Genoa in 1298, did not become widely available until the invention of printing towards the end of the 15th century. By this time people in southern Italy had long been devouring '*maccheroni*', which is what all pastas, of whatever shape, were called in Naples and Sicily. It seems reasonable to suppose that the idea of making something as simple as pasta dough would occur to all people able to grind wheat sufficiently finely. Making bread by adding yeast seems a positive stroke of genius in comparison.

Something approximating pasta is said to have been identified on Etruscan funerary plaques. And it is now accepted that the Arabs, who knew about durum wheat before the Italians, used to cook thinly rolled sheets of dough. The technique of rolling wheat paste into thin sticks in order to dry it in the sun and thus preserve it has also been attributed to the Arabs. Is that how the hole got into macaroni? The origin of documents in the Museum of Pasta – once located in Pontedassio, a town on the Ligurian Riviera, and now in Rome – is still uncertain. What is curious, however, is that the ancient Romans, on the evidence of recipe collections that have come down to us, do not seem to have prepared any pasta dishes. Perhaps they were simply unsuited to the

cuisine of the polite society of that time, whose eating habits were detailed in the writings of both Petronius and Apicius.

Spaghetti eating as a spectator sport

In fact, pasta has never been polite or refined. The *lazzaroni* of Naples, a horde of good-for-nothings and idlers, are said to have subsisted largely on pasta. The scope this offered for showing off can well be imagined: until the 16th century few people used table cutlery, least of all forks, so diners would take long strips of pasta in their hands, tilt their heads backwards, and let the pasta slide into their mouths; often they did not even chew it, but simply swallowed it whole. Such artistry was undoubtedly congenial to those of an exhibitionist temperament.

For rich and poor

So we are in Italy. Where else? It was only in that country, not in China or Japan, that pasta became a cult object, the focus of culinary attention, comparable in status with rice in the Far East. The dumplings of Germany can lay no claim to such a success story, and in France there has never been a food of such fundamental, to a certain extent 'national', importance. Pasta dishes even reflected the social order in Italy: egg noodles and meat encased in sheets of pasta were available for the rich, while the poor had to make do with pasta made from just flour and water, the so-called *pasta asciutta*.

Cutters for making a wide range of stuffed pastas were developed by manufacturers, providing cooks with tools that made it simpler to produce a variety of shapes.

Interior view of a pasta plant around the turn of the century. In this machine room, the dough ingredients were first combined in a mixing machine and then kneaded in a sort of press into a smooth dough before further processing.

Pasta wheels reflect the Italian love of detail. Made of wood, iron and brass, they cut decorative edges on pasta strips and shapes.

What about the tomatoes?

Nowadays we think of the marriage of pasta and tomatoes as authentically Italian. Of course the combination cannot be very deeply rooted in the past, since tomatoes were not cultivated in Italy until the 19th century. The abundance and powerful flavour of this solanaceous plant, which includes the deadly nightshade among its relatives, have made it both cheap and popular. However, the tomato was not available all year round until it became an industrial product, first as a concentrated paste in cans or tubes and then peeled, chopped or whole, in cans. Prior to this, the only way of preserving tomatoes was to dry them and keep them in oil, or to seal a ready-made sauce in glass jars specially made for the purpose.

But the producers have not been idle. *Pomodori* – literally, golden apples – now ripen all year round. However, their flavour and texture often leave something to be desired, even in Italy.

The industrial age

The wide range of pasta shapes familiar to us today became possible only through industrial production, which is a relatively recent phenomenon. It is true that, at an early stage, the pasta-obsessed people of

Naples developed various means of hastening the production process, but it wasn't until the early years of the 20th century that the attractively grooved or curved pasta shapes, with their highly imaginative names, were first produced. Large, high-speed presses, designed by inspired engineers in France, Switzerland and Italy, made this possible.

The French have a saying: there is no cooking without cooks, meaning that culinary discoveries are always made in the kitchen. But this is not the case with dried pasta: certainly as far as shape is concerned, it is a purely industrial product. The Italians do not consider this to be a flaw in any way. Even while fresh pasta continued to be made in many households, factory-made spaghetti, at least, absolutely straight and incredibly long, soon replaced the home-made variety. Older people will remember

that the commercial spaghetti of their youth was bent at one end, as if it had been dried on a rail – a notion that still made sense during the transition from manual to machine production. (You still see some of this spaghetti today.) Italians are not at all suspicious of machines. Indeed, the pride and joy of many Italian restaurateurs is still a device that produces noodles or presses and shapes ravioli. Of course, there are many connoisseurs who are persuaded of the quality of hand-made pasta. They avoid machines and willingly accept that making pasta by hand requires extra time and effort.

Pasta spreads throughout the world

The spread of pasta beyond Italy is also part of its history. It is very difficult to explain why the French have never really taken to pasta, even though French cuisine is said to have its roots in the Italy of Catherine de' Medici. She introduced the cooking of her native country to the court of Henri II – and pasta was undoubtedly known in late Renaissance Italy. The reason why Catherine did not bring pasta with her can only be that it was a food for the poor and therefore not suitable for the court. Even Escoffier, who is said to have revitalized 20th-century cooking, includes no pasta dishes in his *Guide Culinaire*, apart from a few Italian-style

Spaghetti can be dried in the open air in Naples thanks to its mild climate; in the damper north of Italy, heated drying rooms are required.

Pasta shapes given their traditional local names. These pages are from catalogues dating from 1916.

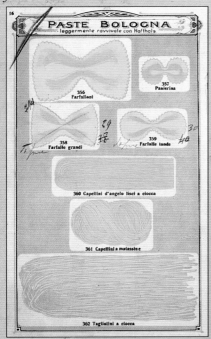

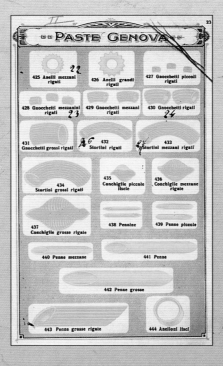

gnocchi and macaroni recipes. It is interesting to note, however, that it was in France that Thomas Jefferson first encountered pasta; he took some macaroni back to the United States in 1786.

All other countries north of the Alps proved to be more receptive, though mainly to industrial pasta which was cheap and very popular with children. Only in southern Germany and in Alpine regions was there any resistance: the traditional types of German pasta, such as Spätzle and Maultaschen, a sort of large ravioli, were not completely ousted, not even by really good egg noodles, which are not dissimilar to Spätzle in flavour.

Apart from the Chinese, the Italians are the most successful exporters of their national cuisine. Everywhere they open a restaurant – and where are there no Italian restaurants? – they also spread their pasta culture, from North America to Australia, from northern Europe to South Africa. Their most popular export, pizza, is so far ahead in the race as to be unbeatable, but spaghetti is hot on its heels. Even the French are now beginning to learn how to wrap the long strands round their forks and raise them to their mouths. Asian noodles, like the colourless cellophane or bean-thread noodles, for example, or soba buckwheat noodles, are gaining in popularity, but they are eaten most often in restaurants, where diners fish the slippery strands out of soups or, when they are served fried, enjoy their crunchiness.

Astonishingly, the development of stuffed pasta followed virtually the same path in Italy and in China. Chinese ravioli differ only slightly from the Italian version. Who learned what from whom remains unclear to this day. The only thing the Italians have never tried their hand at, despite their passion for things artistic, is the technique of repeatedly stretching a ball of dough until it forms thin noodles.

Pasta makes it to the top

The multi-cultural cuisine of our time has certainly muddled everything up. The Japanese now eat spaghetti, the Italians eat cellophane noodles, and the top cooks in all countries have discovered that pasta stuffed with various fillings is a great delicacy, regardless of whether it is called 'raviolis', as in France, or wonton, or whether it is boiled, steamed, or fried. And a few paper-thin noodles – home-made of course – enliven the ambitious menus of leading chefs everywhere. Fresh pasta, whether commercially prepared or home-made, has even penetrated the domestic kitchen, with more and more cooks trying to emulate the Italian pasta specialists.

Pasta beyond Italy

Everyone is now aware that pasta is treated differently at mealtimes in Italy. The Italians have always considered pasta to be worthy of a course in its own right, the *primo*, which comes before the *secondo*, or main course. The three-course meal, consisting of *antipasti* (hors d'oeuvres), *primo* (pasta or risotto), and *secondo* (meat or fish, possibly accompanied by vegetables), has remained more or less unchanged, even in the upper reaches of Italian gastronomy, while to the north of the Alps, and elsewhere in the world, different customs have emerged. There, pasta is either used as an accompaniment to meat and as a vehicle for sauces of all kinds, or it forms the main course, whether as a dish of spaghetti or other pasta with various ingredients or as part of a dish baked in the oven.

There is not a great deal to be said about noodles as a side-dish, and every cook knows they are delicious simply dressed with a little melted butter or extra virgin olive oil. Egg noodles are the favourite choice as a side-dish for roasts and their gravy. And for those seeking a little more variety in their side-dishes, the imaginatively shaped products of the pasta industry, such as bow ties (farfalle) or wagon wheels (rotelle), can be recommended, as can the combinations of yellow, red, green, and other coloured pastas that are now available.

One-dish meals for hungry families include the familiar and well-loved macaroni cheese, lasagne of all kinds, manicotti and cannelloni, spaghetti and meatballs, an endless variety of pasta casseroles, and traditional German types of pasta, such as Spätzle, that are often served with browned onions and rich, melting cheese.

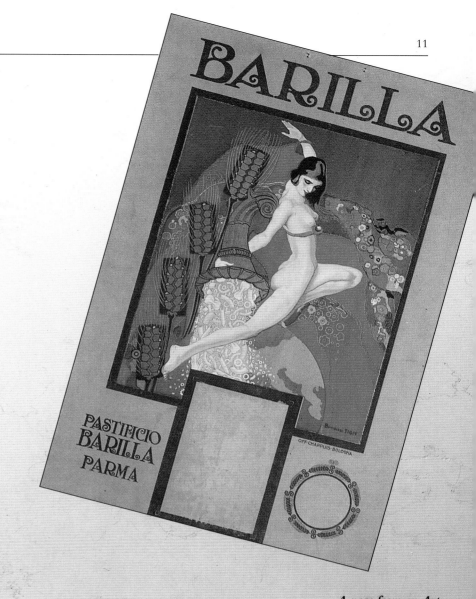

A page from an Art Nouveau calendar – *an allegorical representation of Ceres, the Roman goddess of agriculture. She is fertilizing the Earth with a cascade of golden pasta.*

North of the Alps *noodles are often served separately as a side-dish, for example, as an accompaniment to meat stews. They are a delicious way of soaking up the gravy.*

The grain

This is the basis of pasta; water is all that is necessary to make dough from flour

From a botanical point of view, the term 'cereal' denotes cultivated or semi-cultivated plants that belong to the grass family (Gramineae, Poaceae). The fruits of these plants are called grains, and are an important food for both human beings and animals. Other plants with grain-like fruits, such as buck-wheat, a member of the genus *Fagopyrun*, are usually defined as sub-orders of the cereals. Cereals are the most important agricultural crops in the world. In addition to their use in the production of bread, they are used all over the world to make pasta. Wheat and rice play a particularly important role in this respect.

A BOTANICAL STUDY

The grain of cereals is a monospermous, or one-seeded, fruit that belongs botanically to the group of indehiscent fruits, because on ripening it does not automatically split open in order to release the seed. Since the three layers of the pericarp (the epicarp, mesocarp and endocarp) not only form a hard woody husk but are also so tightly fused to the testa, or seed coat, that they cannot be separated, the fruit is a 'caryopsis'.

The grains of the various cereals are similar in appearance and structure. They consist of the outer covering or husk (the pericarp and seed coat), the endosperm, and the embyro or germ. The grains of barley, oats, rice and millet have glumes with pointed, needle-shaped projections tightly fused to the pericarp, known as awns; these are not detached from the grain even during threshing. Wheat and rye, however, have no glumes. The diagram on page 13 uses the example of wheat to depict the structure of a cereal grain. Bran, which is rich in fibre or roughage, an aid to digestion and thus of great importance to the human diet, consists of the outer covering and the aleurone layer. The endosperm – to which the aleurone layer belongs in botanical terms – contains starch grains, which are enclosed in a thin layer of protein. The embryo or germ is the primary store of substances essential to a newly developing plant, and contains everything required for building new life. This unique combination of foodstuffs is also of value to human beings, since it provides everything needed for a nutritious diet. The high-quality store of nutrients can be made available for human use either by grinding (milling) the whole grain to make flour or by waiting for germination to start and then eating the grains and the shoots growing from them. Flour obtained solely from the endosperm is best suited to making dough and for baking, but it lacks the nutrients contained in the bran and germ.

Wheat (*Triticum*). Various forms of wheat have been the most important cereal in many parts of the world for thousands of years. It is native to Eurasia. Breeding and selection have led to the development of cultivated forms whose different qualities are used in a variety of ways in the kitchen. Commercial pasta is produced mainly from hard durum wheat (*Triticum durum*). As a summer wheat, it prefers warmth and can survive with little rain, conditions that prevail especially throughout the summer in Italy and North America. The gluten-rich flour it provides produces a firm dough ideally suited to being kneaded or cut into shape. Mixed with starchy soft wheat (*Triticum aestivum*), it also fulfils all the demands made by baking. **Spelt** (*Triticum spelta*) is closely related to soft wheat. Unlike soft wheat, however, the grains of spelt are enclosed by glumes. Its gluten-rich flour was for a long time the basis for the flour-based desserts and baked goods of parts of Germany. **Green spelt grain**, called *grain de blé vert* in France, is spelt that has been harvested while it is still unripe and green. It is dried in kilns, which gives it a robust, full-bodied flavour.

Rice (*Oryza sativa*) is the staple food of many parts of Asia. Rice grows in the humid tropics and sub-tropics. Because of its high rate of transpiration it requires a plentiful supply of water. For this reason, it is grown mainly in paddy fields which are flooded for a large part of the growing period. There are many different species of rice, divided according to the shape and size of the grain into long-grain, medium-grain, and short or round-grain rice.

Buckwheat (*Fagopyrum esculentum*). A close relative of sorrel and rhubarb, buckwheat produces reddish-brown, triangular seeds, 4–6 mm/⅛–¼ in in length and similar in appearance to beechnuts. The flour obtained by grinding the seeds is used in breads and pancakes, including blini, and to make noodles.

Millet (*Panicum miliaceum*). The term millet denotes a number of tropical and subtropical cereals that produce small seeds or grains on drooping, loosely branched flower clusters. Millet flour lacks gluten, so is usually mixed with wheat flour for baking breads.

Barley (*Hordeum vulgare*) is not of great importance in the production of pasta. In many countries, barley flour is used on its own, to make round, flat loaves, but it is usually mixed with durum wheat for noodles and similar products, since it contains no gluten. Malting barley is of great importance throughout the world as a basic ingredient for beer.

Oats (*Avena sativa*) are also of little significance in the manufacture of pasta. However, wholegrain products made from oat bran and durum wheat are available commercially.

Maize (*Zea mays*) is a basic foodstuff for millions of people, particularly in the Americas and parts of Italy. The different varieties of maize are classified according to the starch content of the grains. The

LONGITUDINAL SECTION THROUGH A WHEAT GRAIN

Labels: Pericarp, Seed coat, Aleurone layer, Endosperm, Cylindrical epithelium, Scutellum, Plumule, Radicle, Coleorhiza, Micropyle

Parts of the grain (% of whole grain)	Contents and functions
Outer layers	Fibre, minerals, vitamins
Pericarp (6%)	Tightly fused to seed coat
Seed coat (1%)	Tightly fused to pericarp
Endosperm	
Aleurone layer (8%)	Proteins, enzymes, vitamins, minerals
Endosperm (80%)	Nutritive tissue, stores food reserves, contains proteins derived from gluten
Embryo	Enzymes, vitamins, minerals, fats
Cylindrical epithelium	Outermost layer of the scutellum
Scutellum	During germination, acts as a conduit for stored food reserves between the endosperm and the embryo
Radicle	The first root to appear on germination
Coleorhiza	A protective structure shielding the delicate radicle in the embryo
Micropyle	The point at which the radicle breaks out of the grain on germination
Plumule	Contains the first leaf, which begins to photosynthesize after germination

various types include dent corn, in which the inner part of the endosperm is soft; flint corn, which has a hard endosperm; sweetcorn; and waxy corn. Sweetcorn is used in a great variety of ways in the kitchen, including as a vegetable, in breakfast cereals, as a coarse or fine meal used in breads and muffins and in polenta and grits, and as cornflour, corn syrup and corn oil. It is also widely used as an animal feed.

GLUTEN

The endosperm of a grain of wheat contains special proteins that make the wheat suitable for baking, even though they have no particular nutritive properties. Gluten, as these proteins are called, gives wheat flour the right 'feel' and influences its baking performance; it also gives pasta, breads, and cakes the right texture because the proteins turn thready and sticky on contact with water. The most important of these proteins, in volume terms, are gliadin and glutelin. As soon as the flour comes into contact with water, the proteins swell. They bind the liquid in the dough and at the same time combine with the fats in the wheat itself. During the baking of bread, for example, the liquid bound by the gluten turns into steam. The air contained in the dough expands, thus producing an open, porous texture. At about 70°C/158°F, the gluten coagulates and combines with the starch in the flour to form the desired crumb texture.

Wheat contains a considerably higher proportion of gluten than rye or other cereals, which is why wheat has been known for hundreds of years as the best cereal for baking. Rye contains little gluten, thus rye flour needs to be supplemented with a leaven of fermented wheat dough in order to make a dough that is sufficiently elastic to be worked and remain in shape. Corn or maize, rice, millet and buckwheat contain no gluten and therefore cannot be used on their own to make flour for baking bread. Nevertheless, the starch they contain makes them

suitable for gluten-free products, which are important in the diet of people who suffer from coeliac disease, a disorder of the small intestine triggered by cereal protein.

Gluten content is of great importance in the manufacture of pasta. Durum wheat, being very high in gluten, makes the best pasta flour, which is why it is often added to other flours in order to improve their structure for pasta-making. Thus noodles made with soy or millet flour will contain a high proportion of semolina flour milled from the endosperm of hard durum wheat.

FROM GRAIN TO FLOUR

The various types of flour made from each cereal can be clearly distinguished from each other at a glance: light-coloured flours are produced solely from the white endosperm, while darker flours also include the outer coverings of the grain (it is the bran that gives colour). A dark flour is a 'wholefood' product in the truest sense of the term, since it contains not only the starchy part of the grain but also the nutritionally important bran and germ, i.e. the aleurone layer, the pericarp and seed coat, and the highly nutritious embryo. However, since the fat in the embryo becomes rancid and bitter very soon after crushing, wholemeal flour does not have a very long shelf life.

The process of milling flour begins by cracking the wheat kernels, and separating the bran and germ from the endosperm. For white flours, all of the bran and germ are sifted out and the endosperm only is ground to the desired degree of fineness. As a result, white flour retains only about 25 per cent of the original nutrients.

UK law requires that any wheat flour not containing the germ must have certain nutrients added back (niacin, riboflavin, thiamin, and iron, as well as vitamins A and D in some cases); this flour is labelled 'enriched'. In wholemeal flour, 100 per cent of the husked kernel is retained – the bran, germ, and endosperm – by being recombined after grinding.

After milling, white wheat flour is light yellow in colour. It will turn white naturally, through oxidation, in a month or two (such flours will be labelled 'unbleached'), but to speed up the process, flour is often bleached with chlorine dioxide. While the colour is purely an aesthetic consideration, the age of the flour is of importance, because maturation does improve the flour's baking qualities. Again, this natural process is normally hastened by means of chemicals.

White wheat flour type 00 *The type of flour most commonly used for making pasta in Italy.*

Plain flour *Fine-textured blend of hard and soft wheats; suitable for all cooking and for making pasta.*

Cake or pastry flour *Soft-wheat, low-gluten flour; makes tender cakes and pastries, but is not suitable for pasta.*

Semolina flour for pasta *Durum wheat flour, more coarsely ground than normal wheat flours.*

Wholemeal flour *Contains the wheat germ. It makes pasta with a nutty flavour and firm texture.*

Wheat bran *Has the highest vitamin and mineral content. It is often added to breads and breakfast cereals.*

Rye flour *Contains less gluten than wheat flours. It produces pasta that retains a slight chewiness when cooked.*

Cornmeal *When mixed with flour containing gluten, it is suitable for making pasta and noodles.*

Rice flour *An important starch in Asian countries, where it is the basis for noodles and rice-paper wrappers.*

Oat flour *When used in baked goods, it must be combined with a flour that contains gluten.*

Spelt flour *A protein-rich flour. Pasta dough produced from it has a pleasant smell and a mellow, nutty flavour.*

Green spelt flour *Produced from spelt grain harvested when still unripe. It has a more robust flavour.*

Dried pasta

Bakers tend to be somewhat envious of pasta-makers. Bread does not taste at its best unless it is freshly baked. Pasta, on the other hand, can be dried and stored for a long time – but not for years and years, as the 'use-before' dates on the packages would have us believe. Dried egg noodles in particular quickly lose their flavour and should be consumed within six months.

Commercial dried pasta is not only a popular product, it is also very simple, consisting only of durum wheat flour and water, or of durum wheat flour, water and eggs (pasteurized or dried). In recent years, the familiar pale yellow colour has been supplemented by green, red and even chocolate-brown pastas and by the dark brown of wholemeal pastas. The latter are made of coarsely ground flour, from the entire kernel of wheat or other cereals, whose vitamin and fibre content make it more nutritious than pastas made from white flour.

Although fresh pasta is becoming increasingly popular, particularly in restaurants, commercial dried pasta is still the ultimate convenience food. It is cheap, it can be prepared without any great culinary skill, and it is popular with children and adults alike. Italian restaurants are now found almost everywhere, and as a result spaghetti has conquered the world. It is even making inroads in France, a country hitherto unreceptive to pasta. The boom in fresh pasta has done nothing to reduce its popularity. Anyone who has ever been to Tuscany and seen how *pinci* are laboriously rolled and thrown over the shoulder will breathe a sigh of relief the next time they shake the brittle sticks of pasta from their packet into boiling water.

Dried noodles are also a familiar sight in Asia, particularly in China and Japan. Some are made from wheat flour and eggs, as in Europe, while others, like the remarkable cellophane noodles, are fashioned from mung beans. From Japan come milky-white rice noodles and somen noodles, which look as though they have been varnished but lose their sheen when cooked. In Asia it is said that long noodles, whether flat or rounded, promise long life. And who would want to shorten it by eating pasta in the shape of little crescents or ears? However, the real reason for their popularity is probably that long noodles are easier to eat with chopsticks than small, slippery shapes.

Absolutely natural

And yet a wholly industrial product

This seems at first sight to be a contradictory assertion. However, it is accurate to the extent that the ingredients of pasta, namely flour, water and, in some cases, eggs, are natural products that are simply combined with each other and processed into pasta. In this sense, industrial technology is merely an aid to the production of large quantities of this simple yet immensely versatile foodstuff. In Italy, the pasta industry became established in those areas where the best conditions for pasta-making existed, and particularly in regions where climatic conditions meant that pasta could be dried outdoors. Such conditions exist in the Parma area, in Naples, and in Abruzzi. Among the rocky slopes of Abruzzi, there is a small town where nature is still largely undisturbed. The River Verde has its source here, and its fresh, perpetually cool, crystal-clear spring water flows directly into the factories where much of Italy's pasta is made. For decades, amid the magnificent scenery of a national park, a food has been manufactured that is as simple and natural as it is possible to be, although in fact it is a wholly industrial product.

The durum wheat used to make pasta comes mainly from Italy and parts of North America where long, dry summers guarantee a high-quality crop. While

The stream in Fara San Martino *is a picturesque sight. Its water is used in the production of dried pasta.*

the ingredients of pasta are highly standardized, the shapes and names of pasta products are extremely varied. In Italy, the term '*pasta secca*' includes all dried pasta, both '*pasta lunga*', or long pasta, and '*pasta corta*', short pasta. Some names, such as

Durum wheat and eggs, *plus water, are the ingredients of most pasta doughs in Europe and North America.*

with each grade having its own number. As already noted, however, the same numbers are not used by all manufacturers. It is also possible to exploit the elasticity of the Italian language to good effect: thus, among the ribbon noodles, tagliolini are narrower than taglierini, which in turn are narrower than tagliatelle. The confusion is complete when narrow ribbon noodles are also sold as lasagne. As with the numbers, the names for ribbon noodles of varying widths are far from standardized. Consumers should therefore seek reassurance in the following motto: if it tastes good, it is good, irrespective of what it's called. And yet the shape of pasta is more important than is often thought. Simply achieving a balanced combination of texture, taste and sauce turns a pasta meal into an exquisite culinary experience.

Eggs are an important ingredient in certain types of pasta. They make them light and pliable, give them a warm yellow colour, increase their nutritional value and impart a full-bodied taste. Hens' eggs are undoubtedly an important source of food for human beings, but those who would make fresh egg pasta need to take account of the fact that fresh eggs and foods made from them have a limited shelf life. When purchasing eggs, it is necessary to ensure that the shells are clean and undamaged: bacteria and other disease-causing agents contained in dirt, particularly salmonella, can penetrate the porous shell and make the eggs unfit for consumption. The longer eggs are stored, the greater the risk of contamination. Regulations ensure that eggs sold

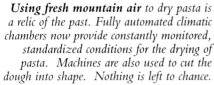

Using fresh mountain air to dry pasta is a relic of the past. Fully automated climatic chambers now provide constantly monitored, standardized conditions for the drying of pasta. Machines are also used to cut the dough into shape. Nothing is left to chance.

spaghetti, macaroni, tagliatelle, fettuccine and pappardelle, are known everywhere, while others are much less familiar.

In order to distinguish their products from those of their competitors, individual pasta manufacturers also give their varieties numbers. Thus various grades of spaghetti are available, ranging from the very fine capellini through spaghettini, spaghetti and spaghettoni to the flatter linguine and fettucelle,

commercially are labelled with the date by which they should be consumed. The same regulations decree that in shops all eggs should be kept under refrigeration. Nevertheless, it is strongly recommended that all home-made pasta containing fresh eggs be consumed immediately and not dried for future use. The pasta industry offers a wide range of perfectly safe products that can be kept in the storecupboard.

- Spaghetti

- Vermicelli

- Capellini

- Capellini

- Fedelini

- Spaghettini

- Spaghettini

- Spaghettini, vermicelli

- Wholemeal spaghetti

- Spaghetti

- Spaghetti

- Spaghetti verdi – with spinach

Spaghetti and macaroni

Shapes synonymous with pasta

Spaghetti is usually round, of variable thickness and normally at least 30 cm/12 in in length. Thicker types with a hole running through them are called macaroni. Pasta shapes made from the same kind of dough taste exactly the same, however they look. Thus it is the shapes – basically the diameter in the case of long noodles –that mainly bring variety to the range of pastas, though diversity is also achieved through different types of dough, some wholemeal, some coloured, some plain.

High-quality pasta demands optimal drying conditions: low temperatures of 60–70°C/ 140–160°F and up to 15 hours' drying time. Spaghetti hangs like a curtain on long iron bars. Tagliatelle and fettuccine are placed in pipes through which currents of air rise, first shaping the pasta into nests and then drying it.

Spaghettoni

Spaghetti alla chitarra

Perciatellini

Bucatini, perciatelli

Perciatelloni

Fusilli lunghi

Mezze zite

Macaroni (Germany)

Zite, mezzanelli

Zite

Infinite care and great attention to detail are essential parts of the production process. In the picture above, dried lumaconi rigati are passing over a belt that shakes and separates them before they are finally weighed and packed.

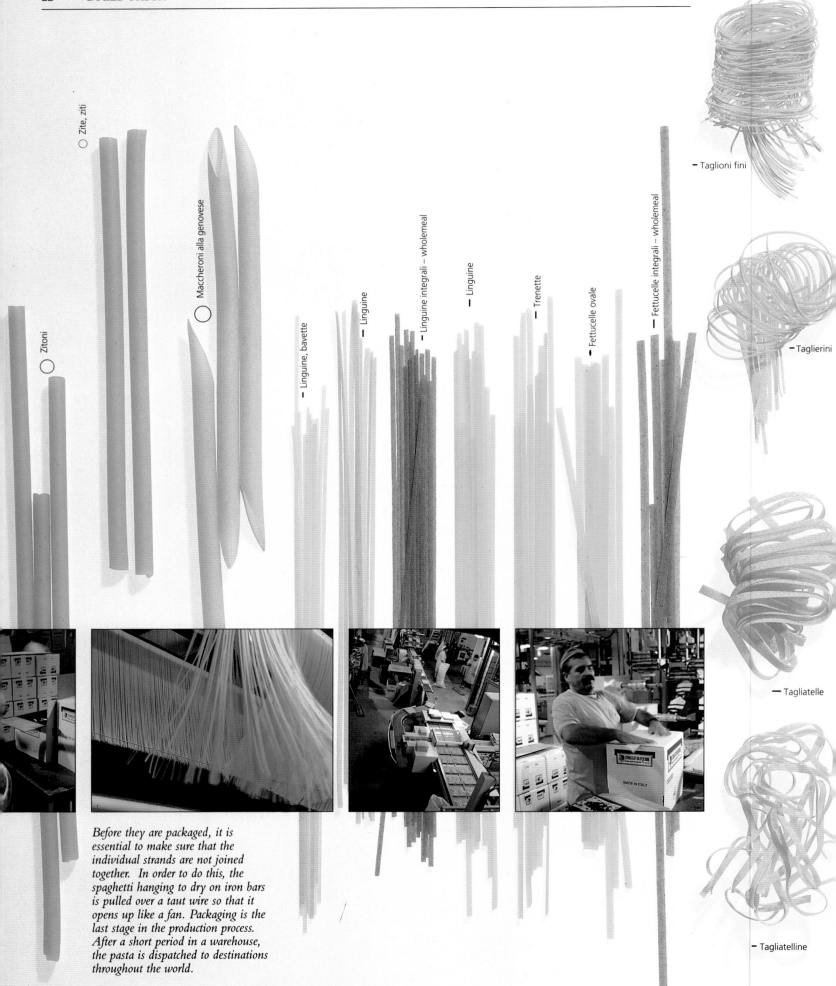

Zitoni

Zite, ziti

Maccheroni alla genovese

Linguine, bavette

Linguine

Linguine integrali – wholemeal

Linguine

Trenette

Fettucelle ovale

Fettucelle integrali – wholemeal

Taglioni fini

Taglierini

Tagliatelle

Tagliatelline

Before they are packaged, it is essential to make sure that the individual strands are not joined together. In order to do this, the spaghetti hanging to dry on iron bars is pulled over a taut wire so that it opens up like a fan. Packaging is the last stage in the production process. After a short period in a warehouse, the pasta is dispatched to destinations throughout the world.

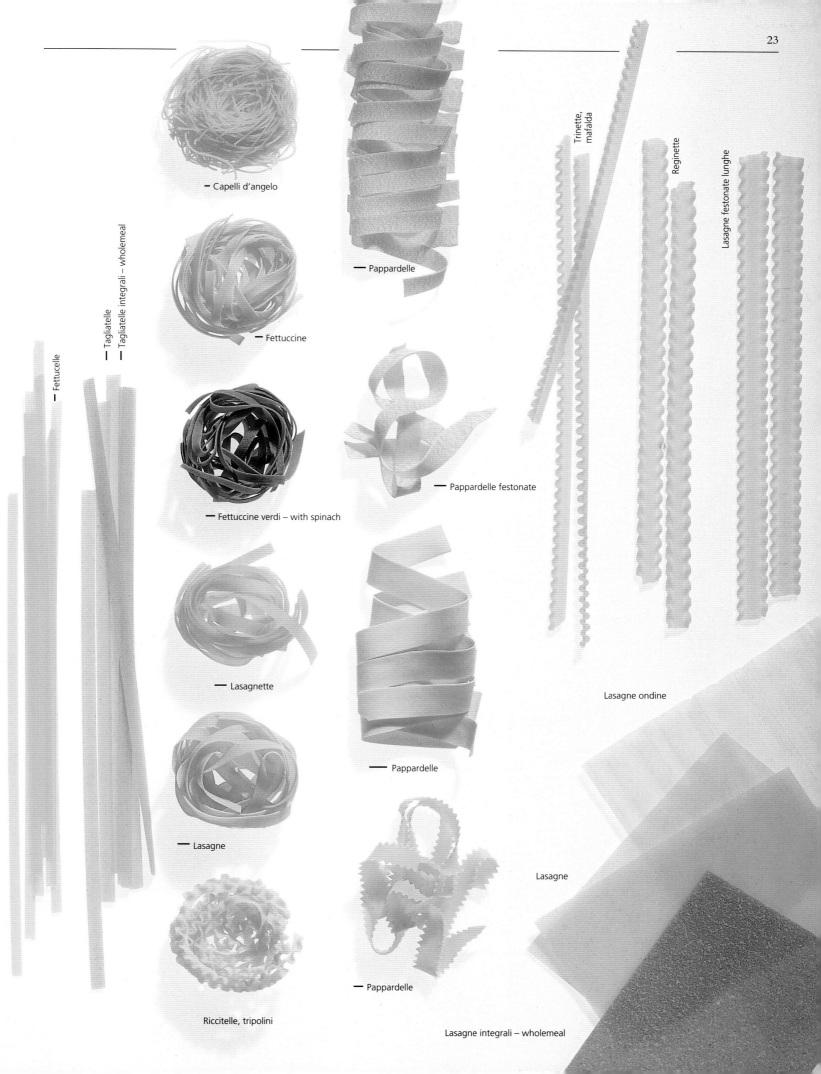

— Capelli d'angelo

— Pappardelle

Trinette, mafalda

Reginette

Lasagne festonate lunghe

— Fettucelle

— Tagliatelle
— Tagliatelle integrali – wholemeal

— Fettuccine

— Fettuccine verdi – with spinach

— Pappardelle festonate

— Lasagnette

Lasagne ondine

— Lasagne

— Pappardelle

Lasagne

— Pappardelle

Riccitelle, tripolini

Lasagne integrali – wholemeal

Tagliardi, green

Tagliardi, white

Sagnarelli

Farfalline
(small bow ties)

Tacconelli

Farfalloni

Maltagliati, large

Nastrini,
farfalline

Tortelli

Maltagliati, small

Farfalle
(bow ties)

Galle rotonde

Cannelloni integrali – wholemeal

Pasta squares
(Israel)

Farfalle
(bow ties)

Canestrini

Cannelloni

Quadrucci

Cravattine

Galle quadre

Riccioli

Casereccie, gemelli

Cappelletti

Banane

Casereccie

Sorprese

Conchiglie (jumbo shells)

Strozzapreti

Conchiglie (small shells)

Conchiglioni da ripieno

Fileia del Calabrese

Panierine

Conchiglie (medium shells)

Conchiglioni

Radiatori

Lumaconi
rigati grandi

Hörnchen – wholemeal
(Germany)

Hütli, trulli (Switzerland)

Gramigna

Tortiglioni, elicoidali

Lumaconi rigati medie

Hörnchen (Germany)

Dischi volanti

Spaccatelle

Rigatini

Pipette, fischiotti,
chiocciole

Creste di gallo

Spiralen (Germany)

Spaccatelle integrali –
wholemeal

Pipette integrali –
wholemeal

Chifferi rigati

Fusilli rigati, cellentani

Fusilli col buco,
fusilli corti

Eliche, thick

Lumacine

Chifferotti rigati

Sigarette mezzini

Eliche, thin

Eliche integrali
– wholemeal

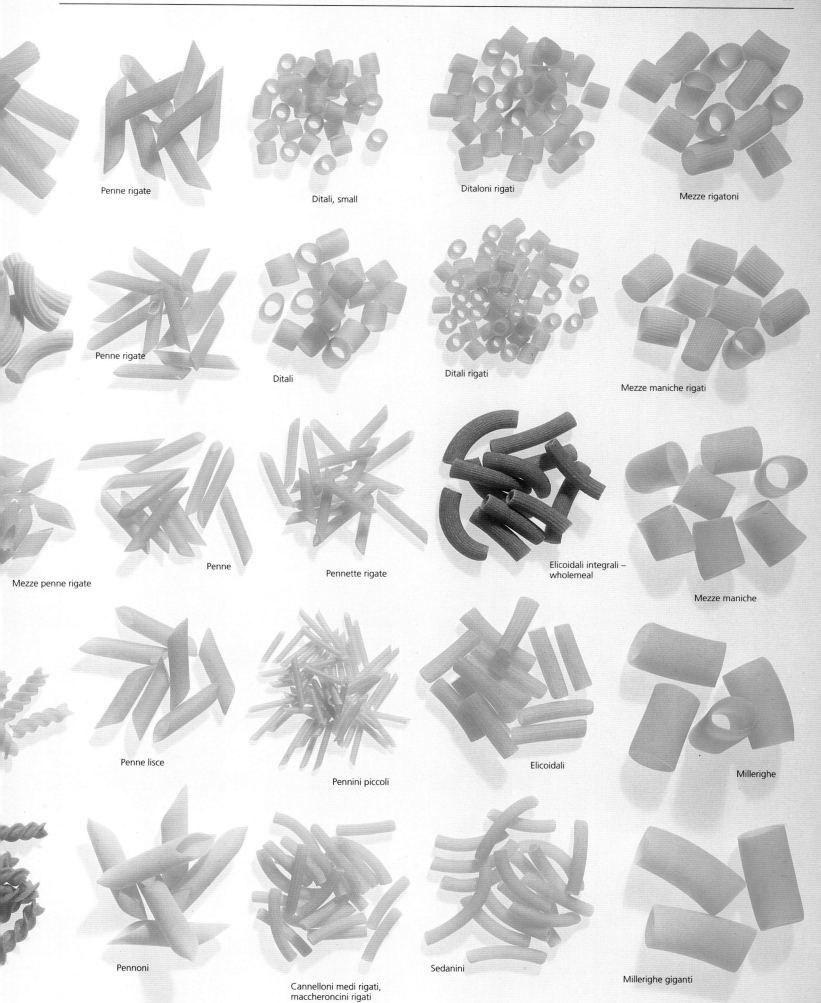

Penne rigate

Ditali, small

Ditaloni rigati

Mezze rigatoni

Penne rigate

Ditali

Ditali rigati

Mezze maniche rigati

Mezze penne rigate

Penne

Pennette rigate

Elicoidali integrali –
wholemeal

Mezze maniche

Penne lisce

Pennini piccoli

Elicoidali

Millerighe

Pennoni

Cannelloni medi rigati,
maccheroncini rigati

Sedanini

Millerighe giganti

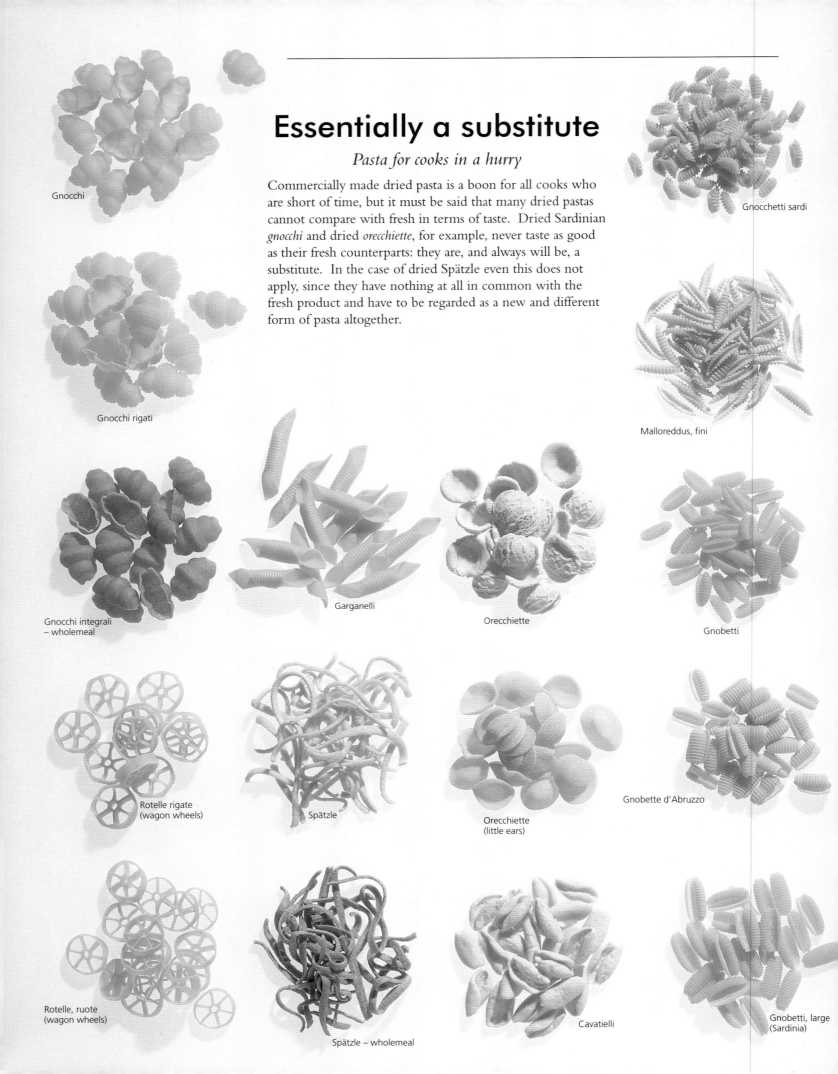

Essentially a substitute

Pasta for cooks in a hurry

Commercially made dried pasta is a boon for all cooks who are short of time, but it must be said that many dried pastas cannot compare with fresh in terms of taste. Dried Sardinian *gnocchi* and dried *orecchiette*, for example, never taste as good as their fresh counterparts: they are, and always will be, a substitute. In the case of dried Spätzle even this does not apply, since they have nothing at all in common with the fresh product and have to be regarded as a new and different form of pasta altogether.

Gnocchi

Gnocchetti sardi

Gnocchi rigati

Malloreddus, fini

Gnocchi integrali – wholemeal

Garganelli

Orecchiette

Gnobetti

Rotelle rigate (wagon wheels)

Spätzle

Orecchiette (little ears)

Gnobette d'Abruzzo

Rotelle, ruote (wagon wheels)

Spätzle – wholemeal

Cavatielli

Gnobetti, large (Sardinia)

Pasta for soups

Small but beautiful

The huge range of small pasta shapes produced by the food industry will enrich any soup. The really tiny varieties, no bigger than grains of rice, are popular additions to clear soups. The somewhat larger types are an indispensable ingredient in any minestrone. The alphabet shapes, little stars and wagon wheels delight children and add variety to the menu.

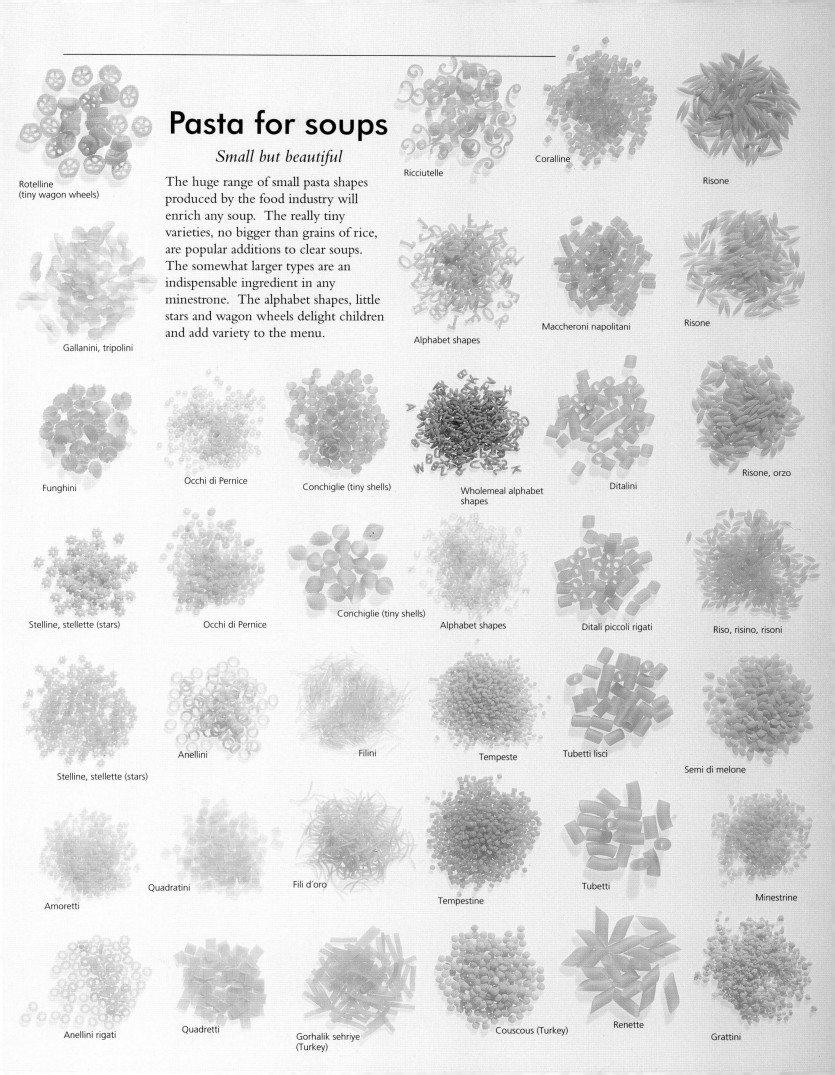

Rotelline
(tiny wagon wheels)

Gallanini, tripolini

Funghini

Stelline, stellette (stars)

Stelline, stellette (stars)

Amoretti

Anellini rigati

Ricciutelle

Alphabet shapes

Occhi di Pernice

Occhi di Pernice

Anellini

Quadratini

Quadretti

Coralline

Maccheroni napolitani

Conchiglie (tiny shells)

Conchiglie (tiny shells)

Filini

Fili d'oro

Gorhalik sehriye
(Turkey)

Risone

Risone

Wholemeal alphabet
shapes

Alphabet shapes

Tempeste

Tempestine

Couscous (Turkey)

Ditalini

Ditali piccoli rigati

Tubetti lisci

Tubetti

Renette

Risone, orzo

Riso, risino, risoni

Semi di melone

Minestrine

Grattini

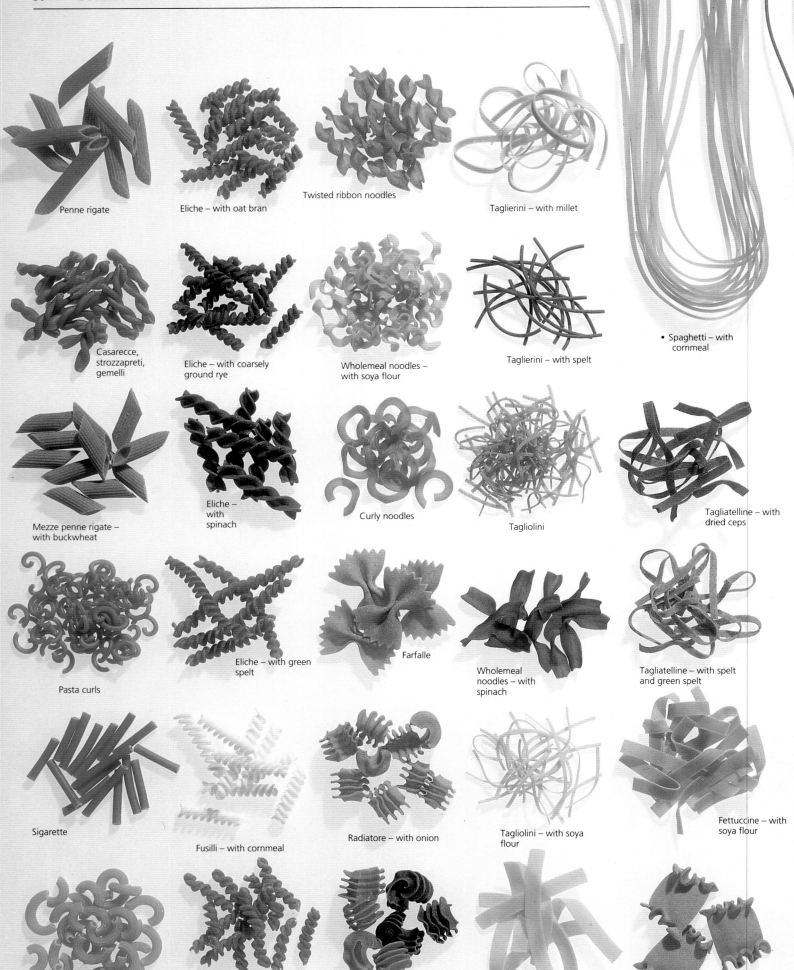

Penne rigate

Eliche – with oat bran

Twisted ribbon noodles

Taglierini – with millet

• Spaghetti – with cornmeal

Casarecce, strozzapreti, gemelli

Eliche – with coarsely ground rye

Wholemeal noodles – with soya flour

Taglierini – with spelt

Mezze penne rigate – with buckwheat

Eliche – with spinach

Curly noodles

Tagliolini

Tagliatelline – with dried ceps

Pasta curls

Eliche – with green spelt

Farfalle

Wholemeal noodles – with spinach

Tagliatelline – with spelt and green spelt

Sigarette

Fusilli – with cornmeal

Radiatore – with onion

Tagliolini – with soya flour

Fettuccine – with soya flour

Gramignina – with soya flour

Fusilli – with cornmeal and spelt

Radiatore – with nettle and carrot

Fettuccine – with soya flour

Wholemeal noodles – with spelt

Wholemeal pasta

A wide range of shapes to choose from

These are mainly made from durum wheat flour and/or durum wheat semolina. There are also wholegrain pastas made from other kinds of flours, but, since wheat flour is the only one that contains the gluten that gives the dough the required texture, it will be included to some degree. Wholemeal pasta is widely available in health food shops and supermarkets.

- Spaghetti – with rye

Linguine

- Spaghetti – with soya flour

- Spaghetti – with cornmeal

- Spaghetti – with wheatgerm

- Spaghetti – with seaweed

○ Spaghetti – with soya flour

○ Spaghetti

○ Macccheroni – with wheatgerm

Lasagne

Tagliatelle – with squid ink

Tagliolini al peperoncino –
with chilli

Fettuccine con spinaci –
with spinach

Spaghetti al
peperoncino rosso
– with red pepper

Tagliatelle with chilli

Nidi di taglioni
– with squid ink

Tagliatelle – with tomato

Tagliatelle con orticia –
with nettle

Lasagne verdi – with
spinach

Nidi di taglioni – with
salmon

Tagliatelle
– with spinach

Penne rigate con spinaci –
with spinach

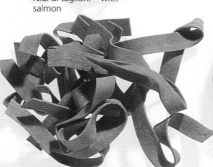

Tagliolino, taglierini – with
spinach

Penne al
peperoncino
– with chilli

Fettuccine – with beetroot

Matasse – with spinach

Matassine
– with spinach

Cannelloni verdi – with
spinach

Orecchiette – with spinach

Coloured pasta

A feast for the eyes

The pasta industry has not only produced a wide range of shapes but also introduced even greater diversity by adding a variety of colours. The main purpose here is to delight the eye. The addition of spinach, tomato, beetroot, squid ink or saffron gives the most familiar pasta shapes an attractive colour; true, it loses intensity during cooking, but it still offers innovative cooks a chance to create pleasing designs on the plate. The taste of these colourings in the finished dish is not generally very noticeable, unless the colouring agent is also added to the water used to boil the pasta or the pasta is cooked in an appropriately flavoured stock.

Cappelletti – plain, with tomato, with spinach

Gnocchetti sardi – plain, with tomato, with spinach, with saffron

Farfallini – plain, with tomato, with spinach

Conchigliette – plain, with tomato, with spinach

Rotelline – plain, with tomato, with spinach

Hearts – plain, with tomato, with spinach

Farfalle – plain, with tomato, with spinach

Malloreddus sardi – plain, with tomato, with spinach

Radiatori – plain, with beetroot, with spinach

Conchiglie – with tomato, with spinach

Eliche – plain, with tomato, with spinach

Creste di gallo – plain, with tomato, with spinach

Hörnchen – plain, with beetroot, with spinach

Sedanini – plain, with tomato, with spinach

Fusilli – with pumpkin, with cornmeal, with tomato

• Spaghetti – with tomato

• Spaghetti – with spinach

Noodles from Asia

A staple foodstuff in Asia

In the cuisines of Asia there are a multitude of pastas and noodles. Unlike pasta in the West, many of these are made from cereals other than wheat and flavourings include green tea and spinach. Soba noodles are made mainly from buckwheat flour, with wheat flour being added simply to improve their cooking performance with its gluten. These noodles look like light grey spaghetti and have a very distinctive taste. Japanese somen noodles, made from durum wheat, are produced by pulling long threads only 1 mm thick from the dough. After drying, they are cut into pieces. Raw somen noodles have a beautiful sheen that is unfortunately lost when they are cooked. Udon noodles, also from Japan, are less than 5 mm/¼ in in diameter, round, squared or flat and often very long. They are available either fresh or partially or fully dried.

Naeng myun – buckwheat noodles (Korea)

Very thin wheat noodles (Japan)

Somen – wheat noodles (Japan)

Thin wheat noodles (Japan)

Chasoba – buckwheat and green tea noodles (Japan)

Buckwheat and wheat noodles (Japan)

Ikeshima shiso somen – wheat noodles with red shiso (Japan)

Ikeshima cha somen – wheat noodles with green tea (Japan)

Zaru soba – buckwheat noodles with yam (Japan)

Aji no udon – wheat noodles (Japan)

Flat wheat noodles (Japan)

Kishimen, sanuki udon – wheat noodles (Japan)

Hime chuka soba – Chinese-style noodles (Japan)

Woh hup longevity noodles (Malaysia)

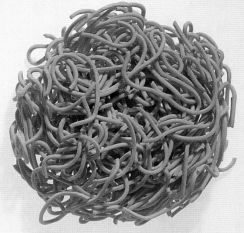

Poh chai mee (Hong Kong)

Longevity noodles, egg noodles (China)

Noodles with spinach (China)

Partially dried noodles (Malaysia)

Mee – wholemeal noodles (China)

Mee (China)

Cantonese noodles (China)

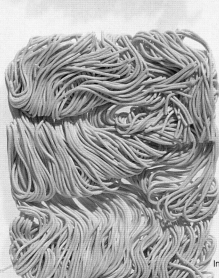

Instant egg noodles (China)

Mee – noodles with spinach (China)

Mee – noodles without egg (China)

Rice noodles, mung bean noodles

Semi-industrial noodle production in Asia

In many Asian countries, in contrast to the fully mechanized and automated production of pasta in the West, most dried noodles are produced by small and medium-sized enterprises. The various doughs are kneaded in large mixing machines and then rolled out and cut by machine or pressed through dies, but the subsequent stages in the production process – hanging the pasta out to dry, cutting it into portions and packaging it – are still carried out by hand. These small firms are wholly specialized, and produce either egg noodles made with wheat flour, rice noodles or cellophane or bean thread noodles. They usually sell these noodles fresh, either direct to the consumer or to small shopkeepers who then pack them in plastic bags and sell them at markets.

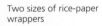

Two sizes of rice-paper wrappers

Flat rice noodles, chantaboon rice sticks (Thai: bánh pho'thu'o'ng hang)

Medium rice noodles, rice sticks (Thai: bánh phó)

Narrow rice noodles, chantaboon rice sticks (Thai: Bánh pho'thu'o'ng hang)

Fine rice noodles, rice vermicelli (Thai: wa wai brand)

Cellophane noodles –
with potato and mung
bean flour (Taiwan)

Mitsukan saifun –
cellophane noodles
with sweet potato
and potato flour
(Japan)

Mitsukan kuzukiri –
cellophane noodles
with arrowroot and
potato flour (Japan)

**Rice noodles being prepared for
drying.** *In a small Chinese factory in
Singapore, this is all still done by hand.
With great skill, the slippery fresh noodles
are hung on rails before being dried in
large ovens.*

Choung soo dang
myun – cellophane
noodles (Korea)

Fresh pasta

'The taste of fresh pasta, made from a pliable dough and cooked for a short time in boiling water, is unsurpassed and cannot be compared with dried pasta.' The enthusings of gourmets are justified, of course, but it is worth remembering that a lot of hard work has been done beforehand, and that the cook's hands and arms will be aching from all the kneading and rolling. There are machines that spare the cook all this effort, but most do not produce pasta as good as that made by hand, at least not in the domestic kitchen. In particular, the machines that claim to both knead the dough and extrude it through nozzles, like the machines in pasta factories, never produce satisfactory results.

Whether the dough should be made from soft wheat flour or durum wheat flour or semolina, or from a mixture of both, whether whole eggs should be used, or more yolk than white or just yolk, whether water should be the only liquid added or whether a spoonful of olive oil is also needed, or even whether it is worthwhile experimenting with wholemeal or highly refined flours – these are all matters of endless dispute. The only thing not at issue is that the ball of dough should, as one chef puts it, be 'kneaded to death' – in other words, worked for as long as is required for it to feel like silk to the touch. Nor is there any doubt that the dough should be wrapped in cling film and left to rest in a cool place before any further handling – though not for days, of course, since fresh eggs cannot be kept indefinitely.

It is difficult to understand why, despite centuries of experience, there are still

problems to be solved in the cooking of pasta. They concern those kinds of pastas to which flavouring and colourings have been added. Most commonly these are spinach, tomato purée or squid ink, although cocoa powder or dried mushrooms, usually ground to a floury consistency, are also used. The boiling water mercilessly extracts the flavour of these additives from the green, red or black pasta, leaving only the colour. The only way of preserving the taste is to cook the pasta in flavoured water – by blanching spinach in boiling water before cooking spinach pasta, or by using dried ceps or porcini to prepare a stock in which to cook pasta containing wild mushrooms. This technique has by no means been fully exploited yet.

Fresh pasta comes in a rather more restricted range of shapes than the commercial dried product. Any cook who is not content with pasta shapes of differing width and thickness, or who would like to offer guests fresh penne or orecchiette, or stuffed pasta of any kind, will have to be prepared to spend half a day in the kitchen.

Asked how the quality of freshly made pasta could be identified, one Italian chef replied, 'If it is so slippery that it seems to slide more easily out of the mouth and back onto the plate than down the throat, then it's perfect.'

Home-made pasta *is*
made fresh every day
for their own restaurants
by pastaie, *Italian*
pasta cooks. This pasta
fresca is made almost
exclusively by women
and is also sold for
consumption off the
premises.

HOME-MADE PASTA DOUGHS

This usually means using eggs

Pasta dough consisting only of flour and water is
made much better in factories than it can ever be at
home. This is due to the selection and mixture of
the right kinds of wheat in the commercial product.
However, the home cook still has to choose among
the various kinds of dough made with eggs, since
different sorts of pasta require doughs made from
specific ingredients. These are determined both by
the kind of flour used and the ratio of egg white to
yolk or of egg to water.

Adding salt to pasta dough is eschewed by some
pasta experts, since it can make white spots in the
dough. This can be avoided by using very fine-
grained salt.

All the ingredients for pasta dough should be
brought to room temperature before mixing, since
only then can flour, eggs and other liquids be
quickly and easily combined to form a smooth
dough. Do not use eggs straight from the
refrigerator.

A solid wooden board is preferred by Italian pasta
experts to a work surface made of any other material,
such as marble or plastic, simply because wood stores
heat well. In a well-heated kitchen, however, this is
not of any great importance.

The flour is crucial to the success of good pasta.
Fortunately, the quality of most kinds of flour does
not vary much. Anyone hoping to guarantee success
under all circumstances will do well to use the
original Italian flours known as '*farina bianca 00*' or
'*Tipo 00*' (type 00) and '*farina di semola fine*' (fine
durum wheat or semolina flour, which should not be
confused with the semolina used in puddings). In any
event, it is worth while paying the closest possible
attention to flour quality and experimenting until
you find the one best suited to your purposes.

PASTA DOUGH NO. 1

This is a standard dough for most kinds of pasta. It
can be used for cut pasta and stuffed pasta shapes.

300 g/10½ oz plain flour, preferably type 00
3 eggs
1 tablespoon olive oil
½ teaspoon salt
1 tablespoon water if required

PASTA DOUGH NO. 2

A dough for 'country-style' pasta that remains firm
when cooked. It owes its characteristic consistency
to the addition of durum wheat semolina.

125 g/4½ oz finely ground semolina flour
125 g/4½ oz plain flour, preferably type 00
2 eggs, 1 egg yolk
½ teaspoon salt

PASTA DOUGH NO. 3

For stuffed pastas, such as ravioli, agnolotti, tortellini,
pansoti and many others.

300 g/10½ oz plain flour, preferably type 00
2 eggs, 4 egg yolks
½ teaspoon salt

PASTA DOUGH NO. 4

A rich dough with a distinctive taste of its own
which swells up on cooking. Ideal for tagliatelle,
fettuccine and other ribbon noodles.

300 g/10½ oz plain flour, preferably type 00
1 egg
7 egg yolks
1 tablespoon olive oil
½ teaspoon salt

1 Sift the flour on to a work surface in a mound and make a hollow in the middle. Break the eggs into the hollow. Add the olive oil and salt to the eggs. With a fork or spoon, first mix the ingredients in the hollow together and then start to mix in the flour from the edge.

2 Gradually incorporate more of the flour until a viscous paste begins to form. Put the fork to one side and, using both hands, heap the remaining flour from the outside over the paste in the middle. Work the flour into the paste. If the paste does not absorb all the flour and if the ingredients cannot be easily worked, add a little water.

3 Work in the water with both thumbs, then press the dough into a ball and work in the rest of the flour. Now the actual kneading begins. Push out the dough with the heel of the hands, then form it into a ball again. Repeat this kneading action until the dough has a firm but slightly elastic consistency and no longer changes shape when you remove your hands. Cover with cling film and leave to rest for about 1 hour.

Wholemeal, cornmeal and chestnut flours

Pasta doughs that offer the cook greater variety – some with a very distinctive flavour of their own

Corn or maize (Zea mays) *is a tropical and subtropical cereal belonging to the grass family. Whether in the form of whole cobs or individual kernels, it has many uses in the kitchen, particularly as a vegetable. Cornmeal or maize flour is used to make pasta and polenta.*

WHOLEMEAL PASTA DOUGH

Wholemeal flour is made from the entire wheat kernel, particularly the highly nutritious embryo (germ) and the husk (bran), which is a good source of fibre. The flour develops its full flavour if used immediately after grinding. All wholemeal flours require the addition of refined white flour to make a dough that is easy to work.

250 g/9 oz wholemeal flour
250 g/9 oz plain flour, preferably type 00
½ teaspoon salt, 2 eggs, 1 tablespoon olive oil
about 200ml/7 fl oz lukewarm water

Preparing wholemeal pasta dough:

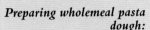

Mix the two types of flour with the salt on a work surface, shape into a mound and make a hollow in the middle. Break the eggs into it.

Measure the tablespoon of olive oil and add it to the eggs in the hollow.

Mix the ingredients in the hollow together, then begin to stir in the flour from the edge.

As soon as a viscous paste begins to form in the hollow, use both hands to heap the remaining flour over the paste.

Mix the flour into the paste, using both thumbs to work in enough water to bind together into a dough. Shape the dough into a ball.

Push out the dough with the heel of the hands and form it into a ball again. Repeat this kneading action until the dough retains its shape.

Roll the dough into a ball, cover with cling film and leave to rest for at least 1 hour.

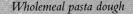

Wholemeal pasta dough

CORNMEAL PASTA DOUGH

The addition of cornmeal or maize flour produces a pasta dough with quite astonishing qualities. First, it is more robust, with a pleasantly firm texture; second, it is easy to mould or cut because it retains its shape and does not stick.

150 g/5½ oz cornmeal
150 g/5½ oz plain flour, preferably type 00
3 eggs, 3 egg yolks
1 tablespoon olive oil, ½ teaspoon salt
freshly grated nutmeg

Preparing cornmeal pasta dough:

Sift the cornmeal and flour on to the work surface, shape into a mound and form a hollow in the middle. Add the remaining ingredients to the hollow.

Mix the ingredients in the hollow with a fork and then begin to stir in the flour from the edge.

Using both hands, work in the remaining flour. Knead the mixture with the heels of the hands into a smooth dough.

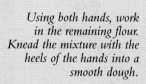

CHESTNUT PASTA DOUGH

Chestnut flour is milled from dried sweet chestnuts, *Castanea sativa*. Its flavour is brought out best if the pasta is served simply with browned butter (*beurre noisette*) and a mild cheese. Chestnut flour can be found in health food stores and Italian delicatessens.

200 g/7 oz chestnut flour
400 g/14 oz plain flour, preferably type 00
4 eggs
5 egg yolks
½ teaspoon salt

Preparing chestnut pasta dough:

Sift the two flours on to a work surface, shape into a mound and form a hollow in the middle. Add the eggs, egg yolks and salt to the hollow.

Mix the ingredients in the hollow with a fork and then begin to stir in the flour from the edge.

Using both hands, work in the remaining flour, then knead the mixture with the heels of the hands into a smooth dough.

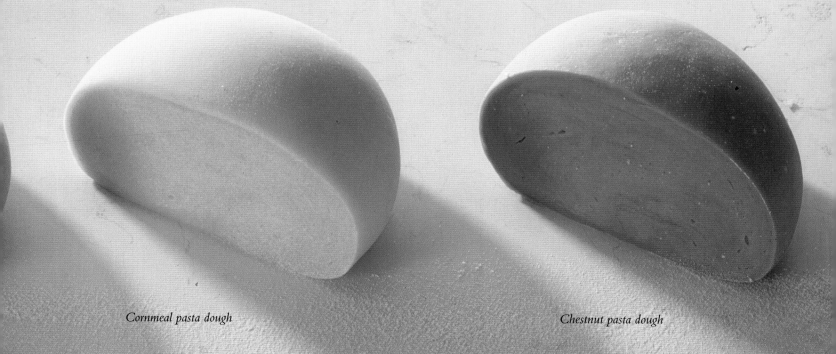

Cornmeal pasta dough

Chestnut pasta dough

Fields of buckwheat are no longer a rarity in Europe: in the trend towards healthy eating, this plant is making a comeback. It is an undemanding crop that thrives even in poor soil.

Soba – buckwheat noodles

Flour made from buckwheat (*Fagopyrum esculentum*) is used to make breads, Russian blini and crêpes in Brittany. In the Balkans and in some parts of Italy, it is also used to make noodles, at least at home.

The situation in Asia is completely different, particularly in Korea and Japan. In these two countries, the making of soba – buckwheat noodles – is a tradition going back more than 400 years. The word *soba* in Japanese denotes both the buckwheat plant and its seeds and the thin, brownish noodles made from them. The continued popularity of these noodles is due to their undisputed nutritional value, as well as to their pleasant, sweetish flavour.

Buckwheat is normally ground quite coarsely when used in Europe and North America. In Japan, on the other hand, there are five or six different grades of buckwheat flour, ranging from coarse, wholegrain flour to the finest white flour, which is ideal for making the most delicate pale noodles. Soba noodles are as popular in hearty dishes during the cold periods of the year as during the heat of summer, when they are served cold with salads or with nothing more than wasabi or a dipping sauce. They can also be served as a dessert, either with fruit or with ice cream. In Tokyo alone, there are 7,000 shops selling soba noodles, and many of them still offer genuine hand-made noodles. There, customers can watch the somewhat complicated process by which soba noodles are made.

There are various means by which one can obtain a smooth dough from buckwheat flour, which, after all, has none of the gluten that is so important for producing a malleable dough. Those wishing to make soba noodles at home are advised to use a mixture containing three or four parts buckwheat flour to one of wheat flour. However, it is possible to increase the proportion of buckwheat flour without the dough becoming impossibly crumbly. In Japan, this is done by using boiling water, which partially compensates for the lack of gluten in buckwheat flour by penetrating the starch in the flour more quickly and thus binding the dough ('*kiko-uchi*', which translates roughly as 'pure buckwheat noodles', is a stamp of quality in Japan). An alternative, very simple method of achieving the same effect is to use an egg. First, whisk it with cold water and then mix it into the dough. This does not alter the taste significantly, but it does make the dough smooth and pliable. The particular flavour of the noodles that can be made with the buckwheat flour available in Europe and North America is full-bodied and earthy, best suited to combinations with vegetables, particularly cabbage, as well as with bacon and strong cheeses.

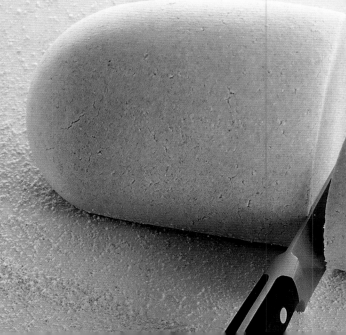

This is the critical phase in the making of buckwheat dough. *After the water has been added to the flour, it must be mixed in quickly in order to avoid hard lumps forming. One tried and tested way of preventing this, used in Europe and in Asia, is to add an egg whisked with water.*

BUCKWHEAT PASTA DOUGH

This dough is always made from a mixture of buckwheat and wheat flours, sifted together into the mixing bowl. By sifting, the two kinds of flour are mixed evenly and are aerated. This is important, since it means that the water can be worked into the flour quickly, thus avoiding the formation of any hard lumps.

300 g/10½ oz buckwheat flour
150 g/5½ oz plain flour, preferably type 00
½ teaspoon salt, 300 ml/½ pt water

Preparing buckwheat pasta dough:

Sift the two kinds of flour and the salt together into a bowl. Stir in the water with a fork.

As soon as the water is absorbed, place the resulting paste on a floured wooden board and knead it into a smooth dough, as described on page 41.

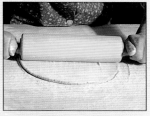

Divide the dough into four equal pieces. Roll out each piece into a disc 2 mm/1⁄16 in thick, sprinkling it frequently with flour while rolling.

Dust the discs with buckwheat flour and allow them to dry out a little. To make noodles, cut the first disc into strips 5 cm/2 in wide.

Stack the cut strips on top of each other, so that the edges are flush. Then cut the strips across into short noodles about 5 mm/¼ in wide.

Place the cut noodles on a clean tea towel. Cut the remaining discs into noodles in the same way.

Pasta with colour and flavour

Colour is not all that is required

In the view of many pasta lovers, pasta should taste of pasta. They prefer to use the sauce to add the flavour of tomatoes or mushrooms or whatever, rather than add it to the pasta itself, and they reject coloured pasta on the same grounds. In fact, coloured pasta offers the creative cook many new opportunities for variations on a theme.

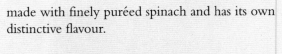

GREEN PASTA DOUGH

Green is the most frequently used colouring for pasta. This may be due to the fact that green is the colour that best sets off a tomato or white sauce. The production process is far from simple, since the colour has first to be taken from the spinach that is the principal colouring agent. This is done by making spinach pulp, which involves extracting chlorophyll from spinach. Chlorophyll has virtually no taste and is therefore well suited for use in sauces, stuffings and even sweet dishes. Green pasta should not be confused with spinach pasta, which is made with finely puréed spinach and has its own distinctive flavour.

Spinach pulp:		
200 g/7 oz spinach, 2–3 tablespoons water		
For the pasta dough:		
160 g/5¾ oz plain flour, preferably type 00		
5–6 egg yolks		
1 tablespoon olive oil, ½ teaspoon salt		
40 g/1½ oz butter		
freshly grated nutmeg, salt		

Making spinach pulp: *Place a few of the spinach leaves in the blender, add the water and blend to a smooth purée. Gradually add the rest of the spinach leaves, blending until smooth. Place the purée in a square of muslin. Squeeze the juice out into a saucepan.*

Heat the spinach juice to about 65°C/150°F, but do not let it boil. Skim off the pulp with a small sieve as it rises to the surface.

Preparing the dough:

Pour the flour on to a work surface, shape into a mound and make a hollow in the middle. Add the egg yolks and the spinach pulp, pressing it through the sieve.

Using first a fork and then your hands, mix all the ingredients into a smooth dough, as described on page 41.

Roll the dough into a ball, cover with cling film and leave to rest for 1 hour.

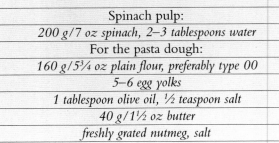

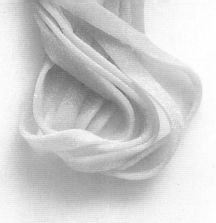

BEETROOT PASTA DOUGH

Very beautiful, almost purple pasta, but with virtually no beetroot taste.

250 g/9 oz plain flour, preferably type 00
2 eggs, 1 egg yolk
2 tablespoons olive oil
½ teaspoon salt
75 ml/2½ fl oz beetroot juice

Prepare the dough as described on page 41. Using a vegetable juicer, extract the juice from fresh beetroot and boil down to 2 tablespoons. Allow to cool. Work the beetroot juice into the dough.

SAFFRON PASTA DOUGH

This is a perfect combination of colour and taste.

1 small sachet saffron threads
250 g/9 oz plain flour, preferably type 00
2 eggs, 1 egg yolk
2 tablespoons olive oil
½ teaspoon salt

Mix the saffron with 2 tablespoons water. Prepare the dough as described on page 41, adding the saffron liquid to the hollow with the other ingredients.

MUSHROOM PASTA DOUGH

The uniquely intense flavour of this pasta makes it a culinary treat.

10 g/½ oz porcini
250 g/9 oz plain flour, preferably type 00
2 eggs, 1 egg yolk
2 tablespoons olive oil, ½ teaspoon salt
1 tablespoon finely chopped fresh parsley
water as required

Finely chop the porcini with a knife or grind them coarsely with a pestle and mortar. Prepare the dough as described on page 41, adding the porcini and parsley to the ingredients in the hollow.

CHILLI PASTA DOUGH

This pasta has very little colour but a hot, spicy flavour.

6 dried red chillies
250 g/9 oz plain flour, preferably type 00
2 eggs, 1 egg yolk
2 tablespoons olive oil
½ teaspoon salt, water as required

Slit open the chillies, remove the seeds and finely chop the pods or grind them with a pestle and mortar. Prepare the dough as described on page 41, adding the chillies to the hollow in the flour.

PRAWN PASTA DOUGH

Aromatic pasta, with a delicate, unmistakable flavour. The recipe uses dried prawns, which should not be confused with the dried shrimp used as a seasoning in Asian cookery.

25 g/1 oz dried prawns
250 g/9 oz plain flour, preferably type 00
2 eggs, 1 egg yolk
2 tablespoons olive oil
½ teaspoon salt
water as required

Finely chop the prawns or grind with a pestle and mortar. Prepare the dough as described on page 41, adding the prawns to the ingredients in the hollow.

BLACK PASTA DOUGH

The colour is the focus of attention here, and can inspire cooks to create dishes full of visual contrast. None of the rich colour is lost during cooking: the water remains completely clear. Squid ink, which has virtually no taste, can be bought in sachets from good fishmongers or extracted from the ink sacs of fresh squid.

300 g/10½ oz plain flour, preferably type 00
2 eggs
2 teaspoons olive oil
½ teaspoon salt
20 g/¾ oz squid ink

Prepare the dough as described on page 41, adding the squid ink with the eggs.

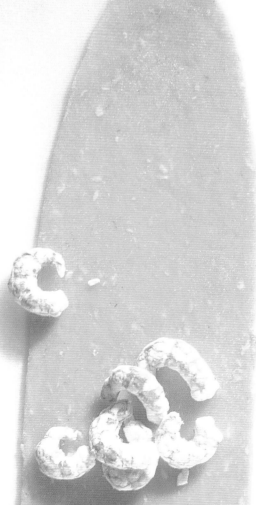

HERB PASTA DOUGH

This pasta has an intense herby flavour. A single herb, such as basil, can be used instead of a mixture.

20 g/¾ oz mixed fresh herbs: sage, thyme, parsley, chives
250 g/9 oz plain flour, preferably type 00
2 eggs, 1 egg yolk
2 tablespoons olive oil
½ teaspoon salt
water as required

Finely chop the herbs. Prepare the dough as described on page 41, adding the herbs to the ingredients in the hollow.

GARLIC PASTA DOUGH

Garlic makes the most strongly flavoured pasta of all.

3 garlic cloves
½ teaspoon salt
2 tablespoons olive oil
250 g/9 oz plain flour, preferably type 00
2 eggs, 1 egg yolk
2 tablespoons olive oil
water as required

Crush the garlic with the salt and oil in a pestle and mortar. Prepare the dough as described on page 41, adding the garlic paste to the ingredients in the hollow.

TOMATO PASTA DOUGH

Pasta with a delicate, fresh aroma and a striking colour.

250 g/9 oz plain flour, preferably type 00
3–4 egg yolks, 50 g/1¾ clarified butter
½ teaspoon salt
2–2½ tablespoons tomato purée
about 3 tablespoons water

Prepare the dough as on page 41, with the butter replacing the oil and the tomato purée added with the egg yolks.

Pasta fresca all'uovo

In Bologna, the pasta centre of Emilia-Romagna, fresh egg pasta is prized above all else

Hand-made pasta is, of course, to be cherished, but there are certain shapes that absolutely have to be made by machine because they would otherwise not be made at all, or only with great difficulty. These include the various sizes of spaghetti and macaroni and many others. So lovers of fresh egg pasta have no alternative but to resort to a machine if they wish to produce these shapes. Hand-operated machines are available, similar in shape to a mincer. The pasta is propelled along a shaft to a suitably perforated disc and extruded through it. Such simple devices exist for making bigoli, for example, a Venetian wholemeal pasta. There are also electric pasta machines with a very wide range of perforations that can produce all the usual long noodles without any difficulty at all. These machines are as suitable for use in domestic kitchens as in restaurants.

With pasta, 'home-made' is still synonymous with 'good quality'. Home-made pasta is good pasta. This applies not only to the making of the dough but also to the subsequent stages of the process – the rolling out and cutting, the stuffing and shaping. And yet in Italy, particularly in Emilia-Romagna, fresh pasta does not necessarily mean home-made pasta.

Rolling out the dough into a sfoglia *– a thin sheet of even thickness – is exhausting work and requires years of experience.*

To make tagliatelle, the sfoglia *is left to dry slightly and then folded over and cut to size. At Gigina's in Bologna, Italy, the whole process is performed with machine-like accuracy.*

Loosely curled bundles of tagliatelle are placed in a small bowl and then turned out carefully on to a board. The pasta 'nests' are then left to dry.

The choice in Italian pasta shops is not very wide, but everything is guaranteed fresh, from the ribbon noodles of varying widths to the house specialities. The picture shows, from left to right, passatelli, gramigna and strozzapreti.

There are still specialists there, the so-called '*pastaie*', who produce fresh pasta day in, day out, whether for their own restaurants or for consumption off the premises. It is advisable to order in advance if you want to be certain of having your fresh tortellini or tagliatelle the next day, since nobody in the pasta region around Bologna will voluntarily forego their *pasta fresca*. And it can be expected that in every good restaurant the pasta '*fatta in casa*' is indeed home-made.

The interesting thing is that the vast majority of *pastaie* are women. Pasta-making is not something to be entrusted to men or to machines; it is the province of the female pasta cook, who kneads the dough and, with incredible speed and skill, rolls it out into *sfoglie*. These thin sheets are then hung on rails and dried for a precisely defined time, since the dough should be neither too soft nor too dry when it is folded over for cutting. With machine-like precision, it is cut into the desired width for tagliatelle and taglierini or into broad strips for pappardelle. Loosely curled into nests, the pasta is then ready for the cooking pot.

Fresh pasta should always be cooked on the day it is made, since it is then dry enough to retain its shape while it cooks but also soft enough to need only a short cooking time. This is just as important for the various forms of cut pasta as it is for the stuffed varieties, which are in any case highly perishable if they have a meat filling.

'Alla chitarra' *is the term used to describe noodles cut with the device shown above, the* chitarra *or 'guitar'. These noodles, known as 'pasta alla chitarra', 'spaghetti alla chitarra' or 'spaghetti quadrati' ('square spaghetti'), come from the Abruzzi region of Italy and are still produced there today. The* chitarra *consists of a wooden frame with thin wires stretched across the top. A sheet of pasta dough, rolled out to a thickness approximately equal to the distance between the wires, is laid over the top of the* chitarra *and a rolling pin is used to press the dough down through the wires. The strips of cut pasta, which now have a square cross section, drop through the wires on to the board that forms the bottom of the frame.*

With knife or machine

Method makes no difference to taste, but it is important for consistent results

With a knife:

Dust the work surface evenly with flour and roll out the dough into a sheet, rolling from the centre alternately in both directions.

For ribbon noodles, fold the sheet of dough over several times. Dust it with flour first, so that the layers do not stick together.

Pappardelle, lasagnette *are cut in broad strips 1.5–2 cm/ 5/8–3/4 in across. Unfold immediately so they do not stick together.*

Tagliatelle *are cut in strips about 5 mm/1/4 in across. Fettuccine are a little wider: 8 mm/3/8 in across.*

Tagliolini or taglierini *are narrow ribbon noodles less than 3 mm/1/8 in in width. In Piedmont they are sold under the name 'tajarin'.*

Fresh pasta can be cut by hand or by machine. By hand means the pasta is cut with a knife. However, this should be done only if you can achieve results similar to those produced by machine. Thus the pasta has to be rolled out evenly and cut into strips of approximately the same width. Strips of differing widths and thicknesses would cook unevenly, which would spoil the taste and texture of the pasta.

Proper tools are essential for both methods. For the first one, this is a knife of appropriate length and sharpness with a blade that is not too thick. The ideal material for the work surface is wood, although plastic boards are now very popular. They are easier to keep clean and are also less damaging to a knife than marble or other surfaces.

Anyone whose skill and artistry with a knife do not match those of the professional pasta cook should consider purchasing a pasta machine. They are generally easy to use, and they produce perfect pasta in a huge variety of shapes and sizes. As shown in

By machine:

Put the strip of dough through the machine's smooth rollers several times, narrowing the setting each time, until the desired thickness is achieved.

Pappardelle, lasagnette *are made using a cutting roller to produce 1.5–2 cm/⅝–¾ in strips. Toss with flour and shape into loose nests.*

Tagliatelle and fettuccine *are cut 5 mm/¼ in and 8 mm/⅜ in wide respectively. If they are not to be cooked immediately, curl them into loose nests and store.*

Tagliolini or taglierini, *narrow ribbon noodles, are made using a cutting roller with a width just under 3 mm/⅛ in.*

Drying noodles. *A rack like this can be improvised with wooden spoons, and the pasta hung over their handles to dry.*

the picture sequence above, the dough has first to be rolled out; then, when it has reached the desired thickness, it can be cut into sheets of lasagne or used to make stuffed pasta. Or it can be fed through one of the interchangeable sets of cutting rollers. Most machine manufacturers supply rollers to make all the common pasta shapes. There are also very sophisticated machines designed to produce filled and shaped ravioli.

Pasta-makers *were very quick to appropriate technology for their own purposes, as the photograph above shows. In one process, this machine can roll out the dough to the required thickness and then feed it straight to the cutting roller.*

Pasta shapes

Cutting fresh dough into shape: pasta doesn't get any more individual

Using a pastry wheel and a ruler, cut strips 1.5 cm/¾ in wide. Moisten the edges of the strips.

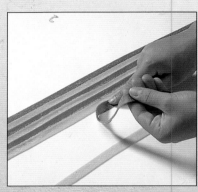

Lay the natural and green strips side by side, alternately and slightly overlapping, and roll to the desired thickness.

Sheets of two-tone dough look particularly attractive, but require a lot of effort to make. A machine makes the rolling easier. Roll out the two batches of dough a little thicker than ultimately required.

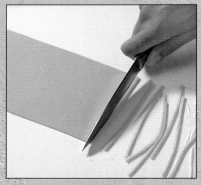

Fusilli *are commercially made in many different forms. Cut strips about 2 mm/ ¹⁄₁₆ in wide and 8 cm/3 in long.*

Wind the strips around a floured wooden stick, then carefully slide the stick out. Allow to dry before cooking.

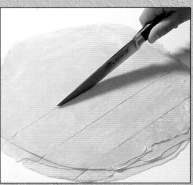

Quadrucci. *Dust thin rounds with flour and allow to dry slightly, then stack and cut into 10 cm/4 in wide strips.*

Cut these long strips across into equal strips of the desired width, then cut them into squares of the desired size.

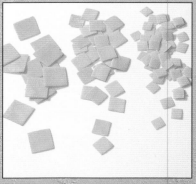

Squares of any size can be cut. The most popular sizes have sides 1, 1.5 and 2 cm/⅜, ½ and ¾ in long.

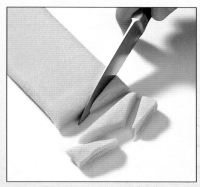

Maltagliati, meaning 'badly cut', is the name of these noodles, so you do not have to be too precise in cutting them.

Sprinkle the dough liberally with flour and fold it over. First cut off the corners and then cut across.

The result will be shapes that taper off at each end. Unfold and leave to dry on a lightly floured surface.

Orecchiette are normally made from a dough consisting only of flour and water. Roll into tubes about 1 cm/⅜ in thick.

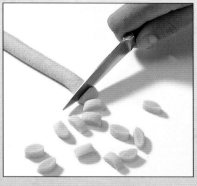

Cut in even-sized pieces about 4 mm/scant ¼ in across, so that all the orecchiette end up the same shape.

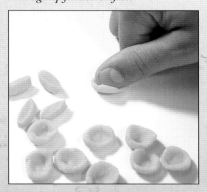

Sprinkle the work surface with flour, then press out each 'ear' shape with your thumb. Leave to dry before cooking.

Garganelli are pasta tubes. Roll 6 cm/2½ in squares of dough around a 5 mm/¼ in diameter wooden stick.

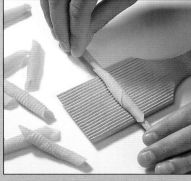

Roll the tube of dough over a grooved board, like that used to shape pats of butter, pressing down firmly.

Carefully slide out the wooden stick without squeezing the tube of pasta. Leave to dry before cooking.

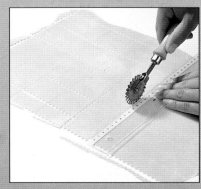

Farfalle, or pasta bows, are made from rectangles varying from 1.5 x 3 cm/¾ x 1¼ in to 3 x 6 cm/1¼ x 2½ in.

Cut long strips of dough with a straight or fluted pastry wheel and then cut these across in rectangles of the desired size.

Pinch each rectangle together in the middle between thumb and forefinger. Leave to dry on a lightly floured surface.

Cantonese noodles

Dexterity and a feel for the quality of the dough are required in order to make noodles as slender as threads of silk

The dough for these noodles consists solely of water and wheat flour. In order to make it, cooks shake flour on to a work surface, add salt and gradually pour on cold water. The dough has the same consistency as normal flour and water dough, but is left to settle only a short time before the next stage of the noodle-making process begins, initially on an unfloured work surface. The dough is stretched into a skein, folded together, stretched out again, folded together again and so on, over and over. At the same time, it is tossed in the air and rotated. As the whole process proceeds, the individual strands begin to emerge, but at this stage they remain stuck together. When they are about 5 mm/¼ in wide, they are sprinkled liberally with flour. The dough is then repeatedly stretched, folded together and twisted into a spiral; from time to time it is rolled in flour, so that the noodles get gradually thinner and thinner and eventually separate from each other. The process continues until the noodles are of the desired thickness. Finally, the thick ends of the skein of dough, which can make up about half its total weight, are cut off with a knife. The noodles are hung to dry over a rail, while the whole process is repeated with the second half of the dough. The surprising thing about these very fine noodles is that, provided they are not cooked too long, they retain a certain degree of 'bite'.

So thin *it can pass through the eye of a needle! Here, Sang Koon Sung, a native of Canton and the noodle specialist at the Pine Court Restaurant in, Singapore's Mandarin Hotel, proudly displays one of the products of his craft. Even the thinnest capelli d'angelo made in Italy cannot compete.*

When a hand is passed through them, *Cantonese noodles look like an evenly draped curtain. It is a real pleasure to watch a Chinese cook making these unbelievably thin noodles, without any tools and almost as quickly as a machine. Having seen the process it is almost impossible to imagine that anyone other than the Chinese could have discovered pasta.*

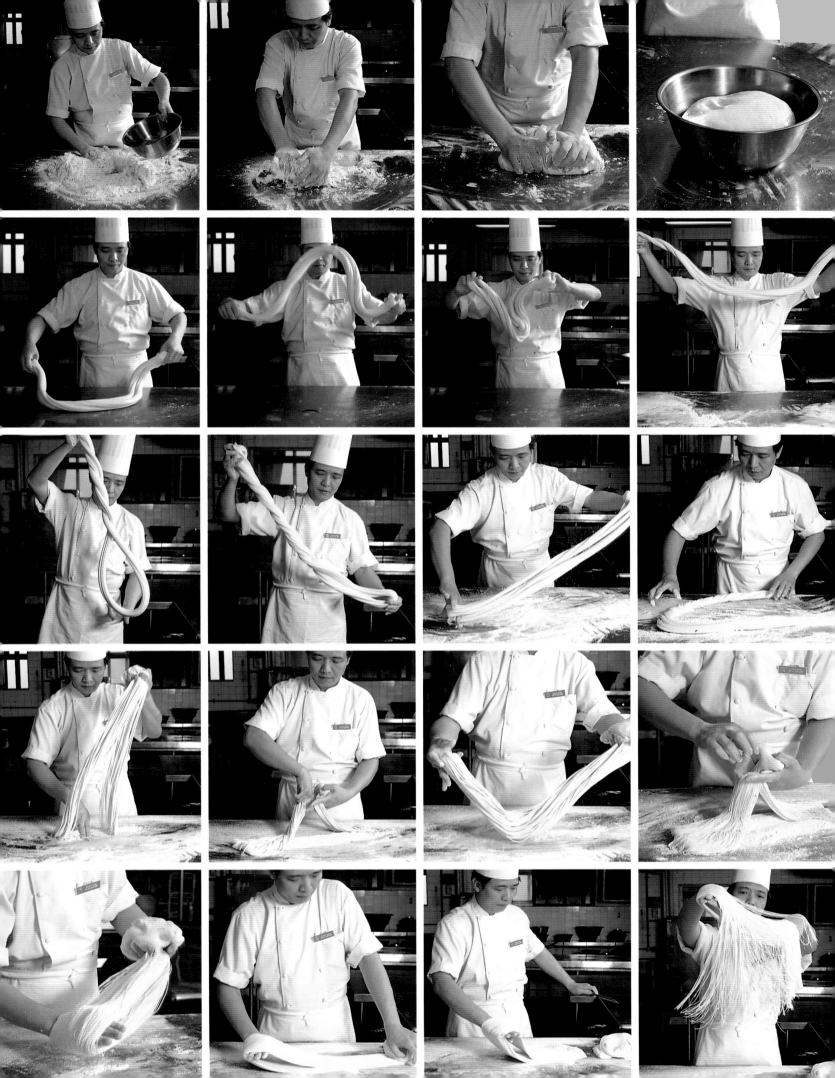

How to cook pasta

It is certainly going too far to suggest that cooking pasta represents a serious challenge for the cook; however, cooking it properly is not such a simple matter

Great attention has to be paid to a few important points. This is why, for pasta experts, cooking pasta is as serious a matter as making the dough. Nothing can be left to chance.

The right pan. The ideal pasta pan should be of good quality, taller than it is wide and big enough to hold sufficient water, and its base must sit flat on the burner. As a rule of thumb, 1 litre/1^3/$_4$ pints of water is required for every 100 g/3^1/$_2$ oz of pasta, whatever shape it may be. This is the minimum water required to cook pasta properly. If the volume of water is increased by 25 per cent or more this can only be of benefit, since pasta requires as constant a temperature as possible during its relatively short cooking time, and this is easier to maintain with a large volume of water. The pasta also cooks more evenly. A tightly fitting lid is necessary in order to cover the pan as soon as the pasta has been added to the boiling salted water. In this way, it will return more quickly to the boil. The lid should then be pushed to one side so that it covers about two-thirds of the pan, thus allowing steam to escape.

Alternatively, the lid can be removed completely so that the cooking process can be monitored more closely. The surface of the water should be at a rolling boil, but it should no longer be bubbling vigorously. In this way, the pasta will automatically swirl around in the large volume of water. Nevertheless, it is a good idea to stir the water occasionally with a wooden spoon or fork in order to avoid clumps of pasta forming that will then cook unevenly.

Al dente – **or the right degree of resistance.** It is not at all simple to predict the exact cooking time for pasta, so frequent testing is required as the end of the assumed cooking time draws close. As it cooks, pasta absorbs water at a variable rate, becoming increasingly soft and swelling up. It is cooked when it feels soft to the touch but is very slightly resistant and firm in the centre (not raw) when bitten into. This is what Italian pasta cooks describe as '*al dente*', or 'to the tooth'. Obviously, the length of time required to achieve this state will vary, according to the shape of the particular pasta and whether it is fresh or dried.

Drain quickly. Some cooking times, particularly

A lot of water is needed. As a rule of thumb, use at least 1 litre/1¾ pints of water for every 100 g/3½ oz of pasta.

Salt the water. Add 1 teaspoon of salt for each litre/1¾ pints of water. This is important for all types of pasta.

Oil is only needed when cooking pasta that tends to stick together, such as large sheets of lasagne and very fresh pasta.

Long pasta should be pushed in gently, and pasta shapes added a few handfuls at a time. The water must be bubbling.

Stir with a wooden fork so that the strands or shapes are separated and do not stick together.

Put the lid on, leaving about a third of the pan uncovered. In this way, steam can escape and the pasta will cook evenly.

The surface of the water should be rolling gently but not bubbling, maintaining a constant temperature.

Testing the pasta should be done frequently towards the end of the cooking time. It should be cooked 'al dente'.

Drain the pasta as soon as it is cooked. Pour it into a colander and shake gently to drain it thoroughly.

Rinse with cold water only if the pasta is to be used in a salad or served as a side-dish.

Rinse with the hot cooking water to keep the pasta warm for a short period. This will keep the pieces separate.

for fresh pasta, are very short, so the pan has to be removed from the heat at exactly the right moment and its contents emptied immediately into a colander in order to bring the cooking process to a halt. If large quantities of pasta are being cooked, this can be a somewhat difficult process; using a fitted draining basket in a pasta pan, as shown in the picture sequence below, makes the task considerably easier.

The cold rinse. The decision as to whether to stop the cooking process by rinsing the pasta in cold water or not depends on what is to be done with it subsequently. Rinsing in cold water removes the glutinous starchy layer from pasta, which is fine if it is to be served cold in a salad, used as a side-dish or browned lightly in butter. However, if it is to be mixed with a sauce and served hot, then the starch layer is necessary in order to prevent the other ingredients simply sliding off the pasta and thus failing to bind properly with it.

Some types of commercial pasta have fluted surfaces – described in Italian as '*rigati*' – to which sauces and cheese adhere particularly well. However, this only works properly if the pasta is really hot and is not sticking together. If it does begin to stick, break it up by pouring the hot cooking water over it,

Cooking pasta in a fitted draining basket has a number of advantages: since the boiling water can circulate between the pan and the basket, the pasta remains in constant motion without sticking to the bottom of the pan. When the pasta is cooked, it can be easily removed from the pan and drained. Large pans with fitted draining baskets are available in good kitchenware shops.

Cooking pasta in a fitted draining basket:
Drop the pasta into the boiling water. The ratio of water to pasta should be the same as usual: 1 litre/1¾ pints of water for every 100 g/ 3½ oz of pasta.

Whether you are cooking long or short pasta, it must be stirred frequently to prevent it from sticking together.

When the pasta is cooked, lift the basket out of the boiling water and hold it over the pan to drain, shaking the basket gently.

Tip the drained pasta into a pre-warmed bowl and mix immediately with butter, olive oil or a sauce.

shaking the colander vigorously as you do so. Pasta and sauce should always be mixed in a pre-warmed bowl immediately after draining.

How much per person? This is a question to which there is no precise answer, since the size of each portion depends on many factors. Unless otherwise indicated, the quantities given in the recipe section are sufficient for 4 servings as a main dish. The rule of thumb is to allow 100 g/3½ oz of pasta per portion. The reason why not all the recipes require 400 g/14 oz of pasta is that the quantities of other ingredients required vary widely and sometimes even exceed the pasta in weight. Since pasta dishes are not only main dishes but are also frequently served as first courses, calculating the quantity of pasta depends in part on how many courses are to be served.

COOKING TIMES

How to decide when pasta is properly cooked is described on page 58. The length of time it must cook before reaching that state cannot be indicated very precisely, so cooking times should always be treated as mere guidelines requiring constant checking.

Fresh pasta is always a problem when it comes to calculating cooking times, since these depend on the extent to which the pasta has been dried. So it makes a big difference whether the pasta is cooked immediately after cutting or several hours afterwards. The thickness of the dough affects the cooking time as well. Fresh dough naturally has a particularly short cooking time which, depending on the thickness and width of the cut pasta, can barely be measured in minutes. This means that thin pasta in particular should be watched constantly as it cooks so that it can be drained as soon as it is ready, bringing the cooking process to an immediate halt. Capelli d'angelo (angel hair pasta), for example, may need just 30 seconds' cooking, taglierini about a minute and stuffed pasta such as tortellini 4–5 minutes.

Commercial dried pasta is less problematic, since cooking times are considerably longer. Thus it is easier to intervene if testing shows the pasta to be ready before the suggested cooking time is up. It is essential to take the time indicated on the packet as a guide, since even with the same shape of pasta the time can vary from manufacturer to manufacturer. The following table is intended as an aid to finding the guideline figure for a given kind of pasta. If the type you are cooking is not listed here, turn to the section of the book on dried and fresh pasta, find a variety similar in shape and size and then use the table to find the recommended cooking time.

Recommended cooking times for dried pasta	
Pasta shape	**Cooking time in minutes**
Alphabet shapes	5
Anellini	5
Banane	8–20
Bavette	4
Bucatini	7–8 (depending on thickness)
Buckwheat noodles (soba)	
• thin, ribbon	4–5
• flat	5
Capelli d'angelo	3–5
Capellini	1–3 (depending on thickness)
Cavatappi	10
Cellophane or bean-thread noodles	3–4
Chinese wheat noodles	
• thin (with egg)	3–5
• thin (without egg)	4–5
Conchiglie, 2.5–3 cm/1–1¼ in	14
Conchiglioni (for stuffing)	8 + 30–40 for baking
Ditali	up to 6 (depending on size)
Farfalle	7–9 (depending on size)
Fedelini	3–5 (depending on size)
Fettuccine	6
Fusilli	11
Gnocchetti sardi	10
Gnocchi	9
Japanese wheat noodles	
• thin (somen)	1
• thick (udon)	10
Lasagne sheets	7–9
Linguine	6–8
• wholemeal linguine	9
Lumaconi	8–9
Maccheroni	10–12
Malloreddus	10–12
Orecchiette	12–15
Pappardelle	4
Penne	11–12
Quadrucci, 1 cm/⅜ in	7–8
Rice noodles	
• long, thin (vermicelli)	3–4
• flat	8
Rigatoni	10
Risoni	5
Sedanini	8
Spaccatelle	9
Spaghetti alla chitarra	15
Spaghetti	12
• wholemeal spaghetti	10–12
Spaghettini	8
Tagliatelle	6–8
Trenette	13–15
Trinette	8
Tubetti	6–7
Ziti	7
Zitoni	9

Spätzle and Knöpfle

Soft-dough pasta specialities from Alsace and the southern Tyrol

If a truly regional variety of pasta exists at all outside of Italy, then it must be Spätzle. It has its origins in southwestern Germany, where it is still made 'by hand' in the traditional way, with each individual Spätzle being cut from a board straight into boiling water. Similar varieties go under the name of Knöpfli in northern Switzerland, Spatzlen in the Tyrol and Pizokel in the Engadine. There is now a commercially produced Spätzle, dried and packed in plastic bags like noodles, but in flavour and texture it has so little in common with the original that it cannot be regarded as a substitute.

SPÄTZLE DOUGH

The same dough is used for all three methods of making Spätzle: scraping, pressing and slicing. However, whether four, five, or even six eggs should be used for each 450 g/1 lb of flour is a question that still gives rise to serious discussion in Germany. In any event, using more water than eggs would be unworthy of even the thriftiest Spätzle cook. The following recipe is a good compromise, and the proper consistency of the dough is actually determined by the little bit of water that is added, for which, even with the best will in the world, it is impossible to specify an exact amount. And Spätzle should be cooked in as much water as possible, so that they can expand properly without sticking.

500 g/1 lb 2 oz plain flour
5 eggs
1 teaspoon salt
about 100 ml/3½ fl oz water

Make the dough as shown in the picture sequence below and use whichever of the three methods you prefer to transfer it to a large pan of boiling salted water. As soon as the Spätzle rise to the surface, lift them out with a slotted spoon. If they are to be served as a side-dish, they can be rinsed in warm water or tossed quickly in fresh butter. If they are to be served with cheese, put the cheese and Spätzle in alternate layers in a dish.

Making Spätzle dough:

Pour the flour into a bowl, make a hollow in the middle and break the eggs into it. Add the salt.

Pour in half the water to start with and mix all the ingredients to a smooth paste using a wooden spoon.

Beat the paste thoroughly until it takes on a smooth, elastic consistency and falls in thick blobs from the spoon. Add more water if necessary.

Cheese Spätzle are enjoyed all over the world. Gourmet tourists who visit southwestern Germany take a Spätzle press home with them as a souvenir, in preference to a cow bell. What makes this simple dish so delicious is the combination of the delicate Spätzle with the melting cheese – Gruyère or Emmental – which stretches into long strings when lifted out of the serving dish. A popular addition is onion rings fried in plenty of butter.

Spätzle scraped off a board by hand *are the really authentic kind. This method requires a board with a tapering front edge. Immediately prior to use, it should be plunged briefly into water. A portion of the Spätzle dough is placed on the dampened board and cut into small pieces with a knife or,*

preferably, a palette knife, which must be repeatedly wetted during the process. These strips of pasta should be of approximately the same thickness so that they require the same cooking time. As they are cut, the strips of dough are 'scraped' off the board into the boiling water.

Partly machine-made Spätzle *might be an accurate description of the strands of dough squeezed into boiling water from the type of Spätzle press that is similar to a potato ricer. The bottom of the press has holes, about 2 mm/1/16 in in diameter, through which the Spätzle dough is squeezed. This*

process produces long threads, similar in appearance to spaghetti, which at first sight seem to have little in common with genuine, 'hand-scraped' Spätzle. However, their lack of resistance to the bite reveals that they are made not from a pasta dough but from the softer Spätzle dough.

Swiss Knöpfli *differ from German Spätzle in their characteristic teardrop shape. Originally, the dough was pressed through a circular sieve with holes about 5 mm/1/4 in in diameter. However, the press shown here, which is similar to a vegetable grater, has been in use for a long time. It*

consists of a long strip of perforated metal on top of which sits a rectangular container for the dough. The container slides to and fro like a sledge along the perforated metal strip. The dough is forced through the perforations and then sliced off immediately as the container is pushed along the metal strip.

Equipment for the pasta cook

1 Machine for rolling out and cutting pasta dough

2 Rollers for cutting ribbon noodles in widths of 2 mm/ ¹⁄₁₆ in (capelli d'angelo), 4 mm/ ¼ in (trenette) and 11 mm/ ½ in (lasagnette) and for making spaghetti

3 Wide wooden spoon

4 Vegetable-grater-type Spätzle press

5 Spätzle board

6 Palette knife

7 Knives of various sizes

8 Shovel-type spatula for serving lasagne

9 Pastry brush

10 Plastic and metal dough scrapers

11 Ruler

12 Pizza cutting wheel, very sharp

13 Fluted pastry wheel

14 Roller for cutting 6 mm/ ¼ in tagliatelle

15 Fluted roller for cutting 4 cm/ 1 ½ in squares

16 Smooth roller for cutting 4 cm/ 1 ½ in squares

17 Roller for cutting 5 cm/ 2 in discs

18 Smooth-edged pastry cutters, 3–8 cm/ 1 ¼–3 in in diameter

19 Fluted pastry cutters, 3–8 cm/ 1 ¼–3 in in diameter

20 Ravioli cutters, 4, 5 and 6 cm/ 1 ¼, 2 and 2 ½ in in diameter

21 Potato-ricer-type Spätzle press

22 Flour sifter

23 Potato ricer

24 Italian rolling pin for pasta

25 Rolling pin with handles

26 Truffle slicer

27 Set of mixing bowls

28 Moulds for stuffed pasta

29 Pestle and mortar

30 Parmesan mill

31 Parmesan grater

1 Large pan for cooking long noodles (*pasta lunga*)

2 Large pan for cooking short pasta (*pasta corta*), stuffed pasta, gnocchi, etc.

3 Collapsible steamer insert

4 Colander and sieve

5 Measuring jugs

6 Ladle

7–9 Slotted or skimming spoons of various lengths and diameters

10 Wire strainer

11 Wide wooden spoon

12 Wooden fork for lifting out pasta for testing

13 Spaghetti server

14 Aluminium foil

15 Ceramic oven dishes for lasagne and other baked pasta dishes

16 Stainless steel tin for lasagne

17 Perforated square spatula for lifting large sheets of pasta from boiling water

18 Cotton tea towel for draining cooked sheets of pasta

19 Chopsticks for Asian cooking

20 Wire strainer for Asian cooking, particularly suitable for removing food from a wok

21 Wok with spatula and cleaning brush

22, 23 Bamboo steamers for Chinese dishes

Pasta sauces

Most Italian cooks have little interest in creating scintillating new sauces for pasta; instead, they are very skilled at adding individual touches to the classics like tomato or bolognese sauce or pesto. Every Italian maintains he can recognize his mother's sauces immediately, and that they are the best he's ever eaten. And they probably are, because they are made at home, from scratch, using the best ingredients available.

For the basic pasta sauces, as for all other dishes, the ingredients are all-important. It is not only foodies who complain that tomatoes in supermarkets nowadays look appetizing but usually taste of nothing. What a joy it is, then, to discover a market stall or greengrocer selling vine-ripened tomatoes that combine the familiar sweetness of tomatoes with a robust acidity. These tomatoes make the most delicious, full-flavoured sauce. When it comes to making a bolognese sauce, the quality of the meat used is

paramount. And it must be freshly minced. Meat of an inferior quality will not give the requisite robustness to this sauce that simmers for hours.

Of course the food industry, with all its energy and competitive zeal, has thrown itself into the sauce business. Until a few years ago, canned tomato concentrate and purée were all the industry had to offer, apart from canned peeled tomatoes, the so-called '*pomodori pelati*', which often have more taste than fresh tomatoes. Today there are sauces of all kinds, both fresh and in cans or cartons. Some are good, but many are not.

In contrast to the basic sauces of classic French cuisine, some of which are difficult to produce in the domestic kitchen, Italian sauces are ideally suited to being made at home. Anyone who owns a heavy cooking pan and shops carefully for the right ingredients can make a pasta sauce as successfully as any professional cook. Because the sauces usually simmer for a long time, there is always an opportunity to correct mistakes – unless, of course, you've been over enthusiastic with the salt. Sauce-making offers plenty of scope for anyone keen to experiment: countless amateur cooks have perfected pasta sauces of their own, of which they are justifiably proud. And don't forget that the delicious aromas permeating the house will whet your family's appetite.

Good, ripe tomatoes

The number one ingredient in Italian pasta sauces

With tomatoes, freshness is not always the most important criterion. If the choice is between freshly picked but green tomatoes from the greenhouse and those picked fully ripe and then canned or dried under the Mediterranean sun, then there's simply no contest.

Fresh tomatoes

The sauce is as simple as the pasta with which it is eaten, and this explains why the quality of the tomatoes is so important. The simplest tomato sauce consists of little more than ripe tomatoes, a little oil and salt. The tomatoes must be really ripe and sweet, brought to maturity on the vine – in the sun, not in a greenhouse. Even in countries with the right climate, such perfection is available only for a limited period. In Italy, the tomato season lasts roughly from August to the end of October. The problem of obtaining good ripe tomatoes is a familiar one for Italian cooks, which is why they bottle sufficient stocks of the best, ripest and sweetest tomatoes during the late summer and early autumn in the form of *conserva di pomodoro*, in order to have a constant supply of this fresh tomato purée.

Making fresh tomato purée

First, plunge the tomatoes into boiling water for a brief blanch and then peel them. Press them through a large-meshed sieve or mouli-légumes, or purée in a blender or food processor (you can then strain out the seeds, if liked). Pack the pulp into sterilized jars or

bottles with wide necks and screw down the lids. Set them in a deep pan, add enough water to come level with the purée in the jars and simmer gently for about 50 minutes. Remove the pan from the heat and allow the jars to cool in the water.

Choosing the right tomatoes

Not all varieties of tomato can be used to make a good sauce, and Italian pasta experts are very choosy. In Italy, the very best tomatoes for sauce-making come from Campania, and it is said that those grown on volcanic soil around Vesuvius are the finest of all. The egg-shaped plum or roma tomatoes are

particularly suitable for sauces. These are the Neapolitan or Roman varieties, very meaty and with few seeds. If they are picked when deep red and really ripe, they have a particularly intense flavour (unfortunately, tomatoes sold in supermarkets are usually picked green and then ripened in a warm room or with ethylene gas, which does nothing for their flavour). When buying tomatoes, choose those with a rich colour and noticeable fragrance. In many greengrocers and supermarkets you can find 'vine-ripened' tomatoes, which will be the most flavourful – as long as the vine grew outdoors, in the sun.

Canned tomatoes

Fresh tomatoes are unlikely to have much flavour if they're not locally grown and in season. If tomatoes have been shipped any distance, they will generally have been harvested when still green in order to stop them spoiling during transport and while they eventually turn red the flavour does not develop to the same extent as when they ripen on the vine. Even greenhouse tomatoes and hydroponic tomatoes (grown in water without soil) generally lack flavour, so it is sensible to keep a stock of canned tomatoes in the pantry. Italian brands, from the tomato-growing areas around Naples and Parma, have an excellent flavour because Italian manufacturers tend to pick riper tomatoes. You can buy canned peeled whole tomatoes, peeled and chopped tomatoes, and tomatoes flavoured with herbs such as basil and oregano, as well as the Italian tomato purée called *passata di pomodoro* or *polpa di pomodoro*. Passata is an ideal base for quick pasta sauces.

Sun-dried tomatoes and tomato purée

Sun-dried tomatoes, sold packed in oil or dry-packed, loose or in cellophane, have a particularly rich, highly concentrated flavour. They are well suited to those *sughi* (sauces) that require little liquid but need a concentrated tomato flavour. Tomato purée, available in cans and tubes, consists of tomatoes cooked down to a concentrate. The best, made from sun-dried tomatoes, is still sold from earthenware pots in some parts of Italy.

FRESH TOMATO SAUCE

Of the many *sugo* recipes, the simplest are the best, as is so often the case. The following sauce is one of these, and it must be made only from the ripest fresh tomatoes. These need not be plum tomatoes – the round varieties are perfectly suitable, as long as they have been ripened in the sun. Their taste comes through pure and unadulterated, because the recipe includes neither onions nor garlic, nor any other dominant flavouring – just basil, which perfectly complements the fresh acidity of the tomatoes.

800 g/1¾ lb ripe, red tomatoes
20 fresh basil leaves
100 g/3½ oz butter or extra virgin olive oil
1 teaspoon salt
freshly ground black pepper

Blanch the tomatoes briefly, then peel them; remove the seeds and dice the tomatoes. Coarsely shred the basil leaves. Add the diced tomatoes to the hot butter or oil and simmer until thick. (The length of time will depend on their moisture content.) Season, stir in the basil and serve.

Preparing the tomato sauce *Fry chopped tomatoes in butter or oil. Add fresh basil after simmering.*

Tomato sauces

From very simple and basic to piquant or luxuriously creamy, tomato sauces are an indispensable element in pasta cooking

BASIC TOMATO SAUCE

In Naples this is called 'La pommarola'. A basic smooth sauce of this kind can be used for many *sughi*, instead of a ready-made sauce from a jar or can. This basic sauce can be seasoned to suit individual tastes, with fresh or dried herbs or as much garlic as you like, and you can replace the olive oil with butter.

50 g/1¾ oz carrot, 100 g/3½ oz onion
100 g/3½ oz celery, 800 g/1¾ lb ripe plum tomatoes
1 teaspoon salt, freshly ground black pepper
4 tablespoons olive oil
1 tablespoon chopped fresh basil

Peel the carrot and cut it first lengthways into strips and then into small cubes. Peel and finely chop the onion. Trim and dice the celery. Prepare the sauce as shown in the picture sequence.

Preparing the tomato sauce:

Wash the tomatoes and trim out the cores. Using a sharp knife, cut the tomatoes in half, then into quarters and finally into dice.

Put the tomatoes and diced carrot into a saucepan. It is important that the tomatoes be on the bottom of the pan as they will exude liquid.

Add the chopped onion and diced celery. Cover the pan and cook on a low heat for about 40 minutes or until all the ingredients are soft.

Put the vegetable mixture into a large-meshed sieve set over a bowl and press through with a spoon. (Or you can use a mouli-légumes.) The sauce will be quite thin.

Scrape all pulp from the base of the sieve and add it to the sauce.

Pour the sauce into a pan and heat. Season to taste with salt and pepper. Add the oil to the sauce and stir in.

Add the chopped fresh basil to the sauce. Check the seasoning, adding more salt and pepper if required.

PIQUANT TOMATO SAUCE

A beautifully thick, rich *sugo*, best suited to tube-like pasta such as macaroni, penne or ziti. If you prefer a thinner sauce, add a little extra meat stock.

500 g/1 lb 2 oz ripe, juicy tomatoes, 85 g/3 oz onion
1 garlic clove, 1 fresh red chilli
5 tablespoons olive oil, 2 tablespoons chopped fresh parsley
1 tablespoon chopped fresh herbs: oregano, sage, rosemary
3 tablespoons meat stock
30 g/1 oz ricotta salata (salted ricotta cheese), salt

Blanch the tomatoes, then peel them. Cut in half, remove the seeds and core and dice. Peel and chop the onion. Peel and thinly slice the garlic. Cut the chilli in half lengthways, remove the seeds and mince. Heat the oil in a wide pan and sauté the onion and garlic until they become translucent. Add the herbs, chilli and diced tomatoes. Pour in the stock and simmer over low heat for about 20 minutes. Press the ricotta through a sieve into the pan and stir in. Season with salt if necessary.

CREAMY TOMATO SAUCE

This is a perfect sauce for spaghetti. Serve with freshly grated cheese – Parmesan or pecorino romano.

800 g/1¾ lb ripe tomatoes
100 g/3½ oz onion
50 g/1¾ oz smoked streaky bacon
1 tablespoon olive oil
4 tablespoons cream
salt and freshly ground black pepper

Wash the tomatoes, cut in half and remove the seeds and core. Cut first in quarters and then in small pieces. Peel and chop the onion. Cut the bacon in small pieces. Fry the bacon with the oil in a saucepan until it begins to brown slightly. Add the chopped onion and sauté until translucent. Add the tomatoes, cover the pan and simmer for 20 minutes.

Purée in a blender or food processor and then press through a sieve. Add the cream and season to taste with salt and pepper.

Ragù alla bolognese

The best example of fine Italian pasta cooking

BOLOGNESE MEAT SAUCE

Italian cooking certainly enjoys an outstanding reputation, but the specialities of Bologna represent a further step up the ladder of culinary excellence. One of these is tagliatelle with meat sauce. This versatile pasta sauce, perhaps the most famous one of all, is very often served in Italy with home-made tagliatelle. Outside Italy, it is indissolubly associated with spaghetti. The sauce must be cooked for a long time – the longer the better – so that all the ingredients can combine to create the unique blend of flavours.

200 g/7 oz carrots, 200 g/7 oz onion
2 garlic cloves, 150 g/5½ oz celery
200 g/7 oz prosciutto, 800 g/1¾ lb fresh tomatoes
2 cans (400 g/14 oz each) whole tomatoes
300 g/10½ oz boned beef, 200 g/7 oz boned pork
4 tablespoons olive oil, 4 tablespoons chopped fresh parsley
85 g/3 oz butter, 6 tablespoons tomato purée
250 ml/9 fl oz meat stock
1 teaspoon salt, freshly ground black pepper
½ teaspoon sugar (optional)

Peel the carrots; cut lengthways in strips and then in small dice. Peel and finely chop the onion and garlic. Finely dice the celery. Cut the prosciutto in small cubes. Blanch the fresh tomatoes, then peel; cut in half, remove the seeds and dice finely. Drain the canned tomatoes and chop coarsely. Mince the meat coarsely. Heat the oil in a saucepan and fry the carrot. Continue as shown in the picture sequence. Then season the sauce with salt and pepper and simmer for at least 1 hour, leaving the lid slightly ajar so that steam can escape. Add sugar, if liked, and simmer for a further 30 minute. Add the rest of the butter and check the seasoning.

Add the minced meat and lightly brown it, stirring and breaking it up so it becomes crumbly.

Add the prosciutto to the meat and vegetable mixture and cook for 5 minutes, stirring constantly.

Add half of the butter and then the diced fresh tomatoes.

Add the canned tomatoes and stir all the ingredients together thoroughly. Simmer briefly, uncovered.

Bolognese sauce *is still made every day in its city of origin, for example at Gigina's, 1 via Stendhal, Bologna, where the traditional recipe is followed scrupulously. The process begins with the selection of the meat; each piece is carefully inspected before purchasing in order to ensure quality, even though it is only going to be put through the mincer. Connoisseurs are agreed that only the best meat should be used, although there is some debate about the ratio of beef to pork, or whether lamb or even rabbit should also be added. Some ragù purists swear by a sauce made just with beef. And just how long it should simmer on the lowest possible heat is a secret that nobody is prepared to divulge.*

Making bolognese sauce:

Add the onion and garlic to the carrots and cook until golden brown, stirring constantly.

Stir in the tomato purée. Let the sauce simmer a little to evaporate excess liquid.

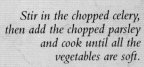

Stir in the chopped celery, then add the chopped parsley and cook until all the vegetables are soft.

Add the meat stock and mix all the ingredients together thoroughly.

The white sauces

Béchamel and velouté, both thickened with flour, are the basis for many pasta sauces

FRESH HERB SAUCE

A creamy sauce is the perfect base for aromatic fresh herbs, delicious with pasta.

25 g/scant 1 oz butter
30 g/1 oz plain flour
500 ml/18 fl oz beef or chicken stock
½ teaspoon salt, freshly ground white pepper
a pinch of freshly grated nutmeg
1 egg yolk
100 ml/3½ fl oz cream
2 tablespoons chopped fresh herbs: chives, parsley, oregano, thyme, sage

Melt the butter in a saucepan over moderate heat, sprinkle in the flour and cook gently, stirring, for 1–2 minutes; do not brown. Pour in the stock, whisking constantly. Season with salt, pepper and nutmeg and simmer for 20 minutes, whisking occasionally. Remove the pan from the heat. Mix together the egg yolk and cream. Add a little of the hot sauce to the egg yolk and cream mixture, then stir into the rest of the sauce. Strain the sauce. Reheat gently (do not boil or the sauce will curdle), then add the herbs and blend thoroughly.

GORGONZOLA SAUCE

The same base can be transformed very simply into a cheese sauce. Just replace the herbs with 85 g/3 oz of gorgonzola or other creamy blue cheese, cut in small cubes, letting it melt into the sauce. Gorgonzola is a particularly good blue cheese to use because it melts well.

This classic Italian blue cheese is available in two strengths – the mild *gorgonzola dolce* ('sweet gorgonzola') and the stronger *gorgonzola piccante* ('sharp gorgonzola').

SAUCE MORNAY

Swiss Gruyère or Emmental can be used instead of Parmesan and fontina.

For the béchamel sauce:
25 g/scant 1 oz butter, 30 g/1 oz plain flour,
500 ml/18 fl oz milk
½ teaspoon salt, freshly ground pepper
a pinch of freshly grated nutmeg
1 egg yolk, 100 ml/3½ fl oz cream
In addition:
30 g/1 oz each Parmesan and fontina cheeses, freshly grated
1–2 heaping tablespoons whipped cream

Make the sauce as shown in the picture sequence.

Making sauce Mornay:

Melt the butter in a saucepan, add the flour and cook gently for 1–2 minutes, stirring. Do not brown.

Add the milk and whisk to a smooth consistency. Add the salt, pepper and nutmeg. Simmer for 20 minutes, whisking occasionally.

Remove the pan from the heat. Mix the egg yolk with the cream and add 2 tablespoons of the hot sauce. Whisk the egg and cream mixture into the rest of the sauce.

Strain the sauce and reheat gently without bringing it back to the boil.

Stir in the cheeses and then the whipped cream.

VELOUTÉ

The quantities given here will produce about 750 ml/1¼ pints of this velvety-smooth sauce.

20 g/scant ¾ oz butter
1 shallot, peeled and finely chopped
20 g/scant ¾ oz plain flour
500 ml/18 fl oz vegetable stock
250 ml/9 fl oz double cream
a pinch of salt, freshly ground white peppper

Melt the butter in a saucepan over moderate heat and cook the shallot until it starts to become translucent. Sprinkle the flour over the shallot and cook for 1–2 minutes, without browning. Pour on the vegetable stock and simmer for 5 minutes, stirring constantly with a whisk. Add the cream and simmer for a further 10 minutes. Season to taste with salt and pepper, then strain the sauce.

Fontina *is a semi-firm yet creamy cheese made from cow's milk. It melts easily and smoothly and is therefore ideal for cooking. It is used in the traditional* fonduta piemontese *(Piedmontese cheese fondue), where its slightly sweet, nutty flavour combines remarkably well with the truffles that garnish the dish.*

Garlic and olives

*These are among the most important ingredients in the
cooking of Liguria and are natural partners for pasta*

PESTO ALLA GENOVESE

This Genoese basil sauce is internationally famous.
There are numerous variations on the theme along
the Ligurian Riviera, but they differ only slightly.
For example, the pine nuts can be toasted before
they are crushed in order to enhance their flavour.

Dry but still fresh – *that's how
the garlic for pesto should be.
Garlic that has dried out too
much and is sprouting will taste
very pungent and sharp, and you
will taste that sharpness in the
sauce.*

4 garlic cloves, 50 g/1¾ oz pine nuts
120 g/4 oz fresh basil leaves
50 g/1¾ oz pecorino cheese, freshly grated
85 g/3 oz Parmesan cheese, freshly grated
salt and freshly ground black pepper
120–150ml/4–5 fl oz extra virgin olive oil

Peel and coarsely chop the garlic. Continue as
shown in the picture sequence (a pestle and mortar is
traditional, but you could also use a food processor).
The finished sauce should have the consistency of
mayonnaise. If the pesto is to be used purely as a
sauce for pasta, it can be thinned down by stirring in
a few spoonfuls of the pasta cooking water.

Making pesto:

*Using a pestle and mortar,
pound the pine nuts with the
chopped garlic.*

*Wash and dry the basil leaves,
then chop them coarsely. Add
them to the garlic and pine
nut mixture and pound
to a paste.*

*Gradually add the finely
grated cheeses and mix in
well. Season to taste with
salt and pepper.*

*Add the olive oil as
when making
mayonnaise –
little by little
and mixing so
that it blends
with the other
ingredients.*

Spaghettini with tapenade: *Cook 400 g/14 oz of pasta in boiling salted water until al dente, drain, tip into a pre-warmed serving dish and toss with the tapenade.*

TAPENADE

This piquant blend of black olives and anchovies comes from Provence. Ready-made tapenade, in jars, is not at all bad, so if you want to prepare a quick olive and pasta dish, the commercial product offers an alternative to home-made.

---

100 g/3½ oz black olives, preferably Niçoise olives
2 anchovy fillets, 3 garlic cloves
125 ml/4 fl oz cold-pressed extra virgin olive oil
salt and freshly ground black pepper

Stone the olives, then chop them. Cut the anchovy fillets in small pieces. Prepare the tapenade as shown in the picture sequence.

Crostini, small rounds of bread rubbed with garlic and then heated in the oven until crisp, are often served with tapenade. But it is equally popular as a sauce for pasta, for example with spaghettini. If the tapenade is too thick to coat the pasta, thin it with 2 tablespoons of the pasta cooking water.

Making tapenade:

Peel and finely chop the garlic and sauté in half of the olive oil until golden. Strain this garlic-flavoured oil and leave to cool.

In a pestle and mortar or in a food processor, pound the olives and anchovies with the remaining oil to a fine paste.

Gradually mix in the garlic-flavoured oil. Season to taste with salt and pepper.

Garlic and good-quality olive oil

First-class pasta requires ingredients of the best quality – this is particularly true of the oil

WITH GARLIC AND OLIVE OIL

'*Aglio e olio*' is one of the standard Italian preparations for pasta, and is a good example of how to conjure up a tasty dish with the minimum of ingredients. This combination also works well with other kinds of long pasta such as bucatini.

5 garlic cloves
2 fresh red chillies
125 ml/4 fl oz extra virgin olive oil
300 g/10½ oz spaghetti or other long thin pasta
salt and freshly ground black pepper

Peel and finely chop the garlic. Cut the chillies in half, remove the seeds and cut in very thin strips. Heat the oil in a small pan, add the garlic and sauté until it begins to brown. (Make sure that the garlic does not brown too much or it will taste bitter.) Add the strips of chilli and sauté briefly with the garlic. Remove the pan from the heat.

While the sauce is being prepared, cook the pasta in boiling salted water until al dente. Drain and place in a pre-warmed serving dish. Pour the sauce over the pasta and mix in thoroughly with two large forks. Season with black pepper and serve immediately.

***Top-quality olive oil** is essential for this dish because, apart from the pungency of the chillies, it is the oil that imparts flavour to the pasta. Indeed, it is the quite distinctive flavour of olive oil, particularly cold-pressed extra virgin oil, that makes this simple dish taste so superb. If you don't like the taste of olive oil you can serve the pasta with butter instead.*

Capers preserved in salt, usually coarse sea salt, are the best to use for this sauce. Capers pickled in vinegar would completely change the character of the dish. Capers in brine could be used, but they must be soaked for an hour beforehand.

WALNUT AND GARLIC SAUCE

'*Alla fornaia*' is how the Italians describe this recipe, which means 'in baker's style'. This distinctive sauce is eaten with long pasta such as spaghetti.

160 g/5¾ oz walnut pieces
100 ml/3½ fl oz extra virgin olive oil
2 garlic cloves, finely chopped
85 g/3 oz white breadcrumbs
½ teaspoon salt, freshly ground white pepper
400 g/14 oz spaghetti or other long thin pasta
1 tablespoon chopped fresh parsley

Chop the walnuts into small pieces. Warm 85 ml/ 3 fl oz of the oil in a saucepan, add the walnuts, garlic and breadcrumbs and sauté gently, stirring constantly, until the garlic is golden brown. Season to taste with salt and pepper.

While the sauce is being prepared, cook the pasta in boiling salted water until *al dente*. Drain, tip into a pre-warmed serving dish, and mix thoroughly with the remaining oil and the walnut and garlic sauce. Sprinkle with the parsley and serve.

CAPER SAUCE

Capers are much used in pasta sauces in southern Italy, which is where caper bushes grow in profusion.

40 g/1½ oz capers preserved in salt
85 g/3 oz black olives, stoned
2 garlic cloves, 2 shallots
12 anchovy fillets, 500 g/1 lb 2 oz ripe plum tomatoes
2 fresh red chillies
6 tablespoons olive oil, salt
400 g/14 oz spaghettini, 60 g/2 oz pecorino romano cheese

Finely chop the capers and olives. Peel and finely chop the garlic and shallots. Cut the anchovy fillets into small pieces. Blanch and peel the tomatoes, remove the seeds and dice. Remove seeds from the chillies, then finely chop. Heat the oil in a saucepan, add the capers, olives, garlic, shallots and anchovies and sauté for 2–3 minutes, stirring constantly. Add the tomatoes and chillies and simmer for 15 minutes.

Meanwhile, cook the spaghettini in boiling salted water until *al dente*. Drain and mix with the sauce. Garnish with thinly shaved pecorino and serve.

Soups

Pity the poor soup! Once it used to be the main meal of the day, sitting steaming in its tureen in the middle of the table while the whole family ate their fill. In our times of plenty, however, soup has been reduced to the role of first course, and the old deep soup bowls have become little bowls and cups, too small to contain anything more than a tasty appetizer. As a result, hearty soups have been relegated to snack meals or lunch, and small pasta shapes designed to be used in soups – such as pretty little stars, melon-seed or rice shapes, or very thin noodles – have been neglected. What a shame! Soups with pasta and noodles can be either robust or elegant, suitable for any dining occasion.

In Italy, *pasta in brodo* (in broth) is eaten as a *primo*, or first course, served before the meat or fish course, or

secondo. Whether ribbon noodles or stuffed pastas are used, the distinctive feature of this dish is that the pasta is not simply tossed, ready cooked, into the hot broth but is actually cooked in it, thereby taking up the flavour of the liquid. If that liquid is just a consommé from a can the culinary effect is not exactly overwhelming, but a home-made stock can make a sublime dish, especially if the pasta has a filling that complements the flavour of the soup.

Soup containing pasta or noodles is extremely popular in Asian cooking. Apart from the indispensable spring onions, a Chinese soup will often contain a cluster of cellophane noodles or the Chinese dumplings known as wontons. Cooks can be seen on every street corner in Hong Kong making wontons, rapidly and with great skill, and then serving them to hungry passers-by in a bowl of clear broth. The solid ingredients are fished out with chopsticks and the broth is slurped down with much enjoyment.

There seem to be two things on which there is universal agreement. First, pasta should be added only to clear soup, such as a consommé, and not to soups thickened with egg yolks or cream. (Italian minestrone, which usually contains pasta, is actually a clear soup.) And, second, fillings for stuffed pasta should be compatible with the soup: ravioli or tortellini stuffed with salmon have no place in a beef or chicken soup, and beef or game fillings have no place in a fish or seafood soup. Some cooks try too hard to be creative, and the results often do not work. In cases of doubt, remember that simple unfilled pasta shapes or noodles will blend with just about everything, even the herbs and seasonings that add zest to a soup.

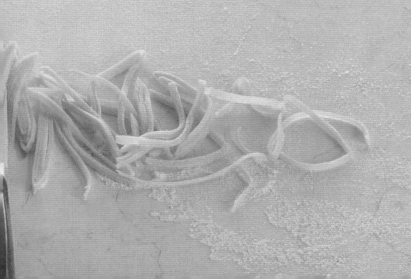

Pasta in clear broth

From capelli d'angelo to thimbles — hand-cut pasta or the fantastical shapes produced commercially

Chicken soup with home-made noodles used to be a special Sunday dish. But once pasta manufacturers gave free rein to their imaginations, cutting the dough into every imaginable shape and size, from those no bigger than a grain of rice to the alphabet shapes so popular with children, soup-making changed forever. Ultimately, however, it is not the pasta that gives the soup its flavour; it is the stock, plus the vegetables, meat and flavourings added. With a little creativity, countless variations on the theme can be produced: flavoursome beef broths, elegant consommés of game or lamb, or chicken soups.

Making beef stock:
Roast the bones, turning them from time to time. As soon as they have all turned golden brown, remove from the oven and drain off the fat. Roast the onion halves until a rich brown.

Place the bones in a large stockpot and cover with cold water.

Bring to the boil, skimming off the scum constantly with a ladle.

Add the roasted onion halves, cloves, peppercorns and bouquet garni. Simmer for 1–1½ hours.

Line a colander with a linen tea towel and set it in a pan. Ladle the stock into the colander.

Let the strained stock cool, refrigerate, then remove the solidified fat from the surface.

BEEF STOCK

Rich beef stock is popular as a basis for soups. The recipe here will produce a good clear stock. It can be made even clearer in the traditional manner by 'clarifying' it with beef and egg white. This also gives the stock a better flavour. Stocks for soup should be prepared without the addition of salt or any other powerful seasonings, since the flavour will become more concentrated when the stock is subsequently reduced and used to make soup. Freshly made stock can be kept for a few days in the refrigerator or up to 6 months in the freezer. The ingredients listed here will make about 1.5 litres/2¾ pints of stock.

2 kg/4½ lb beef bones sawed into chunks
500 g/1 lb 2 oz beef marrow bones
3 tablespoons vegetable oil
1 onion, unpeeled
2 cloves
6–8 white peppercorns
For the bouquet garni:
85 g/3 oz each carrot and leek
85 g/3 oz celeriac
½ garlic clove
a few parsley sprigs, 1 bay leaf

Preheat the oven to 180°C/350°F/gas 4. Rinse the bones, chop into equal-sized pieces and put in a roasting tin with the oil. Put the tin in the oven. Cut the onion in half and put in a small roasting tin, cut side down, without any oil. Put into the oven. Tie the ingredients for the bouquet garni together in a small piece of muslin. Continue as shown in the picture sequence.

CONSOMMÉ
WITH CAPELLINI AND PEAS

A delicate consommé, whose subtle flavour is
perfectly complemented by tender fresh peas and
thin noodles. Cooking the noodles separately keeps
the consommé clear.

100 g/3½ oz capellini
325 ml/11 fl oz beef stock (see opposite page)
150 g/5½ oz shelled fresh peas
salt
freshly ground pepper
2 courgette flowers (optional)

Cook the capellini in boiling salted water until *al
dente*, then drain and rinse briefly with cold water to
prevent the noodles sticking together. At the same
time, bring the stock to a boil, add the peas and
simmer gently for a few minutes. Add the noodles,
season the consommé and simmer for a further 2–3
minutes. Garnish with the courgette flowers.

CONSOMMÉ
WITH DITALINI AND VEGETABLES

Short pasta tubes such as ditalini are ideal for vegetable
or meat soups as they are easy to eat with a spoon.

120 g/4 oz ditalini rigati
150 g/5½ oz kohlrabi, cut into diamond shapes
60 g/2 oz carrot, cut in rounds
85 g/3 oz courgette, cut in short strips
100 g/3½ oz broccoli florets
750 ml/1¼ pints beef stock (see opposite page)
150 g/5½ oz tomatoes, peeled and chopped
salt and pepper, 1 tablespoon chopped fresh chives

Cook the pasta in boiling salted water until *al dente*;
drain and rinse with cold water. Briefly cook the
kohlrabi, carrot, courgette and broccoli in 250 ml/ 9
fl oz of the stock. Add the tomatoes and pour on
the rest of the stock. Simmer for 2–3 minutes. Add
the pasta, bring back to the boil and season to taste
with salt and pepper. Garnish with the chives.

Vegetable soup with pasta and cheese

A popular combination, and not only in Italy

MINESTRONE

This most famous of all Italian soups does not always contain pasta as it is also made with rice. If pasta is used, then a short variety, such as quadrucci, ditalini, tubettini, or gnocchetti sardi, is best.

200 g/7 oz each celery and carrot
300 g/10½ oz waxy potatoes
200 g/7 oz fresh peas in the pod
120 g/4 oz cooked or canned cannellini beans
100 g/3½ oz courgette
200 g/7 oz leeks, 4 tomatoes
20 g/scant ¾ oz butter
1 tablespoon olive oil
150 g/5½ oz small broccoli florets
a pinch of salt
freshly ground white pepper
2 litres/3½ pints chicken stock (see page 86)
120 g/4 oz tubettini rigati
100 g/3½ oz streaky bacon
1 onion, peeled
2 garlic cloves, peeled
1 tablespoon chopped fresh parsley
To serve:
85 g/3 oz Parmesan cheese, freshly grated

Trim and dice the celery. Peel and thinly slice the carrots. Peel and dice the potatoes. Shell the peas. Put the beans in a sieve, rinse under cold water and drain. Cut the courgette in rounds and then cut the rounds in half. Slice the leeks in thin rings. Blanch and peel the tomatoes, then cut in half, remove the seeds and cut the flesh in strips. Heat the butter and oil in a large pan. Add the celery, carrots, potatoes, peas, broccoli and beans. Season with salt and pepper and sauté briefly. Pour on the chicken stock and bring to the boil. Add the pasta. After simmering for 5–8 minutes, add the courgette and leeks.

Finely chop the bacon, onion and garlic and sauté together in a frying pan over moderate heat for 20 minutes. Add to the soup, together with the tomato strips and parsley. Ladle the soup into bowls and serve with the Parmesan.

GREEK TOMATO SOUP
WITH ORZO

A real summer soup, made all around the
Mediterranean. The preparation is basically the same
in the different countries – all that changes is the
shape of the pasta added to the soup. In Greece, it
usually contains orzo, the tiny pasta shaped like
grains of rice. Italian cooks prefer short pasta tubes
such as ditalini or pennini piccoli, although they
sometimes use risoni, as one rice-shaped variety is
called in Italy. It is vital to use really ripe tomatoes
with a fully developed, fruity flavour, otherwise the
soup will be dull and insipid. If good fresh tomatoes
are not available, use canned rather than making do
with unripe fresh ones. The Greek cheeses suggested
in the recipe go particularly well with the soup, but
you could also use a mature pecorino romano.

500 g/1 lb 2 oz red, ripe tomatoes
1 garlic clove, 85 g/3 oz onion
85 g/3 oz carrot, 50 g/1¾ oz celery
½ bunch of fresh parsley with stalks
2 tablespoons extra virgin olive oil
750 ml/1¼ pints veal stock, a sprig of thyme
a handful of lovage or celery leaves
salt and freshly ground black pepper
120 g/4 oz orzo
50 g/1¾ oz kefalotiri or feta cheese

Wash the tomatoes, cut out the cores and chop
coarsely. Peel and finely chop the garlic and onion.
Peel the carrot and trim the celery; cut both in
small pieces. Chop the parsley, including the stalks.
Heat the oil in a large pan and sauté the onion and
garlic until translucent. Add the carrot, celery and
parsley and cook for 4–5 minutes, stirring constantly.
Add the chopped tomatoes and cook for 3–4
minutes, then pour on the veal stock. Add the sprig
of thyme and the lovage leaves and season with
salt and pepper. Simmer over a low heat for about
30 minutes.

Pour the soup through a sieve into a clean pan,
pressing down on the vegetables to extract all the
liquid, and bring to the boil again. In the meantime,
cook the pasta in boiling salted water until *al dente*.
Drain and add to the soup. Sprinkle the crumbled
cheese over each serving.

Chicken stock

A good base for many dishes

Good chicken stock is not only the basis for excellent soups but can also be used in vegetable and meat stews, sauces, risottos and many other dishes. A rich, nutritious stock can be made following the same method as that given for beef stock on page 82. Other kinds of poultry, such as turkey or guinea fowl, could be used instead of chicken.

CHICKEN STOCK

Here, a whole bird is used to make the stock. The meat can be used for soup, salads or sandwiches. This will yield about 3 litres/5¼ pints of stock.

2–2.5 kg/4½–5½ lb stewing fowl, cut in quarters
1 kg/2¼ lb veal bones, chopped in pieces
4 litres/7 pints water, 20 black peppercorns
2 garlic cloves, crushed
1 onion, studded with 4 cloves
For the bouquet garni:
1 carrot, ½ leek, 1 celery stick
2 bay leaves, 2 sprigs of fresh thyme
6 sprigs of parsley

Begin preparation of the stock as shown in the 3-picture sequence left. After skimming off all the scum for the second time, simmer for 3 hours, keeping the liquid just below boiling point. After 2 hours of cooking, add the peppercorns, garlic, onion and bouquet garni, and add more water if necessary. Continue as in the picture sequence below.

Making chicken stock:
Put the chicken and veal bones in a stockpot and cover with hot water. Bring to the boil, skimming off the scum that rises to the surface. Drain the chicken and bones and rinse with warm water. Return to the pot, add the measured quantity of water and bring to the boil, skimming off any scum.

After simmering 3 hours on a very low heat, remove the chicken and reserve for later use.

Strain the stock through a colander lined with a tea towel, letting the liquid run through without pressing.

When the stock has cooled, remove the fat that will have solidified on the surface.

CHICKEN BROTH WITH TAGLIATELLE AND CHICKEN LIVERS

200 g/7 oz tagliatelle, 2 tablespoons vegetable oil
200 g/7 oz chicken livers, carefully cleaned and trimmed
1 tablespoon finely chopped shallot
200 g/7 oz tomatoes, peeled and diced
1 teaspoon chopped fresh oregano
2 tablespoons chopped fresh parsley
salt and freshly ground black pepper
750 ml/1¼ pints boiling chicken stock

Cook the tagliatelle in boiling salted water until *al dente*; drain and rinse briefly with cold water. Heat the oil in a saucepan, add the chicken livers and brown on all sides. Remove and cut into cubes. Return the chicken livers to the pan, add the shallot and diced tomatoes and sauté over high heat, stirring, until the livers are just cooked. Stir in the oregano and half of the parsley and season. Add the noodles. Divide among soup bowls, ladle in the hot stock and garnish with the remaining parsley.

CHICKEN BROTH WITH CAPELLI D'ANGELO AND VEGETABLES

750 ml/1¼ pints chicken stock
85 g/3 oz mange-touts, cut into diamond shapes
50 g/1¾ oz carrot, cut into thin sticks
50 g/1¾ oz celeriac, cut into thin sticks
salt and freshly ground black pepper
100 g/3½ oz capelli d'angelo (angel-hair pasta)

Bring the chicken stock to the boil and cook the vegetables in it until just tender. Cook the mange-touts first, adding the carrot and celeriac after 2–3 minutes and cooking for a further 1–2 minutes. Season to taste. At the same time, cook the pasta in boiling salted water for 1–2 minutes or until *al dente* and drain. Divide the pasta among soup bowls and ladle the stock and vegetables over the top.

BEAN SOUP
WITH PENNETTE RIGATE

'*Pasta e fagioli*' – pasta and beans – is a combination that is served in many regions of Italy, as well as in Greece. It is most popular in Tuscany, where home-made fettuccine or tagliatelle, cut in small pieces, are used. The soup here can also be made with short pasta such as ditali, lumachine, or pennette (small penne).

---

250 g/9 oz dried beans: borlotti, cannellini, navy
2 bay leaves, 6–8 fresh sage leaves
1 sprig of fresh savory, 2 garlic cloves
9 tablespoons olive oil, 100 g/3½ oz celery
150 g/5½ oz each red and green pepper
50 g/1¾ oz each onion and carrot
100 g/3½ oz tomatoes, peeled and chopped

---

1 litre/1¾ pints chicken stock (see page 86)
salt and pepper, 1 teaspoon fresh thyme leaves
2 tablespoons chopped fresh basil
200 g/7 oz pennette rigate
freshly grated Parmesan cheese

Soak the beans overnight. Drain and place in a large shallow pan with the bay leaves, sage leaves and savory. Crush the unpeeled garlic cloves with the side of a knife and add to the pan. Pour in 6 tablespoons of the oil and enough water to cover the beans by about 4 cm/1½ in. Bring to the boil, then lower the heat and simmer gently for about 1½ hours until the beans are very soft.

Meanwhile, trim and dice the celery. Cut the peppers in half, remove the core and seeds and cut in strips. Chop the onion and dice the carrot. Heat the remaining oil in a large pan and fry the onions until translucent. Add all the remaining vegetables and sauté for 2–3 minutes. Add the stock, bring to the boil and simmer for 30–40 minutes.

Remove the herbs and garlic cloves from the beans and discard. Purée half of the beans in a blender or food processor, then press through a sieve. Add the bean purée and the whole beans to the soup and bring it back to the boil. Season with salt and pepper and add the thyme and basil. Cook the pasta in boiling salted water until *al dente*; drain and add to the soup. Serve Parmesan separately.

MOROCCAN VEGETABLE SOUP
WITH VERMICELLI

The Arabs are one of the peoples who claim the discovery of pasta for themselves, noting that pasta would last longer than flour and would be easier to transport on long caravan journeys through the desert. This is a plausible claim, particularly since

there is good evidence that the Arabs introduced pasta into Sicily and southern Italy and since there are pasta dishes of Arab origin. However, today pasta is not much eaten in the Arab countries of North Africa, with the exception of soups, which often contain very thin vermicelli. One of these traditional soups is made with lamb or chicken and vegetables (with chickpeas always in evidence). If you prefer, the pasta can be cooked separately, in boiling salted water, but by cooking it in the soup, it absorbs all the spicy flavours.

400 g/14 oz boned shoulder of lamb
500 g/1 lb 2 oz tomatoes, 200 g/7 oz onion
100 g/3½ oz carrot
200 g/7 oz courgettes, as small as possible
150 g/5½ oz celery, 3 tablespoons olive oil
¼ teaspoon ground cinnamon
a pinch of cayenne, 2 tablespoons paprika
a pinch of ground saffron, salt and pepper
1 litre/1¾ pints lamb stock or chicken stock
(see page 86)

100 g/3½ oz cooked or canned chickpeas
100 g/3½ oz courgette flowers, 200 g/7 oz vermicelli
To garnish:
small fresh coriander leaves

Cut the lamb into 1.5 cm/⅝ in cubes. Blanch the tomatoes, peel them, cut in half, remove the seeds and dice. Peel and finely chop the onion. Cut the carrot into 1 cm/⅜ in cubes and thinly slice the courgettes and celery. Heat the oil in a large pan and brown the cubes of lamb on all sides; remove from the pan. Sauté the onion in the remaining oil until translucent. Add the carrot and fry for a further 2 minutes, stirring constantly. Add the courgettes and celery and sauté briefly. Stir in the diced tomatoes, mixing thoroughly with the other ingredients. Return the lamb to the pan together with the spices and salt and pepper to taste. Add the stock, bring to the boil and simmer gently for about 30 minutes.

After 20 minutes, add the chickpeas. After a further 7 minutes, add the chopped courgette flowers and vermicelli. When the soup is ready, check the seasoning. Ladle into warmed bowls and garnish with coriander leaves.

CHINESE NOODLE SOUP
WITH PORK AND VEGETABLES

One of the attractions of this Chinese soup is the
contrast between different textures: the soft noodles,
the chewy fried pork and the crisp vegetables.

250 g/9 oz pork fillet, salt
2 tablespoons dark soya sauce
2 tablespoons rice wine, 1 tablespoon caster sugar
2 tablespoons vegetable oil
For the noodle broth:
500 ml/18 fl oz chicken stock (see page 86)
100 g/3½ oz Chinese egg noodles, 200 ml/7 fl oz water
2 tablespoons light soya sauce, 2 tablespoons rice wine
For the vegetables:
2 tablespoons vegetable oil
4 spring onions, cut into 4 cm/1½ in pieces
70 g/2½ oz sliced bamboo shoots
1 fresh red chilli, deseeded and cut into rings
100 g/3½ oz spinach, washed and thick stalks removed
salt and freshly ground pepper

Season the pork with salt and pepper. Mix together
the soya sauce, rice wine and sugar. Heat the oil in a
wok over high heat and brown the pork quickly on
all sides. Reduce the heat and cook for a further 15
minutes, turning and basting frequently with the soya
sauce mixture. Wrap the pork in foil and keep warm.

Wipe the wok clean with paper towels. Cook
the noodles in the wok as shown in the picture
sequence below. Drain the noodles, reserving the
cooking liquid, and set aside. Put the liquid in a
saucepan, stir in the soya sauce and rice wine, and
season with salt. Leave this broth to heat gently.

Wipe the wok clean again. Heat the oil and
briefly stir-fry the spring onions. Add the bamboo
shoots and chilli and stir-fry for 1 minute. Add the
spinach and stir-fry until it wilts. Season to taste.

Cut the pork in thin slices. Divide the noodles
among the soup bowls and add the pork and
vegetables. Ladle in the broth and serve.

Cooking egg noodles:
*Pour the stock into the
wok, bring to the boil
and add the noodles.*

*Bring the stock back to the
boil over high heat and break
up the noodles with chopsticks
so that they will cook evenly.*

*As soon as the stock is boiling
again, pour in the water.
Cook, stirring occasionally to
prevent the noodles from
sticking.*

CELLOPHANE NOODLE SOUP WITH MEATBALLS AND VEGETABLES

In Asian soups, cellophane noodles, also called bean-thread noodles, are used to provide a background for other, more strongly flavoured ingredients. They blend well with just about anything, allowing the flavours and texture of ingredients such as meat and vegetables to come to the fore.

100 g/3½ oz cellophane noodles
For the meatballs:
250 g/9 oz lean minced pork
1 tablespoon fish sauce (nam pla)
1 tablespoon soya sauce
1 teaspoon five-spice powder
salt
For the broth:
1 litre/1¾ pints vegetable stock
3 tablespoons fish sauce (nam pla)
For the vegetables:
60 g/2 oz carrot
15 g/½ oz dried tree or wood ear mushrooms, reconstituted in water
100 g/3½ oz white cabbage, shredded
100 g/3½ oz leeks, thinly sliced
2 spring onions, sliced
50 g/1¾ oz bamboo shoots, cut into thin strips
To garnish:
2 garlic cloves, finely chopped
1 tablespoon vegetable oil
fresh coriander leaves

To make the meatballs, mix the minced pork with the fish sauce, soya sauce, five-spice powder and some salt. Shape into balls about 2.5 cm/1 in in diameter. Drop into a pan of boiling salted water and cook for 3–4 minutes, then drain.

Mix the vegetable stock with the fish sauce in a large pan and bring to the boil. Cut the carrot in matchstick-sized strips. Drain and chop the mushrooms.

Add the vegetables to the simmering broth in the following sequence: first the white cabbage; after 2 minutes the carrot; after another 2 minutes the leeks and spring onions; and after a further 1 minute the bamboo shoots and mushrooms. Then reduce the heat, add the cellophane noodles to the soup and cook for 2 minutes to soften. Add the meatballs.

Quickly fry the garlic in the oil in a small pan until golden brown. Ladle the soup into bowls, distributing the ingredients as evenly as possible. Sprinkle each serving with the fried garlic and garnish with coriander leaves.

Crispy wonton soup

Deliciously contrasting textures are one of the delights of Chinese cooking

Wontons are one of the best-known dishes in the southern provinces of China and may be stuffed with pork or seafood, particularly prawns, depending on the region. They are now found all over Southeast Asia, wherever Chinese people have settled – they are part of the Nonya cuisine of Malaysia and of the regional cooking of Indochina. In the Philippines, they are not deep-fried but instead are boiled and served in chicken broth.

Wonton wrappers, which are small squares of paper-thin pasta, are seldom made at home, even in China. In order to make the effort of preparing wontons worthwhile, it is a good idea to make a large quantity. They taste equally good hot or cold, and are an ideal snack and an indispensable part of any selection of dim sum.

NOODLE SOUP

1 tablespoon dried shrimp
150 ml/1¼ pints hot water, 1 tablespoon groundnut oil
20 g/scant ¾ oz piece of fresh root ginger, sliced
1 litre/1¾ pints chicken stock (see page 86)
200 g/7 oz Cantonese or other Chinese noodles
1 small head of Chinese cabbage (pak choi)
1 tablespoon light soya sauce
salt and freshly ground pepper, 1 tablespoon caster sugar
fresh coriander leaves to garnish

Soak the dried shrimp in the hot water for about 30 minutes; drain, reserving the water. Heat the oil in a pan large enough to hold the finished soup and add the sliced ginger and shrimp. Stir-fry for 1 minute, then add the stock and the reserved water. Reduce the heat and simmer gently for about 30 minutes. Meanwhile, cook the noodles in boiling salted water until *al dente*; drain and rinse with cold water.

Add the green parts of the cabbage leaves to the soup and simmer until wilted. Add the noodles and season with soya sauce, salt, pepper and sugar. Ladle into soup bowls and add 3 or 4 deep-fried wontons to each bowl. Garnish with coriander leaves.

WONTONS

200 g/7 oz fresh belly pork
100 g/3½ peeled raw prawns
60 g/2 oz spring onions, finely chopped
2 tablespoons oriental sesame oil
1 teaspoon salt, freshly ground pepper
1 egg yolk, 40–60 wonton wrappers
oil for deep frying

Put the pork and prawns through the fine blade of a mincer, chop in a food processor or finely chop with a large knife or a Chinese cleaver. Combine the pork, prawns, spring onions, sesame oil, salt, pepper and egg yolk in a bowl and mix well. There are two methods of stuffing the wontons: you can use two wrappers for each, as shown below, or just one. In the latter case, stuff and fold the wontons in the same

Stuffing wontons:

Place 2 wonton wrappers on top of each other on your hand and put a little stuffing near one corner of the stacked wrappers.

Fold that corner over the stuffing and then roll up, leaving the top third of the wrapper flat.

Brush the two ends of the roll with a little egg white, then fold them up over the roll and press firmly together.

Pull the top corners of the two wrappers apart. Keep the wontons covered with a damp cloth until ready to cook.

way but do not pull apart the two ends. As the wontons are prepared, keep them covered to prevent them drying out.

Heat the oil to about 180°C/350°F and fry the wontons until light brown. Drain on paper towels.

PANCIT MOLO

This is the Filipino version of Chinese wonton soup. Here, the wontons are boiled rather than deep-fried.

(not illustrated)
For the stuffing:
100g/3½ oz lean boneless pork
100g/3½ oz peeled raw prawns
30 g/1 oz water chestnuts, finely chopped
30 g/1 oz spring onions, finely chopped
½ teaspoon salt, 1 tablespoon light soya sauce
freshly ground pepper, 1 egg white, lightly beaten
about 40 wonton wrappers
For the soup:
200 g/7 oz skinned and boned chicken breast
1 litre/1¾ pints chicken stock (see page 86)
200 g/7 oz peeled raw prawns
60 g/2 oz spring onions, finely chopped
2 garlic cloves, finely chopped, 1 tablespoon light soya sauce
1 tablespoon fish sauce (nam pla)
salt and freshly ground pepper
fresh coriander leaves to garnish

Mince or finely chop the pork and prawns. Mix with the water chestnuts, spring onions, salt, soya sauce, pepper and egg white. Use the mixture to stuff the wonton wrappers, as shown in the picture sequence left. Cook the wontons in boiling salted water for about 4 minutes. Remove with a slotted spoon and place in a bowl of cold water. Drain.

Cut the chicken meat for the soup in thin strips. Bring the stock to the boil, add the chicken, prawns and spring onions and season with the garlic, the soya and fish sauces, salt and pepper. Simmer for 3–4 minutes. Add the stuffed wontons and leave to stand, off the heat, for a few minutes. Garnish with coriander leaves.

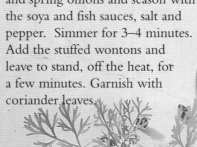

With cheese, herbs and spices

Cheese and pasta have been a successful combination since time immemorial. Virtually all hard or semi-hard cheeses that melt when heated can be used. The best known of these, Parmesan, which comes from northern Italy, is one of the few cheeses that does not form long threads as it melts. As a result, it is the perfect partner for pasta, especially as spaghetti or taglierini coated with grated Parmesan can be eaten more or less decorously.

Perhaps the most sublime dish of pasta and cheese is that created by the legendary Alfredo of Rome. His *Fettuccine all'Alfredo* demonstrates most impressively that a world-class pasta dish can be produced with almost nothing other than cheese. The dish certainly merits a brief description here. After cooking the pasta, a little of the boiling hot cooking water is poured into a warmed gratin dish; some freshly grated *grana padano* (hard grating cheese) and a generous quantity of butter are added to the water and whisked together with a fork until pale and creamy; then the pasta – fresh and home-made of course – is added and stirred with two forks (gold-plated ones in Alfredo's kitchen) until it gleams enticingly. It is recommended that an egg yolk be added to finish off the dish to perfection, but this is optional. However, cream has absolutely no place in this recipe, contrary to the belief still held by many cooks.

There can be no mention of Asian dishes in connection with cheese, since both cheese and butter are wholly alien to that part of the world. Instead, Asian pasta dishes make use of herb and spice mixtures, particularly those containing fiery hot chillies. Hot spices can turn a bland plate of pasta into a real challenge for the taste buds and make the sweat pour from diners' foreheads. Garlic, too, can have an impact. In Italy, garlic often plays the starring role in a simple sauce – in combination with olive oil, it makes up the famous *aglio e olio* sauce. Virtually any herb or spice can be combined with pasta or added to the cooking liquid. Saffron is an excellent flavouring, and gives a delicate yellow colour, too. One well-respected European chef likes to cook his pasta in coconut milk and season it with fresh coriander leaves. The imagination knows no bounds.

One of the more recent innovations in the culinary art is sheets of pasta patterned with fresh herb leaves. The result is very decorative. Despite the impressive appearance, the preparation of this herb pasta is not as difficult as you might think.

With butter and cheese

The simplest is also the most elegant

Adding butter is the simplest way of serving pasta. Butter coats pasta in a thin film, making it glisten and imparting a wonderful taste. It is added when the pasta is cooked and drained but still warm. And by using browned butter (*beurre noisette*), or with the addition of a few fresh herbs, you can impart even more flavour. The brief contact with heat allows the flavour of herbs to develop to perfection. A word of warning: pasta tossed with too much butter becomes very slippery. This is a problem with dishes to be served with a sauce, since the sauce and pasta will not combine readily if the pasta is too buttery.

It is hard to imagine Italian pasta without cheese, and there are so many dishes that make use of this delicious combination. The types of cheese used with pasta range from fontina, which melts readily, to the extra hard, crumbly cheeses of the Parmesan family. Whatever is used, it must be freshly prepared to guarantee the best flavour. Whether chopped into small pieces, sliced, grated, or cut in fine shavings, the cheese is generally mixed into the pasta or sprinkled on top of it just before serving. The melting cheese binds the pasta and gives it a creamy texture, or forms a delicious crust on top of baked pasta dishes or those finished under the grill. The combination of pasta and cheese is found outside Italy as well, namely in the Spätzle of Germany and Switzerland. There, the main types of cheese used are Gruyère and Emmental, which are excellent for grating and melting because of their high fat content.

Emmental cheese, named for Switzerland's Emmental valley, has a mellow flavour that is sweet and nutty. As it matures, its nutty flavour becomes more intense. Made from cow's milk, Emmental is light golden in colour and has marble-size holes.

Gruyère *Produced in Switzerland and France. Made from cow's milk. Rich, sweet, nutty flavour. Ideal for grating.*

Pecorino romano *Sheep's milk gives this cheese its distinctive flavour. Aged pecorino is stronger than Parmesan.*

Pecorino sardo *The embossed rind is due to the basket in which it matures. Ideal for strongly flavoured pasta dishes.*

Sbrinz *A hard, grating cheese from Switzerland. Has a rich, mellow flavour and melts particularly well.*

Idiazabal *from Spain. Made from sheep's milk. A salty, tangy, smoked cheese. Ideal for 'country-style' pasta.*

Provolone piccante *A well-aged, full-bodied grating cheese, preferred by some pasta fans to all other grating cheeses.*

Montasio vecchio *(Montasio piccante) is a flavourful grating cheese. Goes well with bacon and ham.*

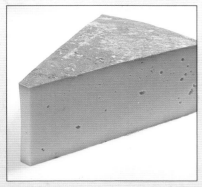

Fontina *from the Aosta valley in Italy, made from cow's milk. A mild, slightly sweet flavour. Creamy when melted.*

Taleggio *A semi-hard slicing cheese from Lombardy. Flavour changes from mild to full-bodied as it matures.*

Tyrolean Graukäse *A lightly blue-veined cheese. Has a sharp, slightly sour flavour.*

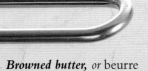

Browned butter, *or* beurre noisette, *is the simplest pasta sauce there is. The melted butter should be only very lightly browned (the colour of hazelnut shells), so that its flavour will be nutty.*

Ricotta *Moist, slightly grainy cheese made from the whey drained off from making other cheeses.*

Mozzarella di bufala *The traditional mozzarella from Campagna and Lazio, made from water-buffalo milk.*

Only the freshest

Cheese should always be freshly grated

Whatever kind of cheese is used, it should always be grated, since this is the only way of ensuring the best and fullest flavour. Under no circumstances buy packets of ready-grated cheese, even though they may be more convenient.

Parmesan is the ideal cheese to accompany pasta. Parmigiano-Reggiano, the original Italian Parmesan, plus the two kinds of *grana padano*, the closely grained cheese from the plain of the River Po made by the same method as Parmigiano-Reggiano, and *grana trentino*, from the region of the same name, are the pre-eminent hard grating cheeses, and not only in Italy. In many other countries Parmesan imitations are produced in vast quantities, but none can compare with true Parmigiano-Reggiano. One way to ensure that you have the genuine article is always to buy the cheese from a block, so that you can check the rind. As shown in the picture sequence opposite, Parmigiano-Reggiano is produced as a cylindrical block between 25 and 30 kg/55 and 66 lb in weight, and with a fat content of at least 32 per cent. It is matured for 2 years before it is brought to market; Parmigiano-Reggianos aged for 3 years are stamped *stravecchio*, and those aged 4 years *stravecchione*. Other good grating cheeses are pecorino – romano, sardo and toscano – and Sbrinz. And well-aged cheeses for slicing, such as provolone piccante, bring their own excellent flavour to pasta.

A simple metal grater, with a very sharp grating surface and small holes, is fine for grating small quantities of hard cheeses and when grating the cheese directly on to pasta. For larger quantities, a hand-cranked or electric grater will make the job easier. The traditional Italian grater shown here is ideal. The cheese is held against a roller fitted with sharp spikes and once grated it falls into the drawer beneath. For softer cheeses, such as Gruyère or Emmental, use a metal grater with larger holes. You can cut wafer-thin slices with a cheese slicing knife, or fine shavings with a vegetable peeler.

***Never grate more** than will be used that day. This way you will ensure that the pasta dish gets the benefit of the full flavour of the cheese. However, if there is some left over, store it in a jar or container with a tightly fitting top – in the refrigerator if possible.*

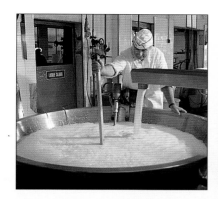   

The storeroom can accommodate up to 100,000 blocks of cheese, neatly stacked on wooden shelves. They will stay in the air-conditioned storage areas until the end of the maturing period (2 years).

  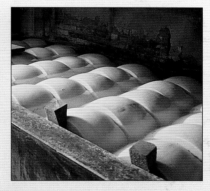

1 *Milk from the evening before is mixed with skimmed milk, then some of the cream is removed: Parmigiano-Reggiano is a relatively low-fat cheese. Whey left over from previous batches is added to encourage fermentation. The milk is heated to 47°C/117°F and rennet is added to make it curdle. The curds are cut into grain-sized pieces using a wire basket and heated to 69°C/157°F, at which point the granular mass of cheese settles to the bottom of the vat.*

2 *The cheese is now lifted from the bottom of the vat with a wooden shovel and linen cloth and eased into the cloth – an operation that requires considerable skill and care. As it is rocked to and fro, the cheese gradually forms a ball. The cloth is tied to a wooden pole suspended over the vat and the ball of cheese is divided up with a large knife. After further processing, each piece will eventually produce a whole block of Parmesan.*

3 *Still in the linen cloth, the cheese is pressed into a wooden or metal mould; the cloth is folded up over the surface. The mould is covered with a heavy wooden lid, which presses the cheese down. Thus secured, the cheese is immersed in a bath of salted water for 20–25 days. After this it is left undisturbed for the next 2 years to mature. Finally, the 'Parmigiano-Reggiano' brand mark is stamped on the rind to guarantee authenticity.*

A fine show

Although extravagant, this makes a real impact

To use half a block of Parmesan as a decorative container for serving pasta might seem just a joke from an eccentric chef, since there are certainly much simpler – and cheaper – ways of adding cheese to pasta. But, in fact, although it is obviously not suitable for a meal for two, it would make a great centrepiece for a pasta party. What is served in the cheese will seem very special indeed, and the half-block of cheese can be used again and again in the same way. If a relatively small amount of pasta is to be served, enough for four or six portions, for example, then the hollow in the cheese does not have to be very big. After repeated use, however, the hollow will become deeper and deeper. Once the pasta has been served, a layer of soft, melted cheese will be left behind and this should be scraped out along with the remaining sauce. Then the half-block of cheese can be kept clean and ready for the next occasion. Use spaghetti or tubular pasta such as macaroni, bucatini, ziti and so on for this presentation, since the pasta has to be turned repeatedly in the hollow to coat it in melting cheese.

BUCATINI SERVED IN A BLOCK OF PARMESAN

The following recipe will produce 4–6 servings, but the quantities can be increased, depending on the number of guests and the capacity of the block of cheese. The highly concentrated veal stock gives the pasta a particularly hearty flavour.

1 litre/1¾ pints veal stock
100 g/3½ oz onion, 1 garlic clove
50 g/1¾ oz each carrot and celery
4 tablespoons extra virgin olive oil
300 g/10½ oz tomatoes
2 small fresh chillies
½ teaspoon salt, freshly ground pepper
500 g/1 lb 2 oz bucatini
3 tablespoons 90% proof alcohol such as grappa

Bring the stock to a boil and simmer gently until only about 100 ml/3½ fl oz remains. Meanwhile, peel the onion, garlic and carrot; trim the celery. Finely chop all these vegetables. Heat the oil in a frying pan and sauté the chopped vegetables until they are quite soft. Blanch the tomatoes, peel, remove the seeds and dice. Cut the chillies in half lengthways, remove the seeds and core and finely chop. Add the tomatoes and chillies to the pan and season with salt and pepper. Cook the pasta in boiling salted water until *al dente*; drain and mix immediately with the reduced stock and the sauce.

Just before the pasta has finished cooking, flame the alcohol in the cheese (see picture sequence, right). Transfer the pasta while still hot to the hollow in the half-block of Parmesan and toss well.

ZITI IN A PIQUANT CREAM AND PANCETTA SAUCE

A combination well suited to 'the cheese treatment'. Pancetta is unsmoked bacon cured with salt and spices. A dry Lambrusco from the region around Modena would accompany the dish to perfection.

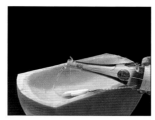

Filling the block of Parmesan:

Pour a generous measure of high-proof alcohol into the hollow cut out of the half-block of cheese.

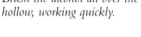

Brush the alcohol all over the hollow, working quickly.

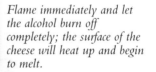

Flame immediately and let the alcohol burn off completely; the surface of the cheese will heat up and begin to melt.

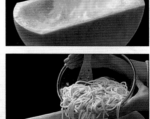

Pour the hot cooked pasta into the hollow in the cheese.

Stir the pasta with a wooden fork to mix it with the melting cheese.

In Italian restaurants *the dish is normally prepared at the table, in huge rounds of Parmesan that have been cut in half crossways.*

(not illustrated)
200 g/7 oz pancetta, cubed, 3–4 tablespoons vegetable oil
85 g/3 oz chopped onion, 2 garlic cloves, chopped
100 g/3½ oz diced celery
½ teaspoon salt, freshly ground pepper
125 ml/4 fl oz double cream
2 fresh chillies, deseeded and finely chopped
a handful of small fresh basil leaves
500 g/1 lb 2 oz ziti

Fry the pancetta, without any additional fat, stirring constantly. Keep warm. Heat the oil in a saucepan and sauté the onion, garlic and celery (including the leaves) until translucent. Add the pancetta and season with salt and pepper. Pour in the cream and boil to reduce by about half. Add the chillies and the basil leaves, whole or coarsely shredded.

In the meantime, cook the pasta in boiling salted water until *al dente*. Drain and mix with the sauce. Transfer to the hollow in the cheese and toss.

Cheese and pasta

Hard cheeses are not the only ones suitable for pasta dishes – soft cheeses also work well

WHOLEMEAL PENNE WITH LEEK AND CHEESE SAUCE

Penne rigate is a fairly 'rustic' kind of pasta, particularly when made from wholemeal flour. It is good with this leek sauce, which gets its tangy flavour from pecorino cheese. For an optional finishing touch, place a slice of ripe taleggio on each serving and melt under the grill.

350 g/12 oz wholemeal penne rigate
For the sauce:
200 g/7 oz leeks, ½ garlic clove
85 g/3 oz butter
125 ml/4 fl oz meat stock, 125 ml/4 fl oz cream
1 teaspoon salt, freshly ground pepper
85 g/3 oz pecorino romano cheese, freshly grated
2 tablespoons chopped fresh chives to garnish

Cut the leeks in half lengthways and remove any traces of grit by washing thoroughly in cold water. Cut across in thin strips. Finely chop the garlic and sauté in the butter with the leek for 2–3 minutes. Add the stock, bring to the boil and reduce by about half. Stir in the cream. Season with salt and pepper and, finally, stir in the pecorino. In the meantime, cook the pasta in boiling salted water until *al dente*; drain and mix immediately with the sauce. Transfer to plates and serve garnished with chopped chives.

*Gorgonzola dolce is a mild variety of this Italian blue-veined cheese. It is less salty than the stronger variety, gorgonzola piccante, and has less blue veining. Another famous blue cheese is the French **Roquefort**. It is made from full-fat sheep's milk and has a rich, creamy texture and pungent flavour. The riper it is, the stronger the flavour will be.*

FRESH TAGLIATELLE WITH GORGONZOLA AND ROQUEFORT

This combination is surprisingly subtle – the sweetish flavour of the gorgonzola contrasts well with the salty tanginess of the Roquefort.

1 recipe of fresh pasta dough no. 4 (see page 40)
For the sauce:
30 g/1 oz butter, 30 g/1 oz shallots, finely chopped
100 ml/3½ fl oz double cream
150 g/5 oz gorgonzola dolce
To finish:
120 g/4 oz ripe Roquefort
120 g/4 oz cherry tomatoes
30 g/1 oz butter, 8 fresh sage leaves
salt and freshly ground pepper

Using a knife or a pasta machine, cut the pasta dough into tagliatelle (see pages 52 and 53). Melt the butter in a saucepan and sauté the shallots until translucent. Stir in the cream. Cut the gorgonzola (minus the rind) in cubes and add to the sauce. Melt the cheese over a low heat, stirring occasionally. Once the

cheese has melted, bring the sauce just to the boil.

In the meantime, cook the tagliatelle in boiling salted water until *al dente*. Drain and mix immediately with the gorgonzola sauce. Divide the pasta among 4 plates. Sprinkle each serving with flakes of Roquefort and place under the grill to melt the cheese. Meanwhile, cut the tomatoes in half and sauté briefly in the hot butter with the sage. Season with salt and pepper and use to garnish the pasta.

CORNMEAL PASTA WITH TOMATOES AND GOAT'S CHEESE

The fresh, tangy taste of goat's cheese combines beautifully with the aromatic tomato sauce, while the cornmeal pasta complements the whole perfectly.

For the pasta dough:
150 g/5½ oz cornmeal
150 g/5½ oz plain flour, preferably type 00
2 eggs, 2 egg yolks
1 tablespoon olive oil, ½ tablespoon salt
grated nutmeg

For the sauce:
300 g/10½ oz tomatoes, 2 garlic cloves
4 tablespoons extra virgin olive oil
60 g/2 oz finely chopped onion
2 tablespoons chopped fresh herbs: thyme, sage, rosemary
½ teaspoon salt, freshly ground pepper
6 tablespoons meat stock, 160 g/6½ oz goat's cheese, cubed

Make the pasta dough, following the directions on page 43. Leave to rest and then cut into thin noodles with a knife or a pasta machine (see pages 52 and 53). Spread out the noodles on a cloth and allow to dry a little so they will not stick together while cooking. To make the sauce, blanch the tomatoes, peel, cut in half, remove the seeds and dice. Peel and finely chop the garlic. Heat the oil and sauté the onion and garlic until translucent. Add the tomatoes and cook for a few minutes until soft but not entirely broken down. Add the herbs, season with salt and pepper and stir in the meat stock. Simmer for 1–2 minutes. Cook the noodles in boiling salted water until *al dente*; drain. Add the cheese to the sauce and mix immediately with the pasta so the cubes do not melt completely.

Pasta with cheese *(from left to right): wholemeal penne, tagliatelle and cornmeal noodles.*

HERB-FLAVOURED SPÄTZLE WITH APPENZELLER CHEESE

The tart fruitiness of Appenzeller cheese makes it a particularly good partner for the intense herby flavour of these Spätzle; onions fried in butter finish the dish off perfectly. Appenzeller, a Swiss whole-milk cheese, is given a wine or cider wash during curing, which is what makes it slightly fruity in flavour. The choice of herbs and greens will vary according to the season. In spring, you might try a mixture such as dandelion leaves, sorrel and borage. In summer, use plenty of young spinach leaves mixed with parsley, oregano, basil and a little lovage or celery leaf.

For the dough:
100 g/3½ oz mixed fresh herbs, chopped
300 g/10½ oz plain flour
6 eggs, 1 teaspoon salt, 1 tablespoon oil
To finish:
150 g/5½ oz Appenzeller cheese
100 g/3½ oz onion
85 g/3 oz butter
8 small tomatoes

Put the herbs in a mortar and pound with the pestle almost to a paste (or purée in a food processor). Sift the flour into a bowl and add the eggs, salt, oil and herbs. Continue as shown in the picture sequence below. Cook the Spätzle in boiling salted water (see also page 63) until they rise to the surface. Lift them out of the water with a slotted spoon, letting them drain thoroughly as you do so. Shred the Appenzeller. Fill a pre-warmed bowl with alternate layers of Spätzle and shredded Appenzeller. Peel the onion and slice thinly. Heat 60 g/2 oz of the butter in a frying pan and fry the onions until golden brown. Pour the onions and butter over the Spätzle. Serve on to 4 plates and garnish each portion with 2 tomatoes sautéed in the remaining butter.

Preparing herb-flavoured Spätzle:

Mix all the ingredients thoroughly with a wooden spoon and beat to a smooth, creamy consistency.

Using a knife or palette knife, scrape the dough, in small portions, from the board into the boiling salted water.

PASTA IN A PIQUANT CREAM SAUCE

Short tubular pasta, such as mezze penne rigate, ditali rigati or lumachine, is best suited to this dish. Use the recipe as a starting point, altering it as you wish by using a different type of cheese or adding vegetables, ham, or left-over roast meat. The pungent chillies will complement almost any other flavour.

1 garlic clove
2 heaping tablespoons nasturtium leaves and flowers
2 small fresh chillies
30 g/1 oz butter
30 g/1 oz shallots, finely chopped
400 g/14 oz mezze penne rigate
For the cream sauce:
250 ml/9 fl oz double cream
85 g/3 oz fontina cheese
50 g/1¾ oz Parmesan cheese, freshly grated
salt
freshly ground white pepper
To garnish:
60 g/2 oz ripe Roquefort
4 nasturtium flowers

Peel and finely chop the garlic. Cut the nasturtium leaves and flowers in thin strips. Cut the chillies in half, remove the core and seeds and finely chop. Heat the butter in a frying pan and sauté the shallots and garlic until translucent. Add the nasturtiums and chillies and remove immediately from the heat.

Boil the cream to reduce by about one third. Gradually whisk in the cubed fontina, letting it melt slowly. Remove from the heat and allow to cool a little, then stir in the grated Parmesan. Cook the pasta in boiling salted water until *al dente*; drain thoroughly, transfer to a pre-warmed bowl and mix with the cream sauce and the sautéed vegetable mixture. Season with salt and pepper and serve on to plates. Cut the Roquefort in small cubes, sprinkle over the pasta and place under the grill until the Roquefort begins to melt, 1–2 minutes at most. Garnish each plate with a nasturtium flower and serve immediately.

Pasta with herbs

These pastas can be served with a meat sauce or other highly flavoured sauces

BASIL-FLAVOURED NOODLES WITH SALAMI SAUCE

Here, the dominant flavour is that of the fresh herbs, even though the dish includes pungent Italian salami. When the pasta is flavoured unmistakably with basil and the sauce is seasoned with thyme, rosemary and parsley, the other flavours take a back seat.

For the pasta dough:
20 g/¾ oz fresh basil leaves, 1 garlic clove, ½ teaspoon salt
300 g/10½ oz plain flour, preferably type 00
3 eggs, 3 tablespoons olive oil
For the sauce:
300 g/10½ oz well-flavoured salami
400g/14 oz tomatoes, peeled and deseeded
25 g/scant 1 oz dried porcini or 250 g/9 oz fresh mushrooms
2 tablespoons olive oil, 1 onion, finely chopped
4 tablespoons red wine
salt and freshly ground pepper
1 tablespoon chopped fresh parsley
½ tablespoon chopped fresh thyme
½ tablespoon chopped fresh rosemary

Make the dough as directed in the picture sequence below and on page 41. Cut the salami and tomatoes into dice. If you are using dried porcini, soak them in 4 tablespoons of warm water; fresh ones should be washed and sliced. Heat the oil and sauté the onion until translucent. Add the salami and porcini and sauté for 10 minutes, stirring constantly. Stir in the tomatoes and wine (with the strained soaking water if dried porcini are used) and season. Simmer, uncovered, for about 50 minutes until the sauce is thick. Check the seasoning and stir in the herbs.

Roll the pasta dough thinly and cut maltagliati from it, as shown on page 55. Cook in boiling salted water until *al dente*; drain. Arrange the noodles immediately on plates and pour the sauce over them.

Making the basil-flavoured dough:

Put the basil leaves, garlic and salt in a mortar and pound to a fine purée with the pestle.

Mound the flour on a work surface, form a well and add the eggs, oil and the basil and garlic purée.

SPRING HERB PASTA

This pasta is made in Liguria and Provence in the spring and is served simply with butter and cheese.

For the pasta dough:
120 g/4 oz fresh spring herbs (see caption, right)
salt and a little freshly ground pepper
1 tablespoon olive oil
350 g/12 oz plain flour, preferably type 00
2 eggs, water as required
To finish:
4 seagull's eggs (optional), 60 g/2 oz butter
100 g/3½ oz Parmesan cheese, freshly grated

Prepare the dough as shown in the picture sequence, kneading it until the flour is evenly coloured green by the herbs. Cook the pasta squares in boiling salted water until *al dente*, about 8 minutes. Meanwhile, boil the seagull's eggs for 8 minutes, then peel. Arrange the pasta and eggs on pre-warmed plates and serve with foaming browned butter and Parmesan.

Sift the flour on to a work surface, form a well in the centre and add the herb mixture and eggs.

Mix and knead to a smooth dough, as described on page 41; add water as required.

Roll out the dough into a sheet 3 mm/⅛ in thick. With a fluted pasta wheel, cut out 4 cm/1½ in squares.

Preparing herb pasta:
First finely chop the herbs (parsley, sorrel, basil, thyme, marjoram, lemon balm, dandelion leaves), then, using a mortar and pestle, pound them to a paste with salt, pepper and the olive oil.

With bacon, spinach and herbs

The simplest combinations are often the best, and this certainly applies to Italian pasta

MALLOREDDUS WITH SPINACH AND PECORINO

It is its simplicity and the combination of strongly flavoured ingredients that make this recipe such a satisfying one. It uses a traditional type of Sardinian pasta.

200 g/7 oz fresh spinach leaves
85 g/3 oz streaky bacon
1 tablespoon olive oil
½ garlic clove
400 g/14 oz malloreddus
30 g/1 oz butter
4 tablespoons freshly grated pecorino cheese

Wash the spinach well, drain thoroughly and chop finely. Cut the bacon in small cubes and cook in a large frying pan with the oil. Peel and finely chop the garlic and sauté briefly with the bacon. Add the spinach and let it wilt. In the meantime, cook the malloreddus in boiling salted water until *al dente*. Drain the pasta and mix in a pre-warmed bowl with the butter and the bacon and spinach mixture. Sprinkle with the grated pecorino and serve immediately.

MALTAGLIATI WITH CHIVES AND BACON

This pasta should be made fresh from dough no. 1 (see page 40), cut in irregular shapes as shown on page 55.

50 g/1¾ oz streaky bacon
400 g/14 oz maltagliati
50 g/1¾ oz butter
salt and freshly ground pepper
4 tablespoons chopped fresh chives
4 tablespoons freshly grated Parmesan cheese

Cut the bacon into small pieces and cook in a large frying pan. Keep warm. Cook the maltagliati in boiling salted water until *al dente*; drain. Put the pasta in a pre-warmed bowl and add the butter and bacon. Season with salt and pepper. Mix all the ingredients together until the butter has melted. Arrange on pre-warmed plates and sprinkle with the chives and grated cheese.

MEZZE MANICHE RIGATE WITH SPRING ONIONS

This short, broad, tubular pasta really demands pungent accompaniments. Plenty of spring onions and aromatic herbs are good choices.

12 spring onions, 75 g/2½ oz butter
½ bunch of fresh parsley, chopped
2 egg yolks, 50 g/1¾ oz Parmesan cheese, freshly grated
300 g/10½ oz mezze maniche rigate
freshly ground black pepper
fresh young lovage or celery leaves, 4 cherry tomatoes

Cut the spring onions in slices (only the white parts should be used). Melt 60 g/2 oz of the butter and cook the spring onions over a low heat for about 15 minutes. If necessary, add a little water to prevent sticking. Remove from the heat. When the spring onions have cooled a little, mix in the parsley and egg yolks and then the Parmesan. In the meantime, cook the pasta in boiling salted water until *al dente*. Drain and toss with the spring onion mixture. Arrange on pre-warmed plates and sprinkle with freshly ground pepper and lovage or celery leaves. Garnish with halved cherry tomatoes that have been sautéed in the remaining butter.

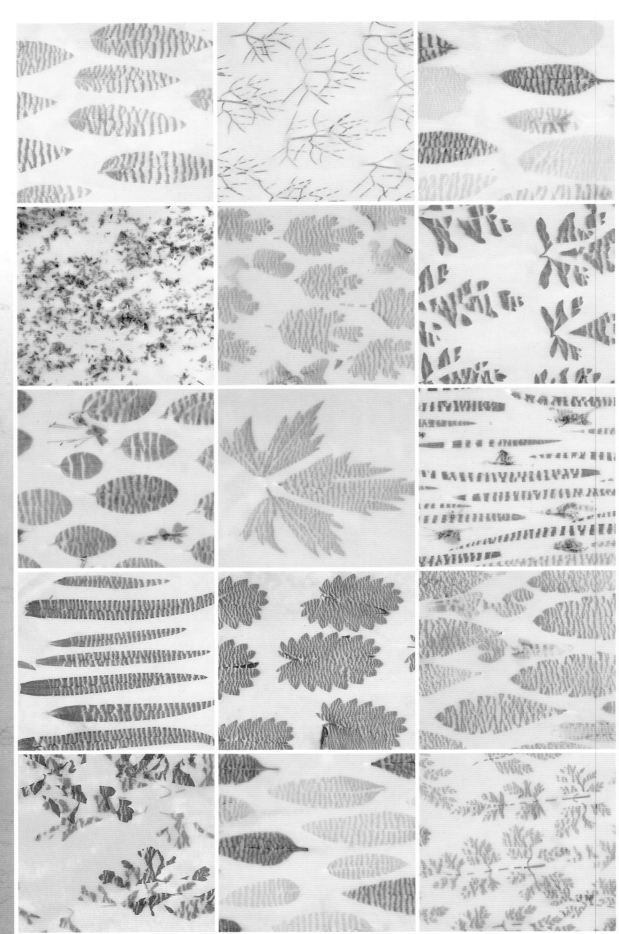

Herb pasta – a delight for creative cooks. Remember, though, that many herbs have an intense flavour, so it is worth giving a little thought to which herbs are best suited to which sauce. The pasta dough can be cut into squares, as shown here, or into pappardelle or thin ribbon noodles.

Herbs in wafer-thin sheets of pasta

Not only does this pasta taste delicious, it looks beautiful, too

225 g/8 oz plain flour, preferably type 00
2 eggs, 1 egg yolk, ½ teaspoon salt
fresh herb leaves

Make the pasta dough as described on page 41. Creating the herb patterns in the pasta dough is actually quite easy: lay the leaves in any arrangement you wish between the thinly rolled out strips of pasta dough and then roll them out again as thinly as possible, as shown in the picture sequence. In this way, the leaves take on quite extraordinary, even bizarre shapes. The rolling can be done in the traditional manner with a rolling pin or using a pasta machine. The latter method is simpler and easier, although the dough is stretched in only one direction and the leaves will be pulled only relatively small distances apart and stretched to more than twice their length. With a rolling pin, a little more effort is needed of course, but this method gives you an opportunity to modify the pattern in all directions and thus produces a quite different result. You can roll the dough alternately from top to bottom and from left to right, thereby pulling the leaves in several different directions. And depending on how much pressure is applied with the rolling pin, it is possible to vary the size of the tears made in the leaves.

Begin by rolling out a strip of dough to a thickness of about 2 mm/¹⁄₁₆ inch. Arrange the herb leaves on it and then place a second thinly rolled strip of dough on top. In order for the herbs to adhere properly, the dough must be very fresh, so if it begins to dry out, mist it with a little water. Roll out the herb-filled dough to the same thickness as before, either using a pasta machine or by hand.

There is a wide range of patterns you can create, since any herb can be used, provided it has thin, flexible leaves. Rosemary with its stiff needles is obviously unsuitable, as is any other plant with inflexible leaves. Nor should the herb have a very powerful flavour, as is the case with rosemary or savory.

The same principle can be applied to making truffle pasta, which although very expensive is truly a special culinary treat. It must be made with fresh truffles, since those from a can would be squashed into an unsightly mess when rolled between the sheets of pasta. First, carefully clean the truffles (peel black ones), then cut into wafer-thin slices, preferably with a special truffle slicer. Lay the slices on the thinly rolled sheet of pasta dough, cover with another sheet of dough and

roll thinly again. The rolling-pin method produces a more attractive pattern than a pasta machine. Both black and white truffles can be used – the white ones do not make such a pretty pattern, but their heavenly taste more than compensates. Truffle pasta needs no more accompaniment than freshly melted, foaming butter, perhaps with a little freshly grated Parmesan.

Rolling out herb pasta:

Put the dough through the smooth rollers of the pasta machine in small batches and roll it out in thin strips.

Lay one strip on a work surface, arrange herb leaves over the surface and place a second strip on top. Press down firmly.

Put the double pasta strip through the machine again and roll out thinly, to more than twice its original length.

In brodo, *which means in broth, is the perfect way to serve herb pasta. Clear chicken or beef broth will not hide the herb patterns as a sauce would. Garnish with the same herbs used in the pasta.*

With vegetables and mushrooms

Tomatoes, of course, top the list of vegetables that are combined with pasta. They are indelibly associated not only with spaghetti but with most other kinds of pasta as well, and all other vegetables pale in comparison, even visually. Nevertheless, virtually any vegetable makes a suitable partner for pasta: humble root vegetables, such as carrots and parsnips; many members of the lettuce family, particularly radicchio; fruiting vegetables such as artichokes, peppers and aubergines; and, of course, leeks, onions and garlic. All impart flavour as well as extra nutritional value to pasta dishes. Some vegetables, particularly spinach and beetroot, can be worked into the dough to produce pasta of different colours. Nor should we forget the fiery hot chillies, so popular in Asian cooking, that can transform the simplest pasta dish when used judiciously.

Whether wild or cultivated, mushrooms are a natural partner for pasta and often give more flavour than other vegetables, meat or fish, particularly when they are used in sauces. In the realm of wild mushrooms and fungi, truffles occupy a special place. Taglierini served with thin shavings of fresh white Piedmont truffle is for many gourmets the *ne plus ultra* of

pasta dishes – and also the most expensive. A number of delicious pasta dishes can also be made with black truffles, although these need to be cooked first: simmer them for a quarter of an hour in a little port and meat stock before cutting into cubes and mixing in with hot pasta. Truffles should never be combined with other edible fungi or mushrooms: they are too precious and expensive. The same is true of fresh morels, ceps and chanterelles, which have highly individual flavours and should always be used by themselves.

Pasta is usually cooked in the standard way in boiling salted water before being combined with vegetables or mushrooms. But creative cooks will know that the flavours of these ingredients can be brought out further and transferred to the pasta by using the vegetable cooking water for cooking the pasta as well. This is not always very effective, but works splendidly with strong-flavoured vegetables such as asparagus, celery and artichokes. Vegetables and pasta can even be cooked together in the same pan of water, while boiling a handful of dried porcini in the cooking water before adding the pasta will impart a most distinctive flavour.

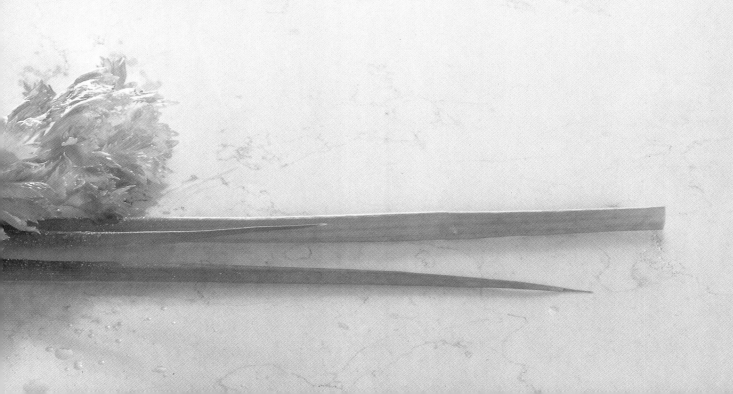

With vegetables and prosciutto

Only air-dried prosciutto has the characteristic flavour that combines so splendidly with vegetables

PENNE WITH PEAS AND PROSCIUTTO

Frozen peas can be used for this recipe – they are very convenient, after all – but the dish tastes so much better when made with peas that are fresh from the pod.

500 ml/18 fl oz veal stock, 750 g/1 lb 10 oz fresh peas
200 g/7 oz prosciutto, very thinly sliced
1 small onion, 1 garlic clove
2 small fresh chillies, 4 tablespoons olive oil
2 tablespoons chopped mixed fresh herbs: thyme, parsley, lovage or celery leaves, sage
¼ teaspoon freshly ground white pepper, salt
400 g/14 oz penne
To serve:
freshly grated pecorino or Parmesan cheese

Bring the veal stock to the boil; turn the heat to low and leave to reduce slowly until only 4–5 tablespoons of stock remain. Shell the peas and put to one side. Cut the prosciutto in small squares. Peel and finely chop the onion. Peel and crush the garlic clove. Cut the chillies in half lengthways, remove the seeds and core, and finely chop. Heat the oil in a large frying pan and sauté the onions and garlic until translucent. Add the prosciutto and fry briefly over a high heat, stirring constantly. Add the peas, herbs and chillies and pour in the reduced veal stock. Season with pepper and, if necessary, salt. Simmer for a few minutes, stirring occasionally. In the meantime, cook the penne in boiling salted water until *al dente*. Drain and mix immediately with the pea and prosciutto mixture. Transfer to 4 pre-warmed plates and sprinkle with grated cheese.

Courgette flowers and baby courgettes *are a popular accompaniment for pasta in many countries, particularly in the Mediterranean region.*

RIGATONI WITH COURGETTES AND PROSCIUTTO

Tender baby courgettes, particularly the very small ones with flowers, work well with a substantial, country-style pasta. Short tubular pasta such as rigatoni or sedanini are particularly suitable.

2 garlic cloves
300 g/10½ oz courgettes
300 g/10½ oz ripe fresh tomatoes or 200 g/7 oz canned whole tomatoes, drained
100 g/3½ oz red peppers
200 g/7 oz prosciutto, very thinly sliced
30 g/1 oz butter
60 g/2 oz shallots, finely chopped
½ teaspoon salt
freshly ground black pepper
400 g/14 oz rigatoni
To finish:
20 g/scant ¾ oz butter
8–10 fresh sage leaves
freshly grated Parmesan cheese

Peel and finely chop the garlic. Wash the courgettes and slice thinly. Blanch fresh tomatoes, peel, cut in half, remove seeds and chop; chop canned tomatoes. Wash the peppers, remove the core and seeds and cut into small cubes. Cut the prosciutto in small squares. Heat the butter in a suitably sized frying pan and sauté the shallots and garlic until translucent. Add the courgettes, tomatoes and pepper. Simmer for 2–3 minutes, then add the prosciutto. Heat through again and season with salt and pepper. In the meantime, cook the rigatoni in boiling salted water until *al dente*; drain. Mix with the vegetables and transfer to pre-warmed plates. To finish, heat the butter in a small pan, toss the sage leaves briefly in it and use to garnish the pasta. Serve with freshly grated Parmesan.

Courgette flowers with tagliatelle This is a particularly sophisticated variation on the pasta and vegetables theme, particularly if the tagliatelle is freshly made using dough no. 4 (see page 40). Take roughly equal quantities of baby courgettes and flowers; wash, dry and cut into pieces. Gently sauté the finely chopped shallots with a little finely chopped garlic and parsley in plenty of butter, add the courgettes and flowers and sauté briefly over a high heat. Then pour on a little reduced veal stock as described in the recipe above and season well with salt and pepper. Cook the tagliatelle in boiling salted water until *al dente*, drain and mix with the vegetables. Serve with freshly grated Parmesan.

Ribbon noodles with vegetables

Beans, cabbage and the more bitter-tasting salad leaves can be combined with any shape of pasta, but they go best with ribbon noodles

PAPPARDELLE WITH RADICCHIO AND ROCKET

Radicchio and rocket are most commonly used in salads. In Italy, however, they are also popular as cooked vegetables and are often combined successfully with pasta.

450 g/1 lb fresh pasta dough no. 4 (see page 40)
1 red onion
100 g/3½ oz streaky bacon
150 g/5 oz radicchio, 100 g/3½ oz rocket
4 tablespoons olive oil, 2 tablespoons dry red wine
salt and freshly ground black pepper
4 nasturtium flowers (optional)

Use a fluted pasta wheel to cut pappardelle from the pasta dough (see page 52), or use dried noodles of a similar size and shape. Peel the onion and chop it coarsely. Cut the bacon rashers across in thin strips. Chop the radicchio finely and the rocket coarsely. Heat the oil in a suitably sized pan and gently sauté the bacon and onion until the onion is translucent. Add the wine and boil for 1–2 minutes. Add the radicchio and let it soften. Season to taste with salt and pepper and turn the heat down very low. In the meantime, cook the pasta in boiling salted water until *al dente*; drain and transfer to a pre-warmed bowl. Mix the rocket into the sauce, then pour it over the pasta and mix thoroughly. Transfer to pre-warmed plates, garnish each plate with a nasturtium flower and serve immediately.

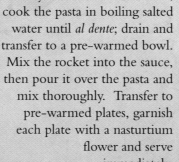

TAGLIATELLE WITH BROCCOLI

The broccoli in this recipe is highly spiced and the result is wonderfully appetizing.

(not illustrated)
400 g/14 oz fresh pasta dough no. 4 (see page 40)
600 g/1¼ lb fresh broccoli
2 garlic cloves
1–2 fresh chillies
6 anchovy fillets, 4 tablespoons olive oil
½ teaspoon salt
freshly ground black pepper

Use a knife or pasta machine to cut tagliatelle from the pasta dough (see pages 52 and 53). Wash the broccoli and divide into florets. Cook in boiling salted water until just tender; drain and keep warm. Peel and finely chop the garlic. Cut the chillies in half, remove the seeds and finely chop. Cut the anchovy fillets in small pieces. Heat the oil in a large frying pan and sauté the garlic, chillies and anchovy

fillets for a few minutes, stirring constantly. Add the broccoli florets and season with salt and pepper. Cook the tagliatelle in boiling salted water until *al dente*; drain and add to the broccoli mixture. Toss together gently and transfer to pre-warmed plates. If the dish is to be served with cheese, choose a mature, highly flavoured pecorino.

FETTUCCINE WITH BEANS AND ROCKET

Pasta and beans are a combination found in several regions of Italy, particularly in the north. With the addition of rocket, you have an interesting, filling dish.

250 g/9 oz dried beans: borlotti, cannellini
350 g/12 oz fresh pasta dough no. 4 (page 40)
1 garlic clove, 2 tablespoons olive oil
60 g/2 oz finely chopped onion
250 g/8 oz canned tomatoes in juice
1 litre/1¾ pints veal or chicken stock
½ teaspoon salt
freshly ground black pepper
100 g/3½ oz rocket
85 g/3 oz Parmesan cheese, freshly grated

Soak the beans overnight; drain. Using a knife or pasta machine, cut fettuccine or tagliatelle from the pasta dough (see pages 52 and 53). Peel and finely chop the garlic. Heat the oil in a large pan and sauté the onion and garlic until translucent. Add the beans, the tomatoes with their juice and the stock. Season with salt and pepper. Cover the pan, leaving the lid slightly ajar so the steam can escape, and simmer gently for 45–60 minutes or until the beans are soft and the liquid is almost completely gone. Add more liquid if necessary. Take out a ladleful of beans and put to one side. Purée everything else in the pan with a hand-held blender (or use a food processor) and then press through a sieve into another pan. Cook the fettuccine in boiling salted water until *al dente*; drain. Add the pasta, the reserved beans and the rocket leaves to the purée and mix everything together. Transfer to 4 pre-warmed plates, sprinkle with grated Parmesan and serve immediately.

Tangy tomato sauce
for orecchiette: fry the
anchovy fillets and then
add the chopped
tomatoes and parsley.
Season well with salt
and pepper.

TAGLIATELLE WITH ASPARAGUS

A pasta dish for the spring, in which tender young asparagus is combined with courgettes and their flowers and fresh herbs.

300 g/10½ oz fresh pasta dough no. 4 (see page 40)
400 g/14 oz thin asparagus spears
40 g/1½ oz butter, 1 tablespoon finely chopped shallot
85 g/3 oz courgette, cut into strips
60 g/2 oz courgette flowers, cut into strips, plus more to garnish
½ teaspoon salt, freshly ground white pepper
1 heaping tablespoon shredded fresh basil leaves
1 tablespoon chopped fresh chives
freshly grated Parmesan cheese to serve

Using a knife or pasta machine, cut tagliatelle from the fresh pasta dough (see pages 52 and 53), or use dried tagliatelle. Trim the tough ends of the asparagus and cut each spear into 4 cm/1½ in pieces. Cook in a large pan of boiling salted water for 3–4 minutes. Lift out with a slotted spoon, reserving the cooking water. Melt the butter in a frying pan and sauté the shallot until translucent. Add the courgettes and courgette flowers and cook for 2–3 minutes. Season with salt and pepper. Add the herbs and the asparagus. In the meantime, cook the tagliatelle in the boiling asparagus cooking water until *al dente*; drain and mix with the vegetables. Transfer to pre-warmed plates, garnish each with a courgette flower and serve with grated Parmesan.

ORECCHIETTE WITH CAULIFLOWER

This simple recipe from southern Italy can also be made with broccoli.

800 g/1¾ lb cauliflower florets, without stalk or leaves
2 unpeeled garlic cloves, crushed
30 g/1 oz butter, 2 tablespoons vegetable oil
8 anchovy fillets, cut into small pieces
250 g/9 oz tomatoes, peeled, deseeded and chopped
2 tablespoons chopped fresh parsley, ½ teaspoon salt
freshly ground black pepper
400 g/14 oz orecchiette (little ears)
freshly grated pecorino romano cheese to serve

Put the cauliflower florets and garlic in a pan of boiling water and cook for 4–5 minutes; drain. Remove the garlic and discard. Heat the butter and oil in a frying pan and sauté the anchovies briefly. Add the tomatoes and parsley and season with salt and pepper. Leave to simmer while you cook the orecchiette in boiling salted water until *al dente*. Drain the pasta and mix with the tomato sauce and cauliflower. Transfer to pre-warmed plates and serve with grated pecorino.

CONCHIGLIE WITH TOMATO SAUCE AND ROCKET

The rocket could be replaced by another bitter salad leaf or with wild spring herbs such as dandelion leaves and wild herb fennel.

400 g/14 oz conchiglie (shells)
400 g/14 oz rocket, coarsely shredded
freshly grated Parmesan cheese to serve
For the tomato sauce:
3 tablespoons olive oil, 100 g/3½ oz chopped onion
40 g/1½ oz diced carrot, 85 g/3 oz chopped celery
1 garlic clove, finely chopped
400 g/14 oz tomatoes, fresh or canned
1½ teaspoons salt, freshly ground pepper
1 small fresh chilli, deseeded and finely chopped

Heat the oil and sauté the onion, carrot, celery and garlic for at least 5 minutes, stirring constantly. Press the tomatoes through a sieve and add to the pan. Season with salt and pepper and add the chilli. Leave the sauce to simmer while you cook the pasta in boiling salted water until *al dente*. After half the pasta cooking time has elapsed, add the rocket to the boiling water. Drain the pasta and rocket and mix with the tomato sauce. Arrange on pre-warmed plates and serve with grated Parmesan.

SPAGHETTI IN PAPER PARCELS

Cooking in greaseproof paper parcels seals in all the flavours and aromas of the ingredients. This recipe will make 12 parcels.

500 g/1 lb 2 oz fresh ripe tomatoes
500 g/1 lb 2 oz spaghetti
20 large black olives (Kalamata)
1 bunch of fresh parsley, finely chopped
2 tablespoons olive oil for brushing
12 slices of pancetta
12 anchovy fillets preserved in salt
12 sprigs of fresh parsley
50 g/1¾ oz butter, melted
freshly grated Parmesan cheese to serve
For the tomato sauce:
3 tablespoons olive oil
1–2 garlic cloves, peeled but left whole
400 g/14 oz can peeled tomatoes, drained
salt and freshly ground black pepper
½ teaspoon dried chilli flakes

First make the tomato sauce. Heat the oil in a heavy-based saucepan, sauté the garlic for 2 minutes and then discard it. Add the tomatoes to the oil and simmer for 15–20 minutes, stirring occasionally. Season with salt, pepper and chilli flakes. Purée with a hand-held blender (or use a food processor), then simmer for a further 10 minutes.

In the meantime, blanch the fresh tomatoes, peel them, cut each in 8 pieces, remove the seeds and place in a large bowl. Cook the spaghetti in boiling salted water until almost *al dente*; drain and add to the tomatoes. Add the olives and parsley and mix well.

Cut out 12 pieces of greaseproof paper, each 25 cm/10 in square, and brush them with olive oil. Proceed as shown in the picture sequence below. Bake the parcels in the oven at 200°C/400°F/gas 6 for 15 minutes. Cut the parcels open with scissors and drizzle the melted butter over the spaghetti. Serve, handing the cheese separately.

Wrapping the parcels:

Put the tomatoes and olives on sheets of greaseproof paper. Wrap some spaghetti round a fork and slide it on to each bed of vegetables.

Flatten the rolled spaghetti into a rectangle and lay a slice of pancetta, an anchovy and a sprig of parsley on top.

Wrap the greaseproof paper over the filling, then fold the ends underneath to make a neat parcel.

PAPPARDELLE WITH A VEGETABLE AND WINE SAUCE

400 g/14 oz fresh pasta dough no. 4 (see page 40)
4 tablespoons extra virgin olive oil
100 g/3½ oz leeks, chopped
300 g/10½ oz courgettes, diced
250 g/9 oz aubergine, diced
400 g/14 oz ripe tomatoes, peeled, deseeded and chopped
125 ml/4 fl oz dry white wine, 1 teaspoon salt
freshly ground black pepper, ½ teaspoon caraway seeds
1 tablespoon chopped fresh basil
85 g/3 oz provolone piccante or Parmesan, freshly grated

Using a knife or pasta machine, cut pappardelle from the pasta dough (see pages 52 and 53). Heat the oil in a pan and cook the leeks, courgettes and aubergine for 6–8 minutes, stirring. Add the tomatoes and wine. Simmer, uncovered, until the sauce is thick. Season with salt, pepper, caraway and basil. Cook the pasta in boiling salted water until *al dente*; drain and mix with the sauce. Serve sprinkled with cheese.

PENNE WITH TOMATOES AND AUBERGINE

9 tablespoons olive oil, 50 g/1¾ oz chopped onion
2 garlic cloves, finely chopped
800 g/1¾ lb fresh plum tomatoes, peeled and chopped
salt and freshly ground black pepper
1 aubergine, weighing about 400 g/14 oz
400 g/14 oz penne rigate, fresh basil leaves
85 g/3 oz freshly grated pecorino cheese

Heat 4 tablespoons of the olive oil in a pan and sauté the onion and garlic until they are translucent. Add the tomatoes, season with salt and pepper and simmer gently until most of the excess liquid has evaporated and the sauce is thick. Cut the aubergine into slices 1 cm/⅜ in thick and season with salt and pepper. Heat the remaining oil in a frying pan and fry the aubergine slices until tender and browned on both sides. Transfer to 4 plates. Cook the pasta in boiling salted water until *al dente*; drain and mix with the tomato sauce. Spoon the pasta on top of the aubergine slices, sprinkle with basil and serve with grated pecorino.

'Pasta alla Norma' – named after Bellini's opera – is how this Sicilian dish of penne with aubergine and tomatoes would be listed on a menu.

The pan can never be too big if Signora Valbuzzi-Gosatti is cooking pizzoccheri for diners at 'La Gatta'. Potatoes, vegetables and pasta must all have room to float.

Buckwheat noodles are an established tradition

Buckwheat has been used for centuries on the southern side of the Alps, in noodles like Spatzlen or pizzoccheri

PIZZOCCHERI

The buckwheat dough for these noodles is not rolled out as thinly as pasta for tagliatelle or fettuccine. For authenticity, Tyrolean 'mountain' cheeses such as casera should be used, but a good substitute is a mixture of equal quantities of creamy fontina and Gruyère. If chard is not available, use spinach instead.

250 g/9 oz potatoes, 200 g/7 oz Swiss chard leaves
300 g/10½ oz casera cheese, 2 garlic cloves
1 quantity of fresh buckwheat pasta dough (see page 45)
200 g/7 oz butter
8 fresh sage leaves, 100 g/3½ oz Parmesan cheese, freshly grated

Peel the potatoes and cut into 1 cm/⅜ in cubes. Cut the chard leaves into strips. Cut the cheese into 1 cm/⅜ in cubes and the garlic into thin slices. Roll out the dough into sheets about 2mm/1⁄16 in thick and cut into strips about 5 cm/2 in wide. Dust the strips with buckwheat flour, stack them on top of each other and cut across in noodles about 5 mm/¼ in wide. Fill a large pan with water, add salt and bring to the boil. Add the cubes of potato to the pan. After 10 minutes of cooking, add the noodles. After a further 8–10 minutes, add the chard and cook for a further 2 minutes. In the meantime, heat the butter in a frying pan and sauté the garlic until translucent, then add the sage leaves. Drain the contents of the pan. Transfer half of the potato and noodle mixture to a pre-warmed bowl, arrange the cubes of cheese on top and cover with the remaining potato and noodle mixture. Pour over the sage and garlic butter, sprinkle with Parmesan and serve.

BUCKWHEAT SPÄTZLE

This type of pasta is known as Schwarzplentene Spatzlen in the southern Tyrol, Schwarzplenten being the Tyrolean term for buckwheat. For a really authentic flavour, use air-dried German ham.

For the Spätzle dough:
150 g/5½ oz buckwheat flour
100 g/3½ oz plain flour
3 eggs, about 100 ml/3½ fl oz water
1 tablespoon oil, ½ teaspoon salt
freshly grated nutmeg
freshly ground white pepper
For the sauce:
250 g/9 oz fresh spinach
120 g/4 oz air-dried German ham or prosciutto
2 tablespoons vegetable oil
1 teaspoon chopped fresh parsley, 250 ml/9 fl oz double cream, 50 g/1¾ oz cold butter
To garnish:
2 tablespoons chopped fresh chives
50 g/1¾ oz Parmesan cheese, freshly grated

Sift the buckwheat and plain flours together into a suitably sized bowl. (It is important to mix the two types of flour thoroughly.) Whisk the eggs in a bowl, adding half of the water and then the oil. Work this liquid into the flour as quickly as possible, either by hand or with a spoon. If necessary, add the remaining water. The dough should be soft enough to be scraped or easily pushed through the Spätzle press. Season the dough with salt, nutmeg and pepper.

Wash the spinach and remove the thick stalks; chop finely. Cut the ham first into slices and then into small cubes. Heat the oil in a suitably sized pan and fry the ham until the fat is rendered. Add the parsley and cream and cook for 3–4 minutes. Cut the cold butter into small pieces and whisk in. In the meantime, add the dough to a pan of boiling water, either by scraping it off a board with a knife or by putting it through a Spätzle press (see page 63). As soon as the Spätzle have all risen to the surface, remove them with a slotted spoon and mix in a bowl with the sauce. Transfer to pre-warmed plates and sprinkle with the chopped chives and grated Parmesan.

Schupfnudeln and Capuns

Some interesting pasta recipes can be found elsewhere in Europe other than Italy. The dishes here are representative of traditional frugal Alpine fare

SCHUPFNUDELN

These noodles are simply fashioned by hand into their characteristic shape – thicker in the middle and tapering at both ends – although if the dough contains potato flour it can also be rolled into thin strands or thick noodles. Of humble origin, Schupfnudeln are delicious with hearty poultry or game stews and with vegetables such as cabbage or sauerkraut. The traditional method of cooking them is first to boil them and then to fry them in plenty of butter, so that they remain soft on the inside but have a crisp, buttery crust. The following dough can be made with wheat flour alone, but the addition of rye flour gives a more robust flavour.

150 g/5½ oz plain flour
70 g/2½ oz rye flour
1 egg, 1 teaspoon salt
about 4 tablespoons water, 50 g/1¾ oz butter
1 tablespoon chopped fresh chives

Schupfnudeln browned in butter. In some regions of Germany, these noodles are eaten with sauerkraut or game stews.

Put both types of flour, the egg, salt and water in a bowl and mix thoroughly together. Turn on to a work surface and knead to a smooth, easily workable dough. Rinse out a bowl with hot water to warm it. Dry the bowl, put in the dough and leave to rest for 15 minutes. Shape the noodles as shown in the picture sequence. Cook in boiling salted water for 8–10 minutes, then drain.

Melt the butter in a frying pan and fry the noodles until they are lightly browned. Arrange on a serving plate, sprinkle with chives and serve.

Shaping Schupfnudeln:

Remove a small portion of dough, keeping the rest covered by the warm bowl, and pull off a small piece.

Roll thinly on a work surface sprinkled with flour. The noodles should be floured so that they do not stick together.

CAPUNS

A variation on the Spätzle theme. These are chard leaves stuffed with Spätzle dough and a spicy salami mixture – an unusual but tasty concoction.

40 Swiss chard leaves
50 g/1¾ oz butter
100 ml/3½ fl oz vegetable stock
100 ml/3½ fl oz double cream
For the Spätzle dough:
300 g/10½ oz plain flour
3 eggs, 5 tablespoons milk
5 tablespoons water
1 teaspoon salt
For the filling:
50 g/1¾ oz smoked back bacon
50 g/1¾ oz salami, preferably German or Swiss
50 g/1¾ oz dry-cured beef, such as Swiss Bünderfleisch
1 onion
a knob of butter
100 g/3½ oz white bread cubes
1½ teaspoons chopped fresh parsley
1 tablespoon chopped fresh chives
a pinch of chopped fresh rosemary
1 tablespoon finely chopped fresh basil

First make the dough. Put the flour, eggs, milk, water and salt in a bowl and mix to form a smooth, soft dough. Beat with a wooden spoon until bubbles form. Cover the bowl and leave the dough to rest for 30 minutes. In the meantime, make the filling. Cut the bacon, salami and beef into small cubes. Peel and finely chop the onion. Heat the butter in a frying pan, add the meats, onion, bread cubes and all the herbs and sauté gently, stirring occasionally. Leave the mixture to cool, then work it into the Spätzle dough.

Briefly blanch the chard leaves in boiling water and spread out on clean tea towels. Put 1 heaping tablespoon of the filling on each leaf and roll up into a tightly sealed parcel. Melt some of the butter in a large frying pan and lightly brown the parcels all over. (There are too many parcels to cook at the same time, so work in batches or use two frying pans.) Pour on the stock, add the cream and simmer gently for about 5 minutes. Serve hot.

TRENETTE WITH
PESTO AND VEGETABLES

In this pesto, Parmesan is replaced by a mature pecorino romano or fiore sardo. Because the pesto is highly flavoured, use it sparingly so that the flavour of the vegetables can be appreciated.

350 g/12 oz fresh pasta dough no. 4 (see page 40)
For the pesto:
2 garlic cloves, 30 g/1 oz pine nuts
50 g/1¾ oz fresh basil leaves
60 g/2 oz mature pecorino romano
salt and freshly ground pepper
5 tablespoons extra virgin olive oil
For the vegetables:
250 g/9 oz tomatoes, 200 g/7 oz courgettes
100 g/3½ oz red peppers
2 tablespoons olive oil
salt and freshly ground pepper
freshly grated Parmesan cheese to serve

Using a knife or pasta machine, cut trenette, which are slightly narrower than tagliatelle, from the fresh pasta dough (see pages 52 and 53), or use dried trenette or tagliatelle. Prepare the pesto as described on page 76. Blanch the tomatoes, peel them, cut in half, remove the seeds and dice. Cut the courgettes lengthways into thin strips. Remove the core and seeds from the pepper and dice finely. Heat the olive oil in a frying pan and sauté the prepared vegetables for 2–3 minutes, stirring constantly. In the meantime cook the pasta in boiling salted water until *al dente*. Drain, mix with the vegetables and pesto and season with salt and pepper if necessary. Serve with freshly grated Parmesan.

Spaghetti with pesto and mussels is a Ligurian version of this dish. Allow about 1 kg/2¼ lb of fresh mussels for 4 people. Scrub the shells thoroughly, then steam open in a little salted water. Remove the mussels from their shells and keep warm. Cook 400g/14 oz of spaghetti in boiling salted water until *al dente*, drain and mix with the pesto. Add the mussels and heat through briefly, then transfer to 4 pre-warmed plates and serve.

Pasta with pesto and vegetables

A perfect blend of tastes for lovers of pasta, garlic and vegetables

TROFIE WITH COURGETTES AND PEAS

This unusual pasta, which is made from flour, water and wheat bran, comes from Camogli on the Gulf of Genoa in Liguria. The bran gives the pasta a rich, full-bodied texture, which combines perfectly with the pesto. Trofie are also good with a fresh tomato sauce and plenty of cheese or *alla carbonara*, that is with pancetta, eggs, garlic and cheese.

For the pasta dough:
300 g/10½ oz plain flour, preferably type 00
50 g/1¾ oz wheat bran
½ teaspoon salt, about 200 ml/7 fl oz water
For the vegetables:
150 g/5 oz yellow courgettes
40 g/1½ oz butter or 4 tablespoons oil
1 tablespoon finely chopped shallots
1 garlic clove, finely chopped
200 g/7 oz shelled fresh peas
4 tablespoons reduced meat stock
50 g/1¾ oz courgette flowers, finely chopped
salt, 1½ teaspoons freshly ground black pepper
1 tablespoon chopped fresh parsley
freshly shaved Parmesan cheese to serve

Make the dough as described in the picture sequence. Cut the courgettes lengthways into thin slices and then cut the slices across in half. Heat the butter or oil and sauté the shallots and garlic until translucent. Add the courgettes and peas, pour on the meat stock and simmer for a few minutes over low heat. Finally, add the courgette flowers and simmer briefly. In the meantime, cook the trofie in boiling salted water until *al*

dente; remove with a slotted spoon and drain in a colander. Mix the pasta with the vegetables in a pre-warmed bowl, season with salt and pepper and stir in the parsley. Serve sprinkled with Parmesan shavings.

Making trofie:

Sift the flour on to a work surface and mix in the bran and salt. Form a well in the middle and pour in three-quarters of the water.

Mix to a dough, adding the remaining water if needed. Shape into rolls as thick as a finger and cut into pieces 1 cm/ ⅜ in across.

Press out the pieces of dough into a slightly elongated shape and curve gently over the back of a fork.

In spring, *in Liguria, trofie are dressed with fresh herbs — mostly basil, plus some thyme, savory and rosemary.*

With mushrooms

*One of the finest pasta dishes is
pasta con funghi*

Pasta cooks should make use of fresh wild mushrooms
whenever they are available. Their flavour and
texture combine particularly well with pasta,
whether mixed with butter and herbs, a béchamel
sauce or just cream. Fresh ceps (*Boletus edulis*) are the
best fungi for a pasta dish, and they taste wonderful
on their own or in a highly flavoured sauce. Truffles
and morels are excellent, too. When you cannot
find fresh wild mushrooms, dried ones make a very
good substitute. They have such a concentrated
flavour that they can be used in small quantities as a
seasoning and can even be added to the pasta
cooking water to give the pasta a mushroom flavour.

PENNE RIGATE
WITH CEPS IN CREAM

The robust tubular pasta contrasts perfectly with the
exquisite flavour of the ceps in a cream sauce.

500 g/1 lb 2 oz fresh ceps
100 g/3½ oz prosciutto, thinly sliced
250 ml/9 fl oz double cream
30 g/1 oz butter, 60 g/2 oz finely chopped onion
6 tablespoons finely chopped fresh parsley
400 g/14 oz penne rigate
salt and freshly ground black pepper

To serve:
freshly grated Parmesan cheese

Clean the ceps thoroughly and trim off the ends of
the stalks. Slice the ceps lengthways. Cut the
prosciutto slices into 1 cm/⅜ in squares. Boil the
cream over low heat to reduce to about half of its
original volume. Heat the butter, add the onion and
sauté gently until the onion is translucent. Add the
ceps and prosciutto and sauté briefly, stirring
constantly. Add the reduced cream and the parsley
and simmer gently until the ceps are tender. This
will take only a few minutes. In the meantime, cook
the pasta in boiling salted water until *al dente* and
drain. Mix the pasta with the sauce and season
with salt and pepper. Transfer to plates and
serve with grated Parmesan.

PAPPARDELLE WITH CEPS

This recipe calls for a lot of fresh ceps. However, it is also delicious made with a mixture of mushrooms, such as field mushrooms, chestnut mushrooms and open cap mushrooms. Only the very best pasta, preferably home-made, should be used for this exquisite mushroom dish.

400 g/14 oz fresh pasta dough no. 4 (see page 40)
about 700 g/1½ lb fresh ceps
1 garlic clove, 300 g/10½ oz ripe tomatoes
50 g/1¾ oz butter
85 g/3 oz finely chopped shallots
85 g/3 oz diced celery
½ teaspoon salt, freshly ground black pepper
2 tablespoons vegetable oil
1 tablespoon chopped fresh parsley
½ teaspoon chopped fresh thyme
4 tablespoons chopped fresh basil

To serve:
freshly grated pecorino or Parmesan cheese

Using a knife or pasta machine, cut pappardelle from the fresh pasta dough (see pages 52 and 53), or use dried pappardelle. Clean the ceps very carefully and trim off the ends of the stalks. Slice the ceps lengthways. Peel and finely chop the garlic clove. Blanch the tomatoes, peel them, remove the seeds and cut into cubes. Heat the butter in a suitably sized frying pan and sauté the shallots, garlic and celery gently for a few minutes. Add the ceps and brown over a high heat. Reduce the heat and cook gently for a few more minutes. Season with salt and pepper. Heat the oil in a second frying pan and sauté the diced tomatoes briefly. In the meantime, cook the pappardelle in boiling salted water until *al dente*. Drain and mix immediately with the ceps, tomatoes and chopped herbs. Check the seasoning and serve with grated pecorino or Parmesan.

Pasta and truffles

This alliance benefits both parties: the humble pasta and the aristocratic truffle

Reto Mathis from St Moritz – a man who knows how to judge the quality of truffles. Many pounds of the 'black diamonds' pass through his hands year after year.

The flavour of truffles is best appreciated when there is little competition from other flavours, so pasta makes an ideal accompaniment for them as it provides a simple backdrop against which the truffle can stand out. Truffles also blend well with butter, cream and mild cheeses, such as the delicately creamy fontina from the Valle d'Aosta. White truffles from Italy's Piedmont region are especially favoured by pasta lovers, used raw, sliced very thinly. White truffles from the area around Alba are considered to be the most fragrant. They are particularly rare and thus very much sought after, so it is no surprise that they change hands at astronomic prices. However, because of their strong flavour, a little truffle goes a long way.

Tagliatelle à la Mathis, a combination that is simple yet sublime. The noodles are first coated with a cream sauce and then with an equal quantity of sauce Périgord. The finishing touch is black truffle, both sliced and freshly grated.

TAJARIN WITH BUTTER AND TRUFFLES

One of the simplest and quickest pasta dishes of all, but certainly also one of the most expensive, comes from Piedmont. Tajarin, the delicate egg noodles of that region, are simply cooked and drained, then transferred to a large bowl and tossed with plenty of melted butter, a little freshly grated Parmesan and pepper. All this has to be done quickly, before the noodles cool down. They are then served on to pre-warmed plates and fresh white truffle is sliced thinly over the top – the more generously the better.

The celebrated Piedmontese *fonduta* makes a wonderful sauce for tajarin. *Fonduta* is made by melting the delicately creamy fontina cheese from the Valle d'Aosta with milk, butter and egg yolks. This rich cheese sauce is poured over the noodles and the whole is topped with plenty of freshly sliced white truffle.

White truffles taste finest when sliced fresh and paper-thin. They are particularly exquisite garnishing noodles in a cream or creamy cheese sauce, or noodles simply tossed with brown butter (beurre noisette).

TAGLIERINI WITH SAUTÉED TRUFFLES

A delightful pasta dish that uses black truffles. These taste superb when sliced paper thin and sautéed briefly in hot butter. Combined with thin, home-made noodles and diced tomatoes, you have a meal ready in no time at all. The trick with this simple dish is to have all three elements – pasta, truffles and tomatoes – ready more or less simultaneously.

350 g/12 oz fresh pasta dough no.4 (see page 40)
100–150 g/3–5½ oz black truffles (fresh or canned)
2 tablespoons olive oil
3 tablespoons finely chopped shallot
120 g/4 oz ripe tomatoes, peeled, deseeded and diced
60 g/2 oz butter
salt and freshly ground white pepper
small fresh basil leaves

Using a knife or pasta machine, cut taglierini from the pasta dough (see pages 52 and 53). Thinly peel the truffles, then cut them into paper-thin slices, using a truffle slicer if you have one. Heat the oil in a small frying pan and cook the shallot until very soft and translucent. Add the diced tomatoes, sauté briefly and remove the pan from the heat. Melt the butter in a second frying pan, add the sliced truffles and fry briefly on both sides. Season with salt and pepper. Cook the pasta in boiling salted water until *al dente*; drain and mix immediately with the truffles and tomato. Transfer to 4 pre-warmed plates and garnish with basil leaves.

Truffle lovers will disapprove, but freshly grated Parmesan makes a perfect accompaniment for this dish.

Vegetables and noodles Chinese-style

Chinese cooks are such masters of the art of cooking vegetables that meat and fish are hardly missed, even in noodle dishes

NOODLES WITH GINGER AND SPRING ONIONS

This noodle dish is quick and simple but surprisingly tasty, largely because of the fresh ginger.

250 g/9 oz dried Chinese egg noodles
For the sauce:
85 g/3 oz fresh root ginger
150 g/5½ oz spring onions
3 tablespoons groundnut oil
salt and freshly ground pepper
2 tablespoons oyster sauce
To garnish:
edible flowers (optional)

Peel the ginger, slice finely and then cut into very thin strips. Trim the spring onions and cut into thin strips. Cook the noodles in boiling salted water until *al dente* (6–7 minutes). In the meantime, heat the oil in a wok. Put the strips of ginger into the wok and stir-fry for 1 minute. Add the spring onions and stir-fry briefly – they should retain a little of their crispness. Season with salt and pepper and put the wok to one side. Drain the noodles and transfer immediately to the wok. Mix everything together thoroughly. Mix in the oyster sauce, check for seasoning and transfer to bowls. Garnish with edible flowers and serve immediately.

VEGETABLES WITH RICE NOODLES

Contrast is an important element in Chinese cooking. Here, the crispness of the fried noodles is set against the moist tenderness of the vegetables.

200 g/7 oz rice noodles, vegetable oil for frying
For the vegetables:
20 g/scant ¾ oz dried shrimp, 85 g/3 oz leek
85 g/3 oz spring onions, 50 g/1¾ oz carrot
50 g/1¾ oz celery
60 g/2 oz each red, green and yellow pepper
2–3 tablespoons groundnut oil
50 g/1¾ oz sliced bamboo shoots, 4 tablespoons rice wine
½ teaspoon salt, 1 tablespoon caster sugar
2 tablespoons dark soya sauce
100 g/3½ oz beansprouts
To garnish:
1 tablespoon chopped fresh coriander

Rinse the dried shrimp, then soak in warm water to cover for about 1 hour; drain, reserving 2 tablespoons of the soaking water. Cut the leek and spring onions into thin rings; dice the carrot; and slice the celery. Remove the core and seeds from the peppers and cut into more or less evenly sized cubes. Heat some oil in a wok and stir-fry the leek, spring onions, carrot, celery, peppers and bamboo shoots briefly in 3 or 4 batches. The vegetables should be tender but still crisp. Set the vegetables aside. Put the rice wine, salt, sugar, soya sauce and reserved shrimp soaking water in the wok and bring to the boil. Return all the vegetables to the wok, together with the beansprouts and shrimp. Heat everything through, tossing well. Check the seasoning. In the meantime, separate the dried noodles and deep-fry in plenty of hot oil until they puff up and are crisp; drain on paper towels. Transfer the noodles to plates or bowls and spoon the vegetables on top, or mix them into the noodles. Sprinkle with chopped coriander and serve.

Fresh root ginger *often promises more than it delivers. Only really fresh ginger is suitable for such a dish. So when buying ginger, check that it is perfectly fresh: it should be firm to the touch and the skin should not have the slightest fold or wrinkle!*

With seafood

In Italy pasta with fish or shellfish is a very common combination, particularly in coastal regions. Here the sea and its produce are omnipresent, even in the pasta itself – in noodles coloured black with squid ink, which are served with every kind of sea creature imaginable. In other parts of the world too, pasta and seafood are a popular partnership, most notably in Asia.

As every cook knows, the cooking of fresh fish is a delicate matter – a few seconds too long and the fish will be overcooked and dry. The heat of freshly

cooked pasta can often be enough on its own: the fish can be cut into very small cubes or strips and then mixed raw into the warm pasta, with a few suitable herbs such as dill and some butter or olive oil. The time required to transfer the dish from kitchen to table will be sufficient to cook the fish so that it is hot but still juicy and translucent inside.

Crustaceans and molluscs are common ingredients in pasta dishes, from juicy prawns to mussels and clams. *Spaghetti alle vongole* (spaghetti with clams) is an Italian classic. Scallops also find their way occasionally into the pasta pot. One unusual speciality from Sicily is *bottarga*, which is pressed and heavily salted tuna roe. It can be grated like cheese over macaroni or spaghetti.

The best of all foods from the sea is lobster, which should always be purchased alive and cooked fresh. Spaghetti or other pasta *all'aragosta* can be cooked in the water used to cook the lobster, or, even better, in a stock in which as much lobster shell as possible has been boiled for half an hour with some white wine and a stick of cinnamon. This lobster-suffused pasta tastes quite extraordinary!

Quick and easy – fish and pasta

Two examples of sophisticated pasta dishes that require little preparation time, using smoked salmon and fresh tuna

Cut the smoked salmon *in 1 cm/⅜ in cubes if you are using the middle of a side of salmon. If the piece has been taken from the thinner tail end, it can be cut into thin strips.*

FETTUCCINE AL SALMONE

You need a thick piece of smoked salmon for this recipe, not thin slices.

350 g/12 oz fresh pasta dough no. 4 (see page 40)
250 ml/9 fl oz double cream
1 small fresh chilli, deseeded and finely chopped
a pinch of freshly grated nutmeg
some grated lemon zest
½ teaspoon salt, freshly ground black pepper
400 g/14 oz piece of smoked salmon, skinned
50 g/1¾ oz butter, cut into small pieces
1 tablespoon finely chopped fresh lemon balm

Using a knife or pasta machine, cut fettucine from the pasta dough (see pages 52 and 53), or used dried fettuccine. Put the cream, chilli, nutmeg, lemon zest, salt and pepper in a large saucepan and boil gently to reduce the liquid by one-third (about 10 minutes). In the meantime, cut the salmon into 1 cm/⅜ in cubes. Cook the fettuccine in boiling salted water until *al dente*. Add the butter, piece by piece, to the cream sauce and stir in well. Remove the pan from the heat and add the cubed salmon. Drain the pasta and mix thoroughly with the sauce. Spoon on to pre-warmed plates and garnish with finely chopped lemon balm.

Swordfish *is an excellent alternative to tuna. It has a similar 'meaty' texture and a mild flavour, which is why many people esteem it particularly highly.*

GARGANELLI WITH TUNA

Garganelli, home-made from a dough with plenty of egg yolk in it, are excellent with this robust tuna sauce, but dried garganelli or other tubular pasta, such as macaroni, ziti, or bucatini, can be used as an alternative.

350 g/12 oz fresh pasta dough no. 4 (see page 40)
300 g/10½ oz fresh tuna steak
salt and freshly ground pepper
about 5 tablespoons olive oil
For the tomato sauce:
500 g/1 lb 2 oz ripe tomatoes
2 garlic cloves
20 black olives, as small as possible
60 g/2 oz sliced spring onions
85 g/3 oz diced celery, 60g/2 oz diced carrot
a pinch of ground ginger
½ teaspoon salt
freshly ground pepper
To garnish:
2 tablespoons finely chopped fresh herbs: thyme, rosemary, parsley

Make garganelli from the pasta dough (see page 55). Cut the tuna in 1.5 cm/⅝ in cubes and season with salt and pepper. Heat the oil in a wide pan and fry the tuna just enough to sear it all over. Remove from the pan and put to one side; reserve the oil in the pan. Blanch the tomatoes, peel them, cut in half, remove the seeds and dice. Peel and finely chop the garlic. Stone the olives; if large, cut them in half. Reheat the oil in the pan, adding a further 2 tablespoons if necessary, and cook the spring onions, celery, carrot, garlic and olives gently until soft. Stir in the tomatoes with the ginger, salt and pepper and cook for about 10 minutes, uncovered; the pieces of tomatoes should be still just recognizable. In the meantime, cook the pasta in plenty of boiling salted water until *al dente*. Add the tuna to the sauce and heat through. Drain the pasta, mix with the sauce and spoon on to pre-warmed plates. Sprinkle with the chopped herbs and serve.

With lobster, sardines and caviar

The ingredients vary enormously, and so do the results — but both these dishes taste wonderful

TAJARIN WITH LOBSTER RAGOUT

This is pasta and seafood cooking at its most elegant and extravagant. Tajarin, a speciality from Italy's Piedmont region, are very narrow tagliatelle-like noodles made from a dough enriched with egg yolks. For a particularly exquisite flavour, cook them in veal stock instead of the court-bouillon. This delicious pasta combines wonderfully with freshly cooked lobster, champagne sauce and caviar.

300 g/10½ oz fresh pasta dough no. 4 (see page 40)
1 whole live lobster, weighing about 800 g/1¾ lb, or
2 lobsters, each about 500 g/1 lb 2 oz
For the court-bouillon:
1 garlic clove
100 g/3½ oz each diced leek, carrot and celery
2 bay leaves, 1 bunch of parsley
2 tablespoons salt, 4 litres/7 pints water
For the sauce:
500 ml/18 fl oz fish stock, 2 sprigs of fresh tarragon
2 sprigs of parsley, 4 black peppercorns
250 ml/9 fl oz double cream, 125 ml/4 fl oz champagne
20 g/scant ¾ oz chilled butter, cut into small pieces
To finish:
4 tablespoons caviar, 4 baby courgettes with flowers
20 g/scant ¾ oz butter

Using a knife, cut tajarin from the fresh pasta dough (see page 55). For the court-bouillon, lightly crush the unpeeled garlic clove with the side of a knife and put it in a large pan with the leek, carrot, celery, herbs, salt and water. Bring to the boil and cook for about 15 minutes. Quickly slide the lobster head-first into the bubbling liquid, cover the pan, turn down the heat, and cook for 15 minutes. (If you are using 2 smaller lobsters, cook for 10–12 minutes.) Lift out the lobster and cool, then cut it open and remove the meat from the tail and claws. Cut the meat in cubes and keep warm. Strain the court-bouillon and return it to the pan.

Heat the fish stock in a saucepan with the sprigs of tarragon and parsley and the peppercorns and simmer gently until reduced to about 5–6 tablespoons. Strain, add the cream and simmer for a few minutes. Add the champagne and simmer again briefly. Mix thoroughly in the pan with a hand blender or hand-held electric mixer, then whisk in the butter to thicken the sauce.

In the meantime, cook the tajarin in the boiling court-bouillon until *al dente*; drain and rinse briefly in hot water. Twist portions of noodles around a 2-pronged fork and transfer to 4 pre-warmed plates. Add the lobster and pour the sauce over the top. Garnish generously with caviar and serve, with baby courgettes and their flowers that have been gently stewed in butter.

PASTA WITH SARDINES

This is the most popular pasta dish in Sicily, although its ingredients would suggest it is of Arabic origin. Absolutely fresh sardines and aromatic fennel are essential to create the distinctive flavour of the dish.

400 g/14 oz macaroni or bucatini
For the sauce:
500 g/1 lb 2 oz bulb fennel
4 tablespoons olive oil
100 g/3½ oz finely chopped onion
2 anchovy fillets, chopped
500 g/1 lb 2 oz fresh sardines
½ teaspoon salt, freshly ground pepper
1 small sachet of dried saffron threads, crushed
30 g/1 oz raisins
30 g/1 oz pine nuts

Trim the fennel, cut out the hard core and cook the bulbs whole in boiling salted water until just tender. Drain thoroughly (if necessary, squeeze gently to remove excess water), reserving the cooking water, and then dice finely. Heat the oil in a frying pan and cook the onion with the anchovies until soft. In the meantime, clean and fillet the sardines (or have your fishmonger do this for you) and cut the fish in small pieces. Add the sardines to the pan and cook for about 5 minutes over a low heat, stirring with a wooden spoon. Season with salt and pepper and stir in the saffron, which in this case is used for its flavour and not for its colour. Add the raisins, pine nuts and fennel and simmer for a further 4–5 minutes. In the meantime, cook the pasta in boiling salted water until al dente. (For a more pronounced taste of fennel, use the fennel cooking water for the pasta.) Drain the pasta, mix with the sauce and serve immediately. In Sicily, this dish is not served with cheese, but the addition of a Sicilian pecorino (such as pecorino pepato, with peppercorns) or ragusano imparts an interesting flavour.

Wild fennel grows in the mountainous regions of the Mediterranean countries. In the late spring, it can be found in markets there, such as this one in Agrigento, Sicily.

Pasta with mussels and clams

There are numerous simple but delicious combinations in Italian pasta cooking

SPAGHETTI WITH MUSSELS, CLAMS AND COCKLES

Versions of this dish are found everywhere, and not only in Italy. The type of pasta varies, and the choice of molluscs is subject to what is available fresh, since all kinds are suitable.

300 g/10½ oz spaghetti
For the seafood:
400 g/14 oz fresh mussels
400 g/14 oz fresh clams
400 g/14 oz fresh cockles
1 bunch of parsley
2 garlic cloves
3 tablespoons extra virgin olive oil
50 g/1¾ oz finely chopped onion
250 ml/9 fl oz dry white wine
For the sauce:
400 g/14 oz ripe tomatoes, 2 tablespoons olive oil
100 g/3½ oz thinly sliced spring onions
1 heaping tablespoon coarsely shredded fresh basil leaves
½ teaspoon salt, freshly ground pepper

Scrub the mussels, clams and cockles thoroughly under cold running water, discarding any that are open or damaged. Coarsely chop the parsley. Peel and finely chop the garlic. Heat the oil in a large pan and sauté the onion, garlic and parsley over moderate heat for about 2 minutes. Put the mussels, clams and cockles in the pan, pour in the white wine, cover and cook for about 8 minutes or until the shells open. (Discard any that remain stubbornly shut.) In the meantime, make the sauce. Blanch the tomatoes, peel them, cut in half, remove the seeds and dice. Heat the oil in a saucepan and sauté the tomatoes and spring onions for a few minutes. Add the basil, salt and pepper and simmer for a further 3–4 minutes. Add the sauce to the mussels, clams and cockles and mix in well. Keep warm. Cook the spaghetti in plenty of boiling salted water until *al dente* and drain. Mix the spaghetti with the mussels, clams and cockles, and serve immediately.

In Italy, this dish is made with venus clams, which are common in the Mediterranean.

BUCATINI ALLE VONGOLE

This dish has become famous outside Italy as *spaghetti alle vongole*, although the traditional pasta to use is bucatini, a sort of thin macaroni. The recipe here uses canned tomatoes, but really ripe plum tomatoes would make the dish even better.

300 g/10½ oz bucatini
For the clams:
800 g/1¾ lb fresh clams
125 ml/4 fl oz white wine
125 ml/4 fl oz water
1 tablespoon olive oil
For the sauce:
2 tablespoons olive oil
50 g/1¾ oz chopped onion
1 garlic clove, finely chopped
400 g/14 oz can tomatoes
½ teaspoon salt
freshly ground pepper
To garnish:
2 tablespoons chopped fresh parsley

Scrub the clams under cold running water, discarding any open or damaged ones. Place them in a large pan, add the white wine, water and oil and heat until the shells open. (Discard any that remain stubbornly shut.) Remove the clams from the pan with a slotted spoon. Leave the cooking liquid to cool a little, so that any grit can settle, then strain the liquid and reserve it. To make the sauce, heat the oil in a suitably large saucepan and sauté the onion and garlic until translucent. Add the canned tomatoes and the liquid in which the clams were cooked. Season with salt and pepper and simmer the sauce for at least 30 minutes or until it is reduced by about half. At this point, the clams can be removed from their shells, making them easier to eat, and added to the sauce. However, the appearance of the dish is enhanced if some are left in their shells. Cook the bucatini in plenty of boiling salted water until *al dente*, drain thoroughly and mix with the sauce. Transfer to pre-warmed plates, sprinkle with the chopped parsley and serve immediately.

PAPPARDELLE WITH SCAMPI AND ASPARAGUS

A successful combination of seafood and crunchy fresh vegetables. The dish comes from Sicily, whose waters teem with scampi (the Italian name for langoustines). Asparagus, too, is found in Sicily, growing wild in the mountainous regions; it is sold at markets on the island in the spring. Only the pasta is not indigenous to Sicily, since pappardelle come from northern Italy. If fresh scampi are not available, you can substitute raw king or tiger prawns.

350 g/12 oz fresh pasta dough no. 4 (see page 40)
10 g/about ⅓ oz squid ink
2 tablespoons olive oil
For the sauce:
1 garlic clove
300 g/10½ oz ripe plum tomatoes
4 tablespoons extra virgin olive oil
60 g/2 oz finely chopped onion
½ teaspoon salt, freshly ground pepper
1 small fresh chilli
125 ml/4 fl oz dry white wine
16 medium-sized scampi
250 g/9 oz thin green asparagus

Make the pasta dough as described on page 41. Before kneading, cut the dough in half and add the squid ink and oil to one half to colour it black. Using a fluted pasta wheel, cut pappardelle from both the plain and the black doughs (see page 52). Lightly crush the unpeeled garlic clove with the side of a knife. Blanch the tomatoes in boiling water, peel them and finely chop. Heat the oil in an appropriately sized pan and sauté the onion until translucent. Add the garlic and the tomatoes and cook for 3–4 minutes over a high heat. Season with salt and pepper. Cut the chilli in half lengthways, remove the seeds and cut into fine strips. Add to the pan with the white wine. Cook for 2 minutes longer, uncovered. Twist the heads off the scampi and peel them, then lay them on their back on a chopping board and cut in half lengthways; devein if necessary. Trim the asparagus and cut into pieces approximately 4 cm/1½ in long. Add the asparagus to the sauce and simmer for 3–4 minutes, then add the scampi and simmer until they are just cooked (about 2–3 minutes). In the meantime, cook the pasta in boiling salted water until *al dente*; drain, mix immediately with the sauce and serve.

TAGLIATELLE VERDE WITH SCALLOPS

This dish is particularly good when made with fresh scallops, but frozen ones are a good substitute.

250 g/9 oz fresh green pasta dough (see page 46)
1 garlic clove, 250 g/9 oz ripe tomatoes
3 tablespoons vegetable oil
85 g/3 oz finely chopped shallots
50 g/1¾ oz diced celery
½ teaspoon salt
freshly ground pepper
½ teaspoon chopped fresh thyme
1 tablespoon chopped fresh parsley
125 ml/4 fl oz dry white wine
300 g/10½ oz scallops, with coral
100 g/3½ oz peeled raw prawns

Using a knife or pasta machine, cut tagliatelle from the pasta dough (see pages 52 and 53), or use dried tagliatelle. Peel and finely chop the garlic. Blanch the tomatoes, peel them, cut in half, remove the seeds and chop. Heat the oil in a suitably sized pan and sauté the shallots, garlic and celery for a few minutes until translucent. Add the tomatoes, season with salt and pepper, sprinkle on the chopped herbs and pour in the white wine. Simmer gently for 2–3 minutes. Cut each scallop in half horizontally and add to the sauce with the prawns. Simmer until the shellfish is just cooked (3–4 minutes). In the meantime, cook the pasta in boiling salted water until *al dente*. Drain, mix immediately with the sauce and serve.

A delightful variation can be made using only mussels. Steam them open in a little extra fish stock, then remove from their shells. Add the strained cooking liquid to the tomato sauce.

POTATO NOODLES WITH TOMATOES AND SEAFOOD

For the dough:
400 g/14 oz baking potatoes
150 g/5½ oz plain flour
50 g/1¾ oz Parmesan cheese, freshly grated
¾ teaspoon salt, freshly ground pepper
2 eggs
For the sauce:
400 g/14 oz ripe tomatoes
1 garlic clove
4 tablespoons olive oil
50 g/1¾ oz finely chopped onion
60 g/2 oz each diced carrot and celery
1 anchovy fillet, finely chopped
½ teaspoon salt, freshly ground pepper
250 ml/9 fl oz fish stock
300 g/10½ oz fresh cockles
200 g/7 oz squid
120 g/4 oz peeled raw prawns
2 tablespoons chopped mixed fresh herbs: basil, parsley, thyme and a little rosemary

Make the potato dough following the directions on page 223, then cut and shape the noodles. Dust them with flour, cover with a cloth and set aside. Blanch the tomatoes, peel them, cut in half, remove the seeds and dice. Peel and finely chop the garlic. Heat the oil in a large saucepan and sauté the onion and garlic until translucent. Add the carrot and celery and sauté gently for 2–3 minutes. Add the diced tomatoes and anchovy and season with salt and pepper. Pour on the fish stock and simmer gently for about 15 minutes. Scrub the cockles and steam them open. Remove the cockles from their shells (discard any that remain closed). Clean the squid, cut the tentacles from the body and cut the cleaned body into rings. Add the cockles, the squid bodies and tentacles and the prawns to the tomato sauce and cook for a further 5 minutes. Cook the potato noodles in a large pan of boiling salted water until they rise to the surface, remove with a slotted spoon and drain thoroughly. Arrange the noodles on 4 plates, pour the seafood sauce over them and sprinkle with the chopped herbs.

TRUFFLE FAZZOLETTI
WITH SKATE WINGS

'Fazzoletti,' which means handkerchiefs, is the Italian name for this pasta dish.

1 quantity of fresh cornmeal pasta dough (see page 43)
1 large fresh black truffle
600 g/1¼ lb skate wings, 40 g/1½ oz butter
85 g/3 oz finely diced carrots
100 g/3½ oz finely diced celery
85 g/3 oz finely chopped spring onions, ½ teaspoon salt
freshly ground pepper, truffle oil
For the sauce:
50 g/1¾ oz each coarsely chopped carrot and sliced leek
500 ml/18 fl oz fish stock, 2 tablespoons dry sherry
125 ml/4 fl oz double cream
20 g/scant ¾ oz chilled butter
To garnish:
fresh chervil leaves

To make the fazzoletti, roll out the dough very thinly in a pasta machine. Following the directions given for herb pasta on page 111, cover half of the strips of dough with paper-thin slices of fresh black truffle and lay the remaining dough on top. Roll out again, preferably with a rolling pin this time. Cut 12 rectangles, approximately 8 x 10 cm/3 x 4 in.

Remove the skin from the skate; take the fish off the bone and cut it in 8 pieces big enough to layer with the pasta rectangles. Brown the fish on both sides in the hot butter and remove from the pan. Sauté the vegetables for 5–6 minutes in the same fat. Season, add a few drops of truffle oil and return the fish to the pan. Keep warm over a very low heat.

Combine the carrot, leek and fish stock in a saucepan and boil until 4–5 tablespoons of liquid remain. Add the sherry. After a minute, stir in the cream and simmer over a low heat for 2–3 minutes. Strain the sauce and return to the pan, then use a hand blender or electric mixer to make the sauce foamy; thicken with the butter. Cook the pasta in boiling salted water until *al dente*; remove with a slotted spatula and drain on a tea towel. Layer the pasta, skate and vegetables on 4 pre-warmed plates and spoon the foamy sauce over the top. Garnish with chervil.

With lobster and crayfish

The special flavour of these crustaceans demands pasta out of the ordinary. Ribbon noodles go particularly well with such sophisticated sauces

BLACK NOODLES WITH CRAYFISH IN CREAM SAUCE

This very elegant pasta dish can also be made with scampi (langoustines) or large prawns and you can substitute plain egg pasta for the pasta coloured black with squid ink. It is a matter of choice as to how wide you cut the noodles.

400 g/14 oz fresh black pasta dough (see page 48)
24 live crayfish, each about 70 g/2½ oz
For the sauce:
4 tablespoons vegetable oil
100 g/3½ oz each coarsely chopped leek, carrot and celery
1½ tablespoons brandy
1 bay leaf, 1 teaspoon salt
½ teaspoon black peppercorns
125 ml/4 fl oz white wine
50 g/1¾ oz each carrot and celery
250 ml/9 fl oz double cream, freshly ground pepper
To garnish:
fresh chervil leaves

Using a knife or pasta machine, cut the pasta dough into ribbon noodles (see pages 52 and 53). Lower the crayfish into boiling water and simmer until cooked (about 6 minutes). Drain and rinse in cold water. Pull off the heads and claws, peel the tails and devein if necessary; set the tail meat aside. If the claws are big enough, remove the meat from them as well. Coarsely chop the heads and shells and reserve.

To make the sauce, heat the oil in a large saucepan, add the chopped vegetables and sauté briefly over high heat. Add the crayfish heads and shells (reserving a few whole heads to garnish) and brown thoroughly over high heat, stirring constantly. Pour in the brandy and add the bay leaf, salt and peppercorns. Pour in enough water to cover the crayfish shells and vegetables. Bring to the boil, then simmer gently over low heat about 40 minutes. Skim off any froth that rises to the surface. Strain the liquid into a clean pan (do not press down on the shells and vegetables in the sieve). Bring the strained liquid to the boil and reduce over low heat to about 125 ml/4 fl oz. Add the white wine and continue to boil until reduced again to about 125 ml/4 fl oz. Cut the carrot and celery into very fine strips, add to the pan and pour on the cream. Simmer for 3–4 minutes. Add the crayfish meat and warm through. Check the seasoning. Cook the noodles in boiling salted water until *al dente*, drain thoroughly and mix with the sauce. Transfer to 4 plates and garnish each with a crayfish shell with claws and chervil leaves.

LOBSTER WITH TAGLIERINI

A luxurious combination that demands the best and freshest ingredients, including home-made pasta.

250 g/9 oz fresh pasta dough no. 4 (see page 40)
For the sauce:
100 ml/3½ fl oz white wine, 1½ tablespoons dry white vermouth
3 tablespoons finely chopped shallot
500 ml/18 fl oz fish stock
200 g/7 oz chilled butter, cut into small pieces
salt and freshly ground white pepper
a few drops of lemon juice
For the lobster:
1 carrot, 1 leek, 1 celery stick
1 garlic clove, salt
2 live lobsters, each weighing 500–600 g/1–1¼ lb
To garnish:
small fresh basil leaves

Using a knife or pasta machine, cut taglierini from the pasta dough (see pages 52 and 53) and spread out on a clean tea towel. To make the sauce, combine the white wine, vermouth and shallot in a saucepan and boil to reduce a little. Pour in the fish stock and boil to reduce the liquid by half.

In the meantime, fill a deep pan with water and add the vegetables, peeled garlic clove and salt. Bring to the boil. Lower the lobsters, head-first, one at a time, into the boiling water, ensuring that the liquid has returned to the boil before adding the second lobster. Cook for about 10 minutes, then remove the pan from the heat and leave the lobsters in the liquid for 5 minutes. Remove the lobsters from the pan. Twist the claws from the body and reserve. With a large knife, cut the body in half lengthways, remove the dark intestinal vein, take the meat from the shell and cut into pieces; keep warm. Arrange the lobster shell halves on pre-warmed plates. Cook the taglierini in boiling salted water until *al dente* and drain. At the same time, add the butter to the sauce, a few pieces at a time, and whisk in. Season and add lemon juice to taste. Toss the taglierini and lobster meat with the sauce and spoon into the shells. Garnish each plate with a lobster claw and a few basil leaves.

Pizokel are made like Spätzle (see page 63), being cut straight from a chopping board into boiling salted water. The only difference is that Pizokel are a little thicker.

SPINACH PIZOKEL WITH SCAMPI IN PROSCIUTTO

Pizokel, a Swiss speciality, look like outsize Spätzle, and they are made in the same way.

For the Pizokel:
125 g/4½ oz plain flour, 2 eggs
150 ml/¼ pint Quark or fromage frais
15 g/½ oz melted butter
salt and freshly ground pepper, freshly grated nutmeg
For the port sauce:
1½ tablespoons finely chopped shallot, a knob of butter
100 ml/3½ fl oz port, 2 tablespoons hollandaise sauce
100 ml/3½ fl oz whipped cream
salt and freshly ground pepper
a little lemon juice
For the spinach:
100 g/3½ oz spinach leaves, 15 g/½ oz butter
salt and freshly ground pepper, freshly grated nutmeg
4 tablespoons cream
In addition:
12 peeled scampi or raw king or tiger prawns
salt and freshly ground pepper
6 thin slices of prosciutto, cut in half
4 tablespoons olive oil for frying

Make a smooth Spätzle-type dough from the Pizokel ingredients (see page 62) and put to one side. To make the sauce, cook the shallot in the butter until soft. Add the port and reduce until almost all the liquid has evaporated. Remove from the heat and stir in the hollandaise sauce. When ready to serve, stir in the whipped cream and reheat gently. Season with salt, pepper and lemon juice.

Wash the spinach and chop roughly. Season each scampi with salt and pepper and wrap in a half slice of prosciutto. Place the dough on a wooden board and, with a palette knife, cut it in thin strips straight into a pan of boiling salted water. As the Pizokel cook, wilt the spinach in the melted butter in a frying pan. As soon as the Pizokel rise to the surface of the water, remove with a slotted spoon and mix with the spinach. Season with salt, pepper and nutmeg and mix in the cream. Heat through. Fry the scampi in the oil until golden brown. Spoon the Pizokel and spinach mixture on to pre-warmed plates and arrange the scampi on top. Serve with the port sauce.

More than just a side-dish

Two shellfish dishes, sufficient in themselves, but complemented to perfection by the addition of pasta

SQUID-INK NOODLES AND COURGETTES WITH SPINY LOBSTER

300 g/10½ oz fresh black pasta dough (see page 48)
1 spiny lobster tail, weighing 500 g/1 lb 2 oz, or 2 tails weighing about 300 g/10½ oz each
For the lobster sauce:
500 ml/18 fl oz rock lobster or fish stock
150 ml/¼ pint double cream
salt and freshly ground pepper
For the courgettes:
180 g/6 oz baby courgettes
30 g/1 oz finely chopped shallot, 2 tablespoons olive oil
1 tablespoon balsamic vinegar
To garnish:
fresh chervil leaves

Using a knife or pasta machine, cut ribbon noodles 1 cm/⅜ in wide from the pasta dough. Cook the lobster tail in boiling salted water or a court-bouillon for about 15 minutes. Drain and let cool, then remove the meat from the shell. Devein if necessary and cut the meat into slices of even thickness. Put back into the original shape, wrap in foil and keep warm. Slowly boil the lobster stock to reduce to about a fifth of its original volume. Stir in the cream, season with salt and pepper and simmer gently for 3–4 minutes. In the meantime, trim the courgettes and cut lengthways in paper-thin slices. (This is most easily done with a mandoline.) Cut the slices in half lengthways. Sauté the shallots in the olive oil until translucent. Cook the noodles in boiling salted water until *al dente*; drain. Add the courgette strips to the shallots and sauté over high heat for 2–3 minutes. Add the balsamic vinegar and then the squid ink noodles and toss well to mix. Arrange on 4 pre-warmed plates with the sliced lobster. Pour over the lobster sauce and garnish with chervil leaves.

From the wok

Stir-frying seafood is an ideal way of preparing it for serving with pasta

Stir-frying is really successful only in a wok because the prepared ingredients can be cooked rapidly over high heat while being constantly moved round at speed, so that all the surfaces of the food come into contact with the hot wok. This cooking method is ideal for vegetables because they retain their crispy freshness and flavour. The same applies to seafood. The scallop dish below and the prawn dishes on pages 152 and 153 are good examples of this Asian cooking technique. The texture of the stir-fried seafood contrasts interestingly with that of the soft noodles.

SCALLOPS WITH EGG NOODLES

400 g/14 oz scallops, without coral
1 green pepper, 1 carrot
2 spring onions, 85 g/3 oz celery
10 g/scant ½ oz fresh root ginger

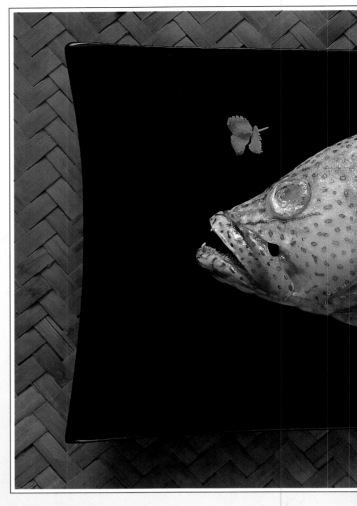

120 g/4 oz Chinese egg noodles
3 tablespoons groundnut oil
2 teaspoons oyster sauce
salt and freshly ground pepper
150 g/5½ oz aubergine cut into 1 cm/⅜ in cubes
1 tablespoon light soya sauce
1 fresh red chilli, cut into rings

Cut the scallops in half horizontally. Cut the green pepper in half, remove the core and seeds and cut into diamonds. Peel the carrot and cut into sticks. Slice the spring onions and celery. Peel and slice the ginger. Cook the noodles in boiling salted water for about 4 minutes, drain and rinse with cold water. Heat 1 tablespoon of oil in a wok and briefly stir-fry the scallops. Add the oyster sauce and season with salt and pepper. Mix everything together, then remove from the wok and place to one side. Heat the remaining oil in the wok and stir-fry the aubergine until lightly browned. Add the carrot, green pepper, celery and spring onions and stir-fry until all the vegetables are cooked but still crisp. Add the soya sauce and chilli rings and mix everything together thoroughly. Add the scallops and the noodles and toss briefly to reheat, then transfer to Chinese soup bowls and serve hot.

FISH WITH
NOODLES AND VEGETABLES

The presentation of food has always been very
important in Asia. Stir-fried dishes are not always
served in individual bowls. An attractive alternative
is to pile them on a long serving dish and then to put
the head and tail of the fish at each end, to give the
appearance of a whole fish. This recipe will serve 2.

700 g/1½ lb whole fish, cleaned and prepared for cooking
salt and freshly ground pepper
1 tablespoon vegetable oil
10 g/scant ½ oz dried cloud ear mushrooms
85 g/3 oz carrot, 2 spring onions, 1 fresh red chilli
2 tablespoons oriental sesame oil
50 g/1¾ oz leek, thinly sliced
70 g/2½ oz courgette, thinly sliced
100 g/3½ oz red pepper, diced
1 tablespoon finely chopped fresh root ginger
50 g/1¾ oz bamboo shoot, cut into strips
1 tablespoon soya sauce
85 g/3 oz Chinese egg noodles
To garnish:
flat-leaf parsley

Season the fish inside with salt and pepper. Lay it in
a suitably sized baking dish, brush with vegetable oil
and cook in the oven at 200°C/400°F/gas 6 for 20
minutes. In the meantime, soak the mushrooms in
cold water. Peel the carrot and cut into thin sticks.
Trim the spring onions and cut into thin rings.
Cut the chilli in half, remove the seeds and core and
cut into thin strips. Remove the fish from the oven;
cut off the head and tail and reserve. Take the flesh
from the fish, discarding skin and bones and cut into
1.5 cm/⅝ in pieces. Heat the sesame oil in a wok
and stir-fry all the prepared vegetables with the
drained mushrooms until just tender. Season with
the soya sauce and salt and pepper to taste. Carefully
mix in the fish pieces. Cook the noodles in boiling
salted water for about 5 minutes, drain and add to
the other ingredients. Arrange the fish and noodle
mixture on a serving dish, with the fish head and tail
placed at the ends so that the fish appears still to be
whole. Garnish with parsley.

A mingling of flavours and textures in the Asian style

Creativity is required when combining ingredients, which in Asia are usually determined by what is available in the market

CANTONESE-STYLE PRAWNS WITH RICE NOODLES

Contrast is a basic feature of the cooking of southern China, and here the crispness of the fried prawns is countered by the softness of the fresh noodles. This recipe is only one of many ways in which shellfish cooked in a wok can be combined with noodles and vegetables. As well as prawns of different sizes, crab meat and lobster can be used, together with egg or cellophane noodles.

400 g/14 oz raw tiger prawns
50 g/1¾ oz fresh shiitake mushrooms
20 g/scant ¾ oz fresh root ginger
100 g/3½ oz Chinese rice noodles
4 tablespoons vegetable oil
60 g/2 oz thinly sliced leek
50 g/1¾ oz bamboo shoot, cut into strips
1 tablespoon chopped fresh coriander to garnish
For the sauce:
2 spring onions
1 fresh red chilli
3 tablespoons light soya sauce
2 tablespoons rice wine
1 teaspoon tomato purée
1 teaspoon rice vinegar
100 ml/3½ fl oz chicken stock (see page 86)
salt and freshly ground pepper
½ teaspoon palm or demerara sugar

Peel the prawns, leaving on the last tail section, and devein. Rinse and dry thoroughly on paper towels. Remove the thick stalks from the shiittake mushrooms and cut the caps in half or quarters, depending on size. Peel the ginger and cut into thin slices. Pour boiling water over the noodles and leave to soak for about 3 minutes, then drain and rinse with cold water. Put to one side. For the sauce, trim and finely chop the spring onions; cut the chilli in half, remove the seeds and finely chop. Mix together the rest of the sauce ingredients.

Heat 2 tablespoons of the vegetable oil in a wok. Season the prawns with salt and pepper and stir-fry until pink and a little crisp. Remove from the wok and put to one side. Heat another tablespoon of oil in the wok and stir-fry the prepared vegetables until just tender – first the mushrooms, then the leek and ginger and finally the bamboo shoots; remove from the wok. Heat the remaining oil in the wok and stir-fry the spring onions and chilli briefly. Pour on the prepared sauce liquid and boil to reduce it slightly. Return all the vegetables to the wok and add the noodles. Toss in the sauce for 1–2 minutes to reheat. Mix in the prawns, sprinkle with coriander and serve immediately.

In Singapore, freshly cooked crab meat is often used instead of prawns and the dish is served in the empty crab body shells.

SEAFOOD WITH EGG NOODLES

While the composition of this dish is flexible – using seafood and vegetables that are the best and freshest in the market – the choice should offer contrasts in both texture and flavour. Cooking in a wok makes it possible to adjust cooking times accordingly. Firm-fleshed fish, such as monkfish or halibut, are the most suitable.

250 g/9 oz Chinese egg noodles
200 g/7 oz squid, 250 g/9 oz raw medium prawns
250 g/9 oz firm white fish fillet
4 dried Chinese mushrooms
3 slices of fresh root ginger
1 garlic clove, 3 tablespoons groundnut oil
100 g/3½ oz mange-touts, 2 tablespoons water
For the sauce:
350 ml/12 fl oz chicken stock (see page 86)
3 tablespoons light soya sauce, ½ teaspoon sugar
2 tablespoons oriental sesame oil
1 teaspoon cornflour, salt and freshly ground pepper
To garnish:
fresh coriander leaves

Soak the noodles in boiling water until they separate from each other; drain. Clean the squid, cut off the tentacles and slit open the squid bodies. Lay the bodies flat and score a diamond pattern in the flesh with a sharp knife; cut into bite-size pieces. Peel the prawns, leaving on the last tail section, and devein. Cut the fish in bite-size pieces. Soak the mushrooms in hot water. Cut the ginger in fine shreds; peel and finely chop the garlic. Heat the oil in a wok and lightly brown the ginger and garlic. Add the drained mushrooms and the mange-touts together with the water. Stir-fry for 1 minute. Remove the contents of the pan and briefly stir-fry the fish pieces. Put the mushroom mixture back into the wok, add the prawns and squid and stir-fry until the squid pieces curl up. Mix the sauce ingredients together, add to the wok and stir until the sauce thickens. Season with salt and pepper. Add the drained noodles and simmer until they have soaked up the sauce (1–2 minutes). Arrange on a pre-warmed serving dish and garnish with coriander leaves.

With meat, poultry and game

Being quite bland, pasta always cries out for sauces and other accompaniments that will impart flavour. A *ragù,* or rich meat sauce, is one of the best ways to give a pasta dish flavour. But it is important to be judicious: the pasta should not be swimming in the sauce. And the sauce must be thick and concentrated, so that it coats the pasta and does not pool on the plate. The same rules are true for a tomato sauce.

In Italy, a full set of cutlery is not provided for the pasta course, just a fork or a fork and a spoon, so any meat to be mixed with pasta is usually cut into small pieces. A *ragù,* then, does not normally contain chunks of meat of the size you might find in a stew, for example, that need to be cut with a knife.

Depending on the meat from which the *ragù* is made, it may be cooked for just a few minutes or simmered for an extended period. Some of the most elegant accompaniments for pasta are

undoubtedly game birds such as quails. Beef, pork, veal and chicken are popular in pasta sauces, as are salami, prosciutto and other preserved meats. Fresh pork sausages, particularly the Italian luganeghe, are wonderful in a sauce for spaghetti or macaroni. In fact, any kind of meat can be used in a *ragù*, mixed with vegetables such as tomatoes, onions, garlic, peppers and chillies.

When making a *ragù*, a better texture is achieved by using a knife to chop the meat finely, rather than putting it through a mincer. This is particularly important for delicate meat, such as quail or pigeon, which always suffers a certain degree of damage when it is minced.

An Italian-style *ragù* is not the only way of serving meat with pasta. Spicy Asian dishes can also lift pasta out of its bland neutrality – whether it be a wholly inauthentic meat curry or a Chinese duck or chicken stew seasoned with soya sauce and a little five-spice powder, the widely used Chinese seasoning that tastes of anise and cinnamon. Pasta provides a flexible basis for many different blends of ingredients. It also offers the imagination plenty of scope, and is a splendid vehicle for the latest creations of those who like to experiment in the kitchen. How else would the myriad combinations that surprise and delight our palates at the dinner table have come into being?

SPAGHETTI ALLA CARBONARA

This spaghetti dish, with its combination of eggs and bacon, is a simple but classic one. You have the choice between the distinctive taste of Italian pancetta (traditionally used in this recipe) and ordinary bacon.

180 g/6 oz pancetta or smoked streaky bacon
1 garlic clove, 400 g/14 oz spaghetti
2 tablespoons vegetable oil, 4 eggs
85 g/3 oz Parmesan cheese, freshly grated
salt and freshly ground pepper

Cut the pancetta or bacon in strips. Lightly bruise the unpeeled garlic clove. Cook the pasta in boiling salted water until *al dente*. In the meantime, continue as shown in the picture sequence below.

Preparing Spaghetti alla Carbonara:

Heat the oil in a large saucepan and fry the pancetta and garlic until the pancetta starts to become crisp.

Break the eggs into a bowl. Add the cheese and whisk thoroughly. Season to taste with salt and pepper.

Add the drained spaghetti to the pan and mix with the pancetta. Remove the pan from the heat, add the egg and cheese mixture and stir in well.

CHESTNUT NOODLES WITH PANCETTA

A very simple dish that requires the best possible ingredients. Pancetta must be used because it is essential to the flavour. Only pancetta has the distinctive taste that combines so well with the chestnut noodles and cheese.

For the dough:
250 g/9 oz plain flour, preferably type 00
150 g/5½ oz chestnut flour
3 eggs
2 egg yolks
½ teaspoon salt
For the sauce:
200 g/7 oz pancetta, sliced thinly
1 tablespoon vegetable oil, 250 ml/9 fl oz double cream
85 g/3 oz Parmesan cheese, freshly grated
salt and freshly ground pepper
To garnish:
2 tablespoons chopped fresh chives

Make the dough following the directions on page 43 and cut it in noodles about 6 mm/¼ in wide. Cut the pancetta into strips. Heat the oil in a frying pan, fry the pancetta until crisp and put to one side. Put the cream in a saucepan and boil to reduce by half, then cool. Add the Parmesan to the cream, season to taste with salt and pepper and mix in the pancetta. Cook the noodles in boiling salted water until *al dente*, drain and mix immediately with the sauce. Sprinkle with the chopped chives and serve on pre-warmed plates.

FARFALLE WITH MEAT SAUCE AND YOGURT

In Turkey, where it is known as '*mankarna mantisi*', this dish is made just with beef, but the addition of pork improves the taste considerably. The quantity of garlic can, of course, be reduced to taste.

400 g/14 oz fresh pasta dough no. 1 (see page 40)
For the meat sauce:
7 tablespoons vegetable oil
250 g/9 oz onions, finely chopped
40 g/1½ oz diced Hamburg parsley (optional)
40 g/1½ oz diced celery, 200 g/7 oz red peppers, diced
200 g/7 oz each minced beef and pork
1 teaspoon salt, freshly ground black pepper
1 tablespoon paprika
½ tablespoon chopped fresh mint, 250 ml/9 fl oz beef stock
For the yogurt sauce:
6 garlic cloves
200 ml/7 fl oz plain yogurt, ½ teaspoon salt
To garnish:
fresh mint leaves

Cut farfalle from the pasta dough (see page 55), or use dried pasta. Heat 4 tablespoons of the oil in a large pan and fry the onions until soft and translucent; add the Hamburg parsley, if using, the celery and peppers and cook for 5 minutes. Heat the remaining oil in a second pan and brown the minced meats, stirring with a wooden spoon to break them up. Mix the meat with the vegetables. Season with salt, pepper, paprika and mint. Pour in the stock and simmer for 10–15 minutes. The liquid should be reduced by about half.

Peel and finely chop the garlic and stir into the yogurt with the salt. Cook the pasta in boiling salted water until *al dente*, drain and divide among 4 pre-warmed plates. Spoon off about half of the liquid from the meat sauce and reserve; pour the sauce over the pasta. Add the yogurt sauce and pour the reserved cooking liquid over the top. Garnish each serving with mint leaves.

Simple pasta dishes

Bacon, ham and cheese make it easy to add flavour to pasta

The 'chitarra' *is a wooden frame on which pasta can be cut. The top and bottom of the frame are strung with wires, like the strings of a guitar. The sheet of dough is laid across the wires and rolled out with a rolling pin. The cut noodles drop into the inside of the frame where they collect on a board.*

SPAGHETTI ALLA CHITARRA

This spaghetti, with its square cross section, is made on a special cutting device known as a *chitarra* (guitar), from which it takes its name. The spaghetti cutters on a pasta machine will give very much the same effect.

400 g/14 oz spaghetti alla chitarra
For the sauce:
1 kg/2¼ lb ripe plum tomatoes
200 g/7 oz pancetta
1 onion
4 tablespoons olive oil
salt and freshly ground pepper
To serve:
100 g/3½ oz pecorino cheese, freshly grated
30 fresh basil leaves

Blanch the tomatoes, peel them, remove the seeds and dice. Cut the pancetta first into slices and then into short strips. Peel the onion and cut into rings. Heat the oil in a pan and lightly brown the pancetta and onion. Add the diced tomatoes and season lightly with salt. Turn the heat down very low, cover the pan and simmer for 15 minutes. Remove the lid and simmer for gently for a further 45 minutes, checking periodically to ensure that all the liquid has not evaporated. Shortly before the end of the cooking time, season the sauce with salt and pepper. Cook the spaghetti in boiling salted water until *al dente* and drain. Immediately mix with some of the sauce. Serve the pasta on to pre-warmed plates and spoon over the rest of the sauce. Sprinkle with cheese and garnish with basil leaves.

Pancetta *is Italian bacon cured with salt and spices (not smoked) and then rolled up into a sausage shape. Its flavour is different from that of ordinary bacon.*

TAGLIATELLE WITH HAM AND CREAM SAUCE

This ham and cream sauce, from the Italian province of Parma, has a quite extraordinary flavour. Prosciutto can be very salty, so taste the sauce before adding any additional seasoning.

400 g/14 oz fresh pasta dough no. 4 (see page 40)
For the sauce:
100 g/3½ oz prosciutto
100 g/3½ oz cooked ham
85 g/3 oz butter
250 ml/9 fl oz double cream
a pinch of freshly grated nutmeg
100 g/3½ oz Parmesan cheese, freshly grated
freshly ground pepper
To garnish:
1 tablespoon chopped fresh parsley
1 tablespoon chopped fresh chives

Using a knife or pasta machine, cut tagliatelle from the pasta dough (see pages 52 and 53), or use dried tagliatelle. Cut the prosciutto and ham in small pieces. Melt the butter in a saucepan, add the prosciutto and ham and cook for a few minutes. Pour in the cream, season with grated nutmeg and stir in half the Parmesan. Simmer over a low heat for about 10 minutes. Season the sauce with pepper. In the meantime, cook the tagliatelle in boiling salted water until *al dente*. Drain and mix immediately with the sauce. Transfer to pre-warmed plates and sprinkle with the remaining Parmesan and the chopped herbs.

Penne with prosciutto and peas is an excellent variation of this dish, to make when fresh peas are available in the summer. Replace the cooked ham with 250 g/9 oz of freshly shelled peas. Add them to the sauce halfway through the cooking time, so that they simmer for only 5 minutes. Cook the penne in boiling salted water until *al dente*, mix with the sauce and garnish just with chopped parsley, omitting the chives.

Prosciutto di Parma gives this dish its characteristic flavour. This salt-cured and air-dried Italian ham can be bought in gourmet markets and many supermarkets.

Pasta with offal

Chicken livers are particularly well suited to pasta sauces, but offal from other animals can also be used

TAGLIATELLE WITH RICH RABBIT SAUCE

Tender white meat of rabbit combined with flavourful offal makes a delicious and quick-to-prepare pasta sauce. Tubular pasta such as penne rigate go well with the sauce, but ribbon noodles with plenty of egg yolk are even better.

300 g/10½ oz fresh pasta dough no. 4 (see page 40)
For the rabbit sauce:
400 g/14 oz boneless rabbit meat
100 g/3½ oz rabbit liver (or chicken livers)
8 rabbit kidneys
2 teaspoons paprika, 2 tablespoons olive oil
30 g/1 oz smoked streaky bacon, chopped
85 g/3 oz chopped onion, ½ garlic clove, crushed
50 g/1¾ oz diced carrot
500 g/1 lb 2 oz tomatoes, peeled, deseeded and chopped
3 sprigs of fresh thyme, 1 small sprig of fresh rosemary
salt and freshly ground pepper
250 ml/9 fl oz dry white wine
4 tablespoons vegetable oil

To finish:
2 heaping tablespoons freshly grated Parmesan cheese
1 heaping tablespoon white breadcrumbs
60 g/2 oz butter, cut into small pieces

Using a knife or pasta machine, cut tagliatelle from the pasta dough (see pages 52 and 53), or use dried tagliatelle. Cut the rabbit meat and liver into small cubes. Trim the kidneys and cut in half lengthways. Sprinkle the meats with the paprika and leave for about 15 minutes so the flavour can soak in. Heat the olive oil in a wide saucepan, add the bacon and brown quickly. Add the onion, garlic and carrot and sauté for 3–4 minutes. Stir in the chopped tomatoes and herbs, season with salt and pepper and pour in the white wine. Simmer for 10–15 minutes longer. Heat the vegetable oil in a frying pan and quickly brown the rabbit meat, liver and kidneys over moderately high heat. Season with salt and pepper and fry for a further 1–2 minutes. Add to the tomato sauce and cook for 2–3 minutes over high heat. In the meantime, cook the tagliatelle in boiling salted water until *al dente*. Drain and mix with the rabbit sauce. Arrange on 4 heatproof serving plates. Mix the Parmesan with the breadcrumbs, sprinkle over the pasta and dot with the pieces of butter. Brown under the grill and serve immediately.

TAGLIERINI
WITH CHICKEN LIVERS

Livers can be used to make marvellous pasta sauces, from inexpensive chicken livers to *foie gras*, the liver of specially fattened geese or ducks. The latter is, of course, expensive, but lightly cooked fresh *foie gras*, with a little pan juice or truffle sauce dribbled over, is indescribably delicious with ribbon noodles.

400 g/14 oz fresh pasta dough no. 4 (see page 40)
For the sauce:
500 ml/18 fl oz chicken stock, 1 small garlic clove
85 g/3 oz shallots, 50 g/1¾ oz butter
250 g/9 oz chicken livers
2 tablespoons port, ½ teaspoon salt
freshly ground pepper
1 tablespoon paprika
To garnish:
1 fresh truffle (optional)
2 baby courgettes with flowers, 30 g/1 oz butter

With a knife or pasta machine, cut taglierini from the pasta dough (see pages 52 and 53), or use dried ribbon noodles. Boil the chicken stock over a low heat until reduced to just under 100 ml/3½ fl oz. Peel and finely chop the garlic and shallots. Melt the butter in a suitably sized pan and gently fry the garlic and shallots until translucent, stirring frequently. Trim the chicken livers and cut into small pieces. Add to the shallots and brown over moderately high heat, stirring constantly. Add the port, stir in the chicken stock and season with salt, pepper and paprika. Simmer for 2–3 minutes over a low heat. In the meantime, cook the taglierini in boiling salted water until *al dente*. Drain and mix with the sauce. Clean or peel the truffle and slice thinly. Cut the two courgettes, including the flowers, in half lengthways. Heat the butter in a pan and brown the truffle slices on both sides, then add the courgettes and brown on both sides as well. Arrange with the pasta on pre-warmed plates. If cheese is to be served with this dish it should be a freshly grated, mature Parmesan.

PASTA SQUARES WITH DUCK

This Greek dish is called '*hilopites me papia*', which translates roughly as 'a thousand pies'. Virtually identical recipes for pasta with duck are found along Italy's Adriatic coast, the only differences being that in the south the duck sauce is served with orecchiette and in the Veneto with bigoli, the Venetian wholemeal spaghetti.

1 quantity of fresh pasta dough no. 1 (see page 40)
For the duck:
1 duck, weighing about 2 kg/4½ lb
2 garlic cloves
3 celery stalks
150 g/5½ oz onion
1 sprig of fresh thyme
1 bay leaf
a few sprigs of fresh flat-leaf parsley
¼ lemon
10 black peppercorns
salt
For the sauce:
thinly pared zest and juice of 1 lemon
2 teaspoons honey
½ teaspoon salt
freshly ground pepper
To garnish:
2 tablespoons toasted sesame seeds
1 tablespoon finely chopped fresh parsley

Roll out the pasta dough very thinly on a floured work surface and cut into 2.5 cm/1 in squares. Lay the squares on cloths to dry. Rinse the duck inside and out, remove all visible fat and pat dry. Place in a large pan, cover with cold water and bring slowly to the boil, skimming off any scum that comes to the surface. Peel and bruise the garlic; coarsely chop the celery and onion. Add these to the pan with all the herbs and seasonings. Simmer until the duck is cooked (about 1 hour). Remove the duck from the pan and keep warm. Strain the cooking liquid, skim off the fat, return to the pan and bring back to the boil. Cook the pasta squares in it until *al dente*. Drain the pasta in a colander set in a bowl and keep warm. Return the cooking liquid to the pan. Add the lemon zest, cut into thin strips, and the honey and season with salt and pepper. Boil over high heat until reduced by half, then add the lemon juice. Take the meat off the duck, discard the skin and cut the meat into 1 cm/⅜ in cubes. Mix with the pasta squares. Pour on the lemon sauce and sprinkle with the sesame seeds and parsley.

FUSILLI WITH
A RAGOUT OF WILD DUCK

A coarse-textured meat sauce goes particularly well with curly pasta such as fusilli, which soaks up the sauce splendidly.

400 g/14 oz fusilli
For the duck ragout:
1 wild duck, weighing about 700 g/1½ lb
50 g/1¾ oz streaky bacon
60 g/2 oz each celery and carrot
60 g/2 oz onion
2 tablespoons vegetable oil
250 ml/8 fl oz red wine (Merlot)
1 tablespoon tomato purée
1½ teaspoons salt
freshly ground white pepper
1 bay leaf
1 sprig each of fresh thyme and rosemary
250 ml/9 fl oz duck or chicken stock
1 tablespoon chopped fresh parsley

Take all the meat off the duck and discard the skin. Finely chop the meat with a knife or mince as coarsely as possible. Cut the bacon into thin strips. Cut the celery and carrot into julienne strips. Thinly slice the onion. Continue as shown in the picture sequence. Cook the fusilli in boiling salted water until *al dente*, drain and transfer to a pre-warmed bowl. Mix the duck ragout with the fusilli and serve immediately.

Preparing the duck ragout:
Heat the oil in a large pan and sauté the bacon until crisp. Add the vegetables and fry briefly, then add the meat from the duck.

Pour in the red wine, stir in the tomato purée and season. Bring to the boil, then reduce the heat to a simmer.

Add the bay leaf, thyme, rosemary and stock and leave to simmer, stirring from time to time.

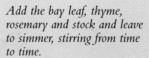

Cook until the meat is tender and the ragout is thick and rich. Add the parsley.

SWEETBREADS
ON MACARONI AU GRATIN

Sweetbreads blend very agreeably with pasta and melted cheese. Be sure to use balsamic vinegar that is at least 10 years old.

500 ml/18 fl oz veal stock
500 g/1 lb 2 oz calves' sweetbreads
3 tablespoons extra virgin olive oil
85 g/3 oz chopped shallots
40 g/1½ oz each diced carrot and celery
½ garlic clove, finely chopped
2 tablespoons balsamic vinegar
½ teaspoon salt, freshly ground white pepper
½ teaspoon paprika
30 g/1 oz butter, 85 g/3 oz mange-touts
4 nasturtium flowers to garnish (optional)
For the macaroni au gratin:
300 g/10½ oz long macaroni, 60 g/2 oz butter
60 g/2 oz Parmesan cheese, freshly grated
2 tablespoons finely chopped fresh herbs: parsley, thyme

Bring the veal stock to the boil and leave to reduce slowly over low heat to just under 100 ml/3½ fl oz. In the meantime, briefly blanch the sweetbreads in boiling water, remove the membrane as carefully as possible and cut into slices about 1 cm/⅜ in thick; set aside. To prepare the macaroni au gratin, cook the macaroni in boiling salted water until al dente; drain. Melt the butter and use some

to grease 4 individual serving plates (they should be deep and heatproof). Arrange the macaroni in a single layer on the plates, starting at the outside edge and spiralling in, curving to fit. Dribble the remaining melted butter over the pasta. Mix the grated Parmesan with the finely chopped herbs and sprinkle over the pasta. To make the sauce, heat the oil in a saucepan and sauté the shallots until soft. Add the carrot, celery and garlic and sauté for a few more minutes. Pour on the balsamic vinegar. Add the reduced veal stock and simmer gently until the liquid is reduced to about half its original volume. Remove the pan from the heat. Season the sliced sweetbreads with salt, pepper and a little paprika. Heat the butter in a frying pan and fry the sliced sweetbreads over high heat for 2–3 minutes on each side. In the meantime, place the plates of macaroni under the grill to brown. Add the fried sweetbreads to the sauce, together with the mange-touts, cut into strips. Heat through, then spoon on top of the macaroni au gratin. Decorate each plate with a nasturtium flower.

Pasta and Roquefort gratin For this variation, use penne, penne rigate or medium-sized conchiglie. Cook in boiling salted water until al dente and drain. Grease the plates with melted butter and make a layer of pasta on each one. Lightly whip 6 tablespoons of cream with 50 g/1¾ oz freshly grated Parmesan, season with a little pepper and nutmeg and pour over the pasta. Cut 40 g/1½ oz of Roquefort into small cubes and dot the pasta with it. Warm under the grill until the surface is light brown and crispy. The Roquefort imparts a very distinctive flavour to the pasta.

BRAISED QUAILS
WITH PARSLEY PASTA

The fresh flavour of parsley is a perfect match for
both the quails and the chanterelles in this dish.
Whole parsley leaves encased in sheets of pasta,
known in Italy as "fazzoletti", add to the subtle
flavour.

12 large squares of pasta with parsley leaves (see page 111)
For the quail ragout:
4 quails, weighing 170 g/scant 6 oz each
salt and freshly ground pepper
2 tablespoons vegetable oil
60 g/2 oz each finely chopped shallots and celery
30 g/1 oz each finely diced carrot and Hamburg parsley (optional)
50 g/1¾ oz smoked streaky bacon, diced, 2 garlic cloves
1 teaspoon flour, 250 ml/9 fl oz chicken stock
2 tablespoons chopped fresh parsley
To finish:
20 g/scant ¾ oz butter
120 g/4 oz small fresh chanterelles

Put the pasta squares between damp cloths to prevent
them from drying out. Cut the quails in half
lengthways. Cut off the legs and wings. Season the
quail lightly with salt and pepper and put to one side.
Heat the oil in a large pan and sauté the shallots until
translucent. Add the celery, carrot and Hamburg
parsley (if using) and sauté briskly for 2–3 minutes;
remove the vegetables from the pan with a slotted
spoon and keep warm. Add the bacon to the pan
and cook until the fat is rendered. Add the quail and
brown over high heat. Bruise the unpeeled garlic
cloves with the side of a knife and add to the pan
with the sautéed vegetables. Sprinkle with the flour
and cook for 3–4 minutes, stirring well. Add the
chicken stock and simmer until the meat is cooked
and the liquid has reduced by more than half. Add
the parsley and adjust the seasoning if necessary.
Cook the pasta squares in boiling salted water until *al
dente*; remove with a slotted spatula and drain
thoroughly. Melt the butter in a small pan and sauté
the chanterelles, adding salt and pepper to taste. For
each serving, layer some quail ragout between 3
squares of pasta. Garnish with sautéed chanterelles.

Pigeon and wild boar

The meat of game animals and game birds is a popular accompaniment for pasta and these dishes are some of the finest that pasta cooking has to offer

LINGUINE WITH PIGEON

This dish is traditionally made with wild pigeons, which have a much stronger flavour than the plump farmed pigeon. However, farmed pigeons with their light, delicate meat impart a subtle flavour to the dish and are well worth trying. The flavour is further enhanced by the addition of prosciutto.

350 g/12 oz fresh pasta dough no. 4 (see page 40)
2 pigeons, weighing about 300 g/10½ oz each
30 g/1 oz carrot, 20 g/scant ¾ oz celery
300 g/10½ oz plum tomatoes, peeled and deseeded
100 g/3½ oz prosciutto, 2 spring onions
2–3 tablespoons olive oil
40 g/1½ oz chopped onion, 1 tablespoon finely chopped fresh parsley

Cut noodles 2–3mm/¹⁄₁₆–⅛ in wide from the pasta dough (see pages 52 and 53), or use dried linguine. Cut each pigeon into quarters. Cut the carrot into thin strips and thinly slice the celery. Chop the tomatoes coarsely. Cut the prosciutto into small cubes and chop the spring onions in rings. Heat the oil in a large pan and sauté the onion, carrot and celery for about 5 minutes, stirring constantly. Add the pieces of pigeon and brown evenly all over. Stir in the tomatoes, cover the pan and simmer for 1 hour. Add a little water from time to time if necessary. Lift out the pigeon, take the meat off the bone and return it to the pan. Add the prosciutto and spring onions to the sauce and warm through. Cook the linguine in boiling salted water until *al dente*, drain and mix with the sauce. Serve sprinkled with parsley.

PAPPARDELLE AL CINGHIALE

Ribbon noodles with a stew of wild boar is a classic dish in Tuscany and the Marches, and there are very similar dishes that use rabbit instead of wild boar. True, the recipe does take time to prepare, but it is richly satisfying.

350 g/12 oz fresh pasta dough no. 4 (see page 40)
500 g/1 lb 2 oz boned shoulder of wild boar (or substitute pork)
4 tablespoons olive oil, 1 tablespoon plain flour
300 g/10½ oz tomatoes, peeled and chopped
salt and freshly ground pepper
For the marinade:
1 small onion, 1 garlic clove
85 g/3 oz diced carrot, 350 ml/12 fl oz red wine (Chianti classico)
12 juniper berries
1 teaspoon black peppercorns
1 piece of lemon zest
1 bay leaf, 1 sprig of fresh rosemary

Cut pappardelle from the pasta dough (see pages 52 and 53), or use dried ribbon noodles. Cut the meat into 1 cm/⅜ in cubes and place in a deep bowl. To make the marinade, peel and slice the onion. Crush the unpeeled garlic clove with the side of a knife. Add the onion and garlic to the meat, together with the remaining marinade ingredients. Cover the bowl and leave to marinate in a cool place for at least 12 hours. Remove the meat and pat dry with paper towels. Strain the marinade and reserve. Heat the oil in a heavy pan over moderate heat and brown the cubes of meat on all sides. Sprinkle with the flour and stir thoroughly. Add the chopped tomatoes and pour in the reserved marinade. Turn up the heat and bring to the boil, stirring to mix in the browned bits on the bottom of the pan. Reduce the heat, cover the pan and simmer until the meat is cooked (about 2 hours, less for pork). Remove the lid and continue simmering to reduce the sauce by about half. Season to taste with salt and pepper. Cook the noodles in boiling salted water until *al dente*, drain and transfer to a pre-warmed bowl. Mix with the boar ragout and serve immediately.

NOODLES WITH CHICKEN AND ASPARAGUS

The crispy vegetables, stir-fried in a wok, are a perfect accompaniment for the chicken and noodles.

300 g/10½ oz Chinese egg noodles
For the chicken:
250 g/9 oz skinned and boned chicken breast
2 tablespoons rice wine, 1 tablespoon light soya sauce
2 teaspoons cornflour, ½ teaspoon sugar
salt and freshly ground pepper
a pinch of ground ginger
For the vegetables:
60 g/2 oz sliced cooked ham
4 dried Chinese mushrooms, reconstituted in water
200 g/7 oz thin green asparagus
4 tablespoons groundnut oil
85 g/3 oz thinly sliced leek
100 g/3½ oz thinly sliced canned bamboo shoots
In addition:
125 ml/4 fl oz chicken stock (see page 86)
1 tablespoon dark soya sauce
1 tablespoon chopped fresh coriander

Cut the chicken breast diagonally into thin slices and place in a bowl. Mix the rice wine and soya sauce together, stir in the cornflour and pour over the chicken. Sprinkle with the sugar, salt, pepper and ground ginger and mix well. Cover and leave to marinate for about 1 hour. Cut the cooked ham in strips about 5 mm/¼ in wide. Drain the soaked mushrooms, squeeze dry and slice. Trim the woody ends from the asparagus stalks, then cut into pieces 4–5 cm/1½–2 in long. Heat the oil in a wok and quickly brown the ham and mushrooms, stirring; remove from the wok and keep warm. Put the leek, bamboo shoots and asparagus in the wok and stir-fry until the asparagus is tender. Remove and keep warm. In the meantime, cook the noodles in plenty of boiling salted water until *al dente* and drain well. Take the chicken from the marinade and drain well, reserving the liquid. Heat the oil remaining in the wok and stir-fry the chicken until lightly browned. Add all the vegetables, pour on the reserved marinade and the chicken stock and toss everything together until piping hot. Add the dark soya sauce and, if necessary, a little more salt and pepper. Add the noodles, mix in and transfer to bowls. Sprinkle with chopped coriander.

FRIED EGG NOODLES WITH PORK

Here the crispy fried noodles and crunchy vegetables contrast perfectly with the moist, tender meat.

300 g/10½ oz lean boned pork, diced
2 teaspoons dark soya sauce, 1 tablespoon rice wine
½ teaspoon cornflour
½ teaspoon each salt, caster sugar and freshly ground pepper, all mixed together
4 dried tree or wood ear mushrooms, reconstituted in water
½ red pepper, 50 g/1¾ oz carrot
100 g/3½ oz spring onions, 2 garlic cloves
250g/9 oz dried thin egg noodles
about 125 ml/4 fl oz groundnut oil
50 g/1¾ oz beansprouts, 100 g/3½ oz peeled prawns
4–6 tablespoons chicken stock
2 tablespoons light soya sauce, 1 tablespoon oyster sauce

Put the pork in a bowl. Mix together the dark soya sauce, rice wine, cornflour and seasoning and add to the pork. Cover and marinate for 1 hour. Cut the drained mushrooms, pepper and carrot into thin strips. Slice the spring onions. Peel and finely chop the garlic. Cook the noodles in boiling salted water until *al dente* and drain well. Leave to dry, then make 4 noodle cakes, as shown below; keep warm. Heat 1½ tablespoons oil in a wok and stir-fry the garlic briefly. Add the pork and marinade and stir-fry over high heat until browned; remove from the wok and keep warm. Put the vegetables, beansprouts and prawns in the wok and stir-fry vigorously. Return the pork to the wok and mix in the stock, light soya sauce and oyster sauce. Taste and add salt if necessary. Spoon on to the noodle cakes.

Spread out the noodles in a dish lined with paper towels and leave to dry completely.

Heat the oil in a large frying pan over moderate heat. Divide the noodles in 4 portions and add one portion to the oil.

Fry until golden brown and crisp, then carefully turn the noodle cake and fry until the other side is lightly browned.

Meat with noodles in the Sichuan style

The cuisine of this Chinese province is renowned for its hearty, pungently flavoured meat dishes as well as for its noodles

SICHUAN PASTE

This spicy mixture is a popular seasoning in Chinese cooking and can be easily made at home. The only unusual ingredient required is fermented black beans, which can be bought in Chinese shops.

2 garlic cloves, finely chopped
2 tablespoons fermented black beans
1 teaspoon chopped fresh red chillies
1 teaspoon chopped fresh root ginger, 1 teaspoon sugar

Using a pestle and mortar, pound all the ingredients together into a paste.

NOODLES WITH SICHUAN MEAT SAUCE

Here is a good example of a pungently spiced meat sauce from the southern part of China, using Sichuan paste.

40 g/1½ oz dried Chinese mushrooms
2 tablespoons groundnut oil
200 g/7 oz flat Chinese noodles, 200 g/7 oz beansprouts
1 tablespoon chopped spring onions
4 fresh red chillies to garnish
For the Sichuan meat sauce:
2 garlic cloves, 1 tablespoon groundnut oil
40 g/1½ oz finely chopped shallots
2 teaspoons Sichuan paste
200 g/7 oz lean minced pork

Soak the mushrooms in 250 ml/9 fl oz hot water for about 30 minutes. Press dry and slice thinly.

Reserve the soaking water. Heat the groundnut oil in a wok and stir-fry the mushrooms for 2 minutes; remove and keep warm. Peel and finely chop the garlic. Add the 1 tablespoon groundnut oil to the oil already in the wok, heat and stir-fry the garlic and shallots until translucent. Add the Sichuan paste and stir-fry for 2 minutes over low heat. Add the pork and stir-fry for 2 minutes more, then pour in about 125 ml/4 fl oz of the mushroom soaking water. Continue to stir-fry until the liquid has evaporated. Remove from the heat and keep warm. Cook the noodles with the beansprouts in boiling water for about 3 minutes; drain, reserving the cooking liquid. Rinse the noodles in cold water, then return to the cooking water and boil briefly to heat through.

Transfer the noodles and beansprouts to 4 bowls and top with the mushrooms and the pork mixture. Sprinkle with the spring onions and garnish each bowl with a red chilli 'flower'.

Marinades containing soya sauce, fish sauce (nam pla), or oyster sauce may not need additional salt as these ingredients are very salty. Wait until the very end, when all the ingredients are mixed together, then check the seasoning.

FRIED RICE NOODLES WITH BEEF

250 g/9 oz flat rice noodles (see page 36)
250 g/9 oz lean tender beef
3 slices of fresh root ginger, 1 small garlic clove
1 teaspoon fermented black beans
1 green pepper
4 tablespoons groundnut oil
100 g/3½ oz beansprouts, 1 tablespoon dark soya sauce
freshly ground black pepper
For the marinade:
2 teaspoons light soya sauce, 2 tablespoons dark soya sauce
1 tablespoon cornflour
2 tablespoons rice wine, 1 teaspoon caster sugar

Cook the noodles in boiling water until almost *al dente*; drain, rinse with cold water and set aside. Slice the meat thinly. Peel and grate the ginger. Finely chop the garlic and fermented black beans.

Remove the seeds and core from the green pepper and cut into pieces. Mix all the ingredients for the marinade in a bowl, add the meat and leave to marinate for 20 minutes. Heat a wok and pour in 3 tablespoons of groundnut oil. As soon as the oil is smoking, pull the noodles apart, put them in the wok and stir-fry for 1 minute. Add the beansprouts and stir-fry for another minute. Remove the noodles and beansprouts from the wok and set aside. Pour the remaining oil into the wok and stir-fry the ginger and garlic. Add the black beans and green pepper and stir-fry for 1 minute. Drain the meat, add to the wok and stir-fry until cooked. Put the noodle mixture back into the wok, with a little more oil if necessary, and toss until piping hot. Stir in the dark soya sauce, season with pepper and serve.

Noodles with meat and prawns

The cooks of Southeast Asia are particularly skilled in creating such combinations

RICE NOODLES WITH PORK AND TOFU

Noodles and meat are often used together in noodle dishes, but the addition of prawns, which rounds off the flavour of this dish perfectly, is most characteristic of Thai cooking. Small quantities of dried shrimp are usually used as a seasoning; fresh prawns are added in more or less equal proportion to the meat.

250 g/9 oz tomatoes, 400 g/14 oz boned pork
150 g/5½ oz firm tofu, 100 g/3½ oz shallots
4 tablespoons oriental sesame oil
400 g/14 oz thin rice noodles (vermicelli), pulled apart
300 g/10½ oz raw prawns, peeled and deveined
300 g/10½ oz fresh beansprouts
750 ml/1¼ pints coconut milk
4 tablespoons Chinese bean sauce
2 tablespoons fish sauce (nam pla)
1 teaspoon caster sugar, salt
2 tablespoons chopped fresh chives

Blanch the tomatoes, peel them, cut into eighths and remove the seeds. Cut the tomatoes into strips about 1.5 cm/⅝ in wide. Cut the pork into strips. Cut the tofu into 2.5 cm/1 in cubes and cut the shallots into thin strips. Heat 2 tablespoons sesame oil in a wok. Add the noodles and stir-fry until they are light brown and crisp. Add the tomatoes and stir-fry briefly. Remove the noodle and tomato mixture from the wok and put on one side. Clean out the wok with paper towels. Heat the remaining oil in the wok and stir-fry the pork. Add the prawns, tofu, beansprouts and shallots and stir-fry for 3–4 minutes. Pour on the coconut milk and add the bean sauce, fish sauce and sugar. Add the fried noodles, mix everything together thoroughly and season with salt. Garnish with chopped chives and serve.

BAMI GORENG

This fried noodle dish is the counterpart to the popular rice dish known as Nasi Goreng and is equally popular, not only in Indonesia. It is now part of the fast-food repertoire in many European countries. Prepared properly, with fresh ingredients, it remains a dish worth eating.

150 g/5½ oz each boned chicken breast and pork
350 g/12 oz thin Asian egg noodles
120 ml/4 fl oz groundnut oil
150 g/5½ oz spring onions, chopped
100 g/3½ oz onion, finely chopped
3 garlic cloves, finely chopped
150 g/5½ oz Chinese leaves, shredded
2 fresh chillies, deseeded and finely chopped
1 tablespoon finely chopped fresh root ginger
100 g/3½ oz small peeled prawns
1 teaspoon salt
1 teaspoon caster sugar
2 tablespoons light soya sauce
To garnish:
strips of very thin omelette (optional)
fresh coriander leaves

Cut the chicken and pork into thin strips. Continue as shown in the picture sequence. It is important that the oil should always be sizzling hot and that cooking times be as short as possible. When everything is ready, check the seasoning and if necessary add a little more salt and soya sauce. Transfer to plates or bowls and sprinkle with the strips of omelette and the coriander.

Making Bami Goreng:
Add the noodles to a pan of boiling salted water and separate them with a fork. Simmer for 1 minute, then drain in a colander and rinse with cold water.

Heat the oil in a wok until it begins to smoke. Stir-fry the noodles until crisp; remove and put to one side.

Add the meat to the wok with the spring onions, onion and garlic and stir-fry until lightly browned.

Add the Chinese leaves and stir-fry briefly. Add the chillies, ginger and prawns and stir-fry for 1–2 minutes.

Season with salt, sugar and soya sauce. Return the fried noodles to the wok and toss to mix with the other ingredients.

Salads – pasta with meat and vegetables

Good examples of how delicious pasta salads can be

Too many recipes for pasta salads use mayonnaise as a dressing, which coats and disguises all the ingredients and makes one pasta salad indistinguishable from another. However, the recipes on these pages are proof not only that pasta can taste excellent in cold dishes but that it can provide a feast for the eyes as well. Because of its neutral taste and soft texture, pasta generally takes a subordinate role in a dish. It is these qualities that make it ideal for salads, where tangy dressings and ingredients with more assertive flavours can be appreciated. For added interest, try serving ingredients such as meat warm, to contrast with cool pasta and vegetables.

WARM SWEETBREADS WITH ASPARAGUS AND NOODLES

Use half plain wheat noodles and half green wheat noodles (coloured with green tea) for added interest in this unusual salad.

100 g/3½ oz Japanese wheat noodles

For the salad:
200 g/7 oz calves' sweetbreads
100 g/3½ oz asparagus tips
1 crisp lettuce heart, 60 g/2 oz mange-touts
8 cherry tomatoes, halved
salt and freshly ground pepper, 15 g/½ oz butter
100 g/3½ oz mushrooms, thinly sliced
For the dressing:
40 g/1½ oz finely chopped red onion, 2 tablespoons garlic vinegar
1 tablespoon truffle oil, 1 tablespoon neutral vegetable oil
salt and freshly ground pepper
To garnish:
½ teaspoon pink peppercorns, crushed
8 nasturtium leaves and 4 flowers (optional)

Blanch the sweetbreads for 2 minutes, then remove the membrane and sinews and slice; put to one side. Cook the asparagus in boiling water for 4 minutes or until tender; drain and refresh in cold water to retain the colour. Tear the lettuce into pieces. Cut the mange-touts in diamond shapes, blanch briefly and refresh. Cook the noodles in boiling salted water for 1–2 minutes; drain. Season the sweetbreads and fry in the butter for 2 minutes each side. Mix the ingredients for the dressing. Put all the salad ingredients in a bowl with the warm sweetbreads and toss gently. Serve on to plates and drizzle with the dressing. Sprinkle with the peppercorns and garnish with the nasturtium leaves and flowers.

SALAD OF JAPANESE WHEAT NOODLES WITH QUAILS

100 g/3½ oz thin Japanese wheat noodles

For the salad:

2 quails, halved

salt and freshly ground pepper, paprika

2 tablespoons vegetable oil, 85 g/3 oz curly endive (frisée)

50 g/1¾ oz each finely diced red, yellow and green pepper

For the salad dressing:

2 tablespoons sherry vinegar, 2 tablespoons walnut oil

salt and freshly ground pepper, a pinch of caster sugar

1 spring onion, cut into thin rings

1 tablespoon chopped fresh chives

To garnish:

fresh herb leaves

Season the quails with salt, pepper and paprika. Heat the oil in a roasting tin and brown the quails all over. Transfer the tin to the oven at 200°C/400°F/gas 6 and roast until cooked (about 10 minutes), basting occasionally with the oil in the pan. Mix the vinegar, oil, salt, pepper and sugar for the dressing. Add the spring onions and chives and check the seasoning. Cook the noodles in boiling salted water for 1–2 minutes, drain and rinse with cold water. Cut the warm quail pieces in half again and arrange on plates with the noodles, curly endive and peppers. Pour the dressing over and garnish with herb leaves.

RABBIT, AUBERGINE AND NOODLE SALAD

100 g/3½ oz Japanese wheat noodles with red shiso

For the salad:

150 g/5½ oz boned rabbit, 8 rabbit kidneys (optional)

salt and freshly ground pepper, 20 g/scant ¾ oz butter

paprika, 4 baby aubergines, 2 tablespoons vegetable oil

8 yellow tomatoes, quartered

20 g/scant ¾ oz lamb's lettuce (mâche)

For the dressing:

4 tablespoons vegetable oil, 1 garlic clove, finely chopped

2 shallots, finely chopped, 3 tablespoons light soya sauce

2 tablespoons balsamic vinegar

1 small fresh red chilli, deseeded and cut into rings

salt, 1 teaspoon palm or light brown sugar

Cut the rabbit into thin strips and the kidneys in half and season both. Brown the rabbit and then the kidneys in the butter. Sprinkle with paprika and fry for 2–3 minutes. Slice the aubergines thinly lengthways, sprinkle with salt and leave to drain for 10 minutes. Fry the aubergines in the oil until golden brown. Cook the noodles in boiling salted water for 3–4 minutes, drain and rinse with cold water. To make the dressing, heat 1 tablespoon oil and sauté the garlic and shallots until soft. Transfer to a bowl and mix in the remaining dressing ingredients. Arrange the salad on plates and pour the dressing over.

Unusual pasta salads can be made by combining thin Japanese noodles with quails and salad leaves, or rabbit, aubergine and tomatoes.

Stuffed pasta

It is said that stuffed pasta was invented by monks as a means of presenting meat in the guise of vegetables during periods of fasting. However, since stuffed pasta is also found in Chinese cooking, we cannot take any of this too seriously. Whatever the origins, the variously shaped packets and parcels, encasing the most delicious stuffings, mark a high point in the art of pasta making. Inventive cooks are proving daily that virtually anything that can be finely chopped or that is naturally soft and tender can be used as a stuffing for pasta. In northern Italy, which is widely assumed to be the home of ravioli, tortellini and agnolotti, there is a long tradition of wrapping all kinds of left-overs in pasta dough.

Cutting, stuffing and sealing pasta to achieve the desired shape is one of the most time-consuming of all kitchen tasks, but it is also extremely rewarding. Anyone wishing to serve a plate of delicious ravioli for dinner needs a rainy afternoon and a whole army of assistants. Fresh, hand-made stuffed pasta is, of course, a unique pleasure, and the only enhancement it requires is a little butter and, perhaps, some freshly grated cheese. There is nothing wrong with tomato sauce, but good ravioli do not need it.

French chefs, who otherwise have little time for pasta, probably came to experiment with stuffed pasta through the influence of Asian cuisines. They were aided in their efforts by the availability of frozen wonton wrappers. These are stuffed and then often sealed at the top with a thin strand of chive or leek, to make little coin purses. Chinese dumplings are steamed or fried in oil, or deep fried, to be served as part of a selection of appetizers called *dim sum*.

A great deal of commercially made stuffed pasta is available today. Some of it is fresh and is of acceptable quality, but too much is uneatable – the dough is too thick, the stuffing is insipid or the sauce tastes synthetic. Because making pasta at home is very laborious, many cooks resort to the commercial product. But it just cannot compare with fresh, hand-made stuffed pasta and will be a disappointment to those who have tasted the real thing.

fast that the eye does not have time to register it. The reason why pasta cooks in Bologna do not entrust the entire operation to machines, which can, of course, do everything much more quickly, is that they are concerned not only about maintaining quality but also want to keep alive a splendid culinary tradition. The cost of enjoying a hand-made product is accepted by diners, who recognize that they are paying for craft and skill. However, this is not limited to gourmets dining in luxury restaurants – in Bologna, hand-made tortellini are regarded as good plain cooking.

The pasta dough is paper thin when rolled out by skilled hands, such as those of the pastaie, *or pasta cooks, in Bologna. The dough acquires its silky, smooth texture as a result of long kneading and even rolling with a long wooden rolling pin. Once rolled out, it is fashioned with incredible speed into vast quantities of tortellini.*

Tortellini

Dexterity is needed to shape these little stuffed rings

A maximum of stuffing in a minimum of dough is the secret of hand-made tortellini from Bologna. Hundreds and hundreds of these tiny rings of stuffed pasta are freshly prepared every day by *pastaie* in family businesses. This requires great skill, starting with rolling out the dough as thinly as possible, thin enough to read a newspaper through it. The small pasta squares are cut out quite simply with a knife, without the aid of a ruler, and yet they all turn out the same size, which also applies to the quantity of stuffing used for each one. All hands are then required to fold the squares into triangles and roll them into shape over the index finger. The whole process of pressing them together, turning over the ends and pulling them off the finger again happens so

TORTELLINI ALLA BOLOGNESE

As with all classic recipes, the search for the original will turn up quite a number of versions claiming to be the authentic one. Ingredients change over time and the proportions are also determined to a certain extent by cost. However, the basis for the stuffing is usually veal or pork, or possibly chicken or turkey. Mortadella also plays a part in a genuine Bolognese stuffing, not only for the flavour it imparts but also because its fat serves to bind the stuffing together. The addition of calves' or lambs' brains makes the meat stuffing particularly rich and smooth and prosciutto can add a distinctively different flavour.

1 quantity of fresh pasta dough no. 3 (see page 40)
For the stuffing:
100 g/3½ oz each boned pork and veal
85 g/3 oz skinned and boned chicken breast
50 g/1¾ oz butter
60 g/2 oz calves' brains (optional)
125 g/4½ oz mortadella
60 g/2 oz prosciutto
3 egg yolks
100 g/3½ oz Parmesan cheese, freshly grated

salt and freshly ground pepper
freshly grated nutmeg
To serve:
1 quantity of fresh tomato sauce (see page 69)
freshly grated Parmesan cheese

Cut the pork, veal and chicken into cubes. Heat the butter in a pan over moderate heat and lightly brown the cubes of meat. Continue frying until the meat is cooked (about 10 minutes longer). Remove the meat and set aside. Quickly brown the brains and mortadella in the pan. Now mince all the meats, together with the prosciutto, in a mincer or food processor. Add the egg yolks and Parmesan and knead to form a smooth paste. Season with salt, pepper and nutmeg. Cover and refrigerate for 2–3 hours. Roll out the pasta dough as thinly as possible and cut into 4 cm/1½ in squares. Take balls of stuffing about as big as a hazelnut and put one in the middle of each square. Form the tortellini as shown in the picture sequence. (The edges of the squares do not need to be sealed with water or egg white, as is advisable with ravioli, since with tortellini it is the folded-over ends that prevent the filling from bursting out.) Spread out the stuffed pasta on a well-floured surface and dry briefly before cooking it in boiling salted water. Tortellini can be served *in brodo*, that is in a clear chicken or beef broth. They can also be served with nothing more complicated than melted butter and finely chopped fresh herbs or, as in the picture below, with fresh tomato sauce and freshly grated Parmesan.

Shaping tortellini:

Fold the pasta square over into a triangle, enclosing the ball of stuffing, and press the edges together to seal. Do not press too hard or the tortellino will lose its neat shape.

Wrap the triangle, apex down, around the index finger and press the ends together tightly so that they stick firmly to each other.

With the fingers of the other hand, fold down the points forming the apex of the triangle. In the same movement, slide the tortellino off the finger.

Stuffed with ricotta

Di magro (lean) is the Italian name for the classic combination of ricotta and spinach, or another leafy vegetable or herb

RAVIOLI WITH RICOTTA AND SPINACH

Pasta stuffed with this mix of ingredients is called *agnolotti* in Piedmont and *ravioli* in Bologna and the surrounding area. The ricotta mixture is used to stuff both the large ravioli and the tiny raviolini. It is also found in tortellini and tortelli, proving that the same stuffing can be used in many different pasta shapes.

1 quantity of fresh pasta dough no. 3 (see page 40)
1 egg white, lightly whisked with a fork
For the stuffing:
300 g/10½ oz young spinach leaves
200 g/7 oz ricotta cheese
½ teaspoon salt, freshly ground pepper
freshly grated nutmeg
100 g/3½ oz Parmesan cheese, freshly grated
2 egg yolks
85 g/3 oz butter, 6 fresh sage leaves
freshly grated Parmesan cheese to serve

Put the spinach in a large pan of lightly salted boiling water and cook until starting to wilt – 2 minutes at most. Drain and plunge into ice-cold water, then drain thoroughly, pressing out as much of the water as possible. Chop the spinach coarsely and mix with the ricotta. Season with salt, pepper and nutmeg and stir in the Parmesan and egg yolks.

If the ravioli are to be stuffed without the aid of special moulds (see pictures), proceed as follows: roll out the dough as thinly as possible and cut into 2 sheets, each about 50 x 30 cm/20 x 12 in. Using the back of a knife and a ruler, score a grid of 5 cm/2 in squares on one of the sheets. Put an equal amount of stuffing on each of the squares. If this process takes a long time, the dough will start to dry out, so you will need to brush a little egg white around each bit of stuffing, so that the second sheet of dough will stick. Lay the second sheet loosely over the first one and press down lightly around the stuffing so that the edges are well sealed. Using a ruler and a fluted pastry wheel, cut out the squares and lay them on a lightly floured cloth. Cook the stuffed pasta in boiling salted water for 4–5 minutes, remove with a slotted spoon and arrange on plates. Melt the butter until clear, briefly toss the shredded sage leaves in it and pour over the pasta. Sprinkle with Parmesan and serve.

Making ravioli in a mould:

Put all the ingredients for the stuffing into a bowl and mix together to a smooth paste.

Lay one thin sheet of dough on the ravioli mould and put a little stuffing in each indentation. If necessary, moisten the dough around the stuffing with a little egg white.

Lay a second sheet of dough over the top. Roll lightly with a rolling pin to cut the pasta squares and seal the edges. Lift from the mould.

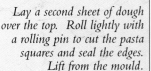

Ricotta cheese has a moist, slightly grainy texture. In Italy, it is made from the whey drained off while making other cheeses and is set either in the traditional baskets or, more usually nowadays, in plastic or stainless steel moulds.

TORTELLONI WITH RICOTTA AND HERBS

1 quantity of fresh pasta dough no. 3 (see page 40)

For the stuffing:

250 g/9 oz ricotta cheese, 1 egg, ½ teaspoon salt

freshly ground pepper

1 tablespoon chopped fresh parsley

1 teaspoon each chopped fresh lovage or celery leaves, thyme and sage

a few rosemary needles

85 g/3 oz Parmesan cheese, freshly grated

For the sauce:

400 g/14 oz ripe tomatoes, 1 garlic clove, 1 fresh red chilli

3 tablespoons extra virgin olive oil, 60 g/2 oz finely chopped onion

½ teaspoon salt, ½ teaspoon sugar

To garnish:

freshly pared Parmesan cheese

Thoroughly mix together all the stuffing ingredients. To make the sauce, blanch the tomatoes, peel them, remove the seeds and dice. Finely chop the garlic. Remove the seeds from the chilli and finely chop. Heat the oil in a saucepan and sauté the onion and garlic until translucent. Add the tomatoes and chilli and season with salt and sugar. Simmer until the

tomatoes have broken down and the sauce is thick (10–15 minutes). Cut out and stuff the tortelloni as shown in the picture sequence. Cook in boiling salted water for 8–10 minutes, then remove with a slotted spoon and transfer to plates. Pour the sauce over and sprinkle with Parmesan shavings.

Preparing the tortelloni:

Roll out the dough thinly and use a fluted cutter to cut out discs 6–7 cm/2½–2¾ in in diameter.

Put 1 teaspoon of stuffing on each disc of dough, positioning the stuffing exactly in the centre.

Fold each disc over into a half-moon shape and press the edges together to seal (moisten the edges with a little water, if necessary).

RAVIOLI WITH BEETROOT STUFFING

Beetroot is a popular vegetable in northern Italy and here it is used in a stuffing for ravioli, called *casonsei*.

1 quantity of fresh pasta dough no. 3 (see page 40)
1 egg white, lightly whisked with a fork
For the beetroot stuffing:
400 g/14 oz fresh beetroot, 1 teaspoon fennel seeds
1 teaspoon salt, 85 g/3 oz butter
30 g/1 oz finely chopped shallots
85 g/3 oz white breadcrumbs
½ teaspoon salt, freshly ground pepper
a pinch of ground ginger, 1 egg yolk
To finish:
85 g/3 oz butter, 30 g/1 oz ground poppy seeds
50 g/1¾ oz Parmesan cheese, freshly grated

Carefully peel the beetroot, cut into quarters and put in a pan of water with the fennel seeds and salt. Cook until tender, then drain. Put through a mincer or purée in a food processor. Allow to cool. Heat the butter and sauté the shallots until translucent. Add the breadcrumbs and fry until golden, stirring constantly. Combine this mixture with the beetroot purée and season with salt, pepper and ginger. Finally, mix in the egg yolk. Roll out the pasta dough thinly and cut out discs about 6 cm/2¼ in in diameter. Put a little stuffing in the middle of each disc and brush the edge with egg white or water. Fold each disc over into a half-moon shape and press the edges firmly together to seal. Cook the ravioli in boiling salted water until they rise to the surface. In the meantime, heat the butter in a small pan and stir in the ground poppy seeds. As soon as the ravioli are done, remove them with a slotted spoon to pre-warmed plates. Pour the poppy-seed butter over them and sprinkle with grated Parmesan.

RAVIOLI STUFFED WITH LAMB

1 quantity of fresh pasta dough no. 3 (see page 40)
1 egg white, lightly whisked with a fork
For the stuffing:
300 g/10½ oz lean boned lamb, trimmed
3 tablespoons olive oil, ½ garlic clove, finely chopped
1 onion, finely chopped, 125 ml/4 fl oz lamb stock
½ teaspoon salt, freshly ground black pepper
a pinch of freshly grated nutmeg
4–6 fresh sage leaves, chopped
½ teaspoon each chopped fresh rosemary and thyme
To finish:
85 g/3 oz butter
85 g/3 oz Parmesan cheese, freshly grated
black olives to garnish

Mince the lamb using a mincer or food processor. Heat the oil in a pan and sauté the garlic and onion until soft. Add the lamb and brown over high heat, stirring to break it up. Pour in the stock and season with salt, pepper and nutmeg. Simmer over moderate heat for about 20 minutes. If necessary, add a little more stock. Stir in the herbs and leave the stuffing to cool. Roll out the pasta dough into two thin sheets. Mark 4 cm/1½ in squares on one sheet. Place a little

stuffing in the centre of each and brush the pasta round the stuffing with egg white.   Lay the second sheet loosely over the first and press down lightly round the stuffing so that the edges are well sealed. Using a ruler and a fluted pastry wheel, cut out the squares and lay them on a lightly floured cloth. Leave to dry for 1–2 hours. Cook in boiling salted water until *al dente* and remove with a slotted spoon to drain. Melt the butter in a pan and toss the ravioli in it. Sprinkle with Parmesan and garnish with olives.

RICOTTA TORTELLINI WITH SAVOY CABBAGE

The texture and flavour of crunchy cabbage offer a pleasant contrast to the tortellini.

1 quantity of fresh pasta dough no. 3 (see page 40)
For the ricotta stuffing:
40 g/1½ oz finely chopped shallots, 30 g/1 oz butter
200 g/7 oz ricotta cheese, 4 egg yolks
50 g/1¾ oz fine white breadcrumbs
1 tablespoon chopped fresh basil
salt and freshly ground pepper, freshly grated nutmeg
For the vegetables:
30 g/1 oz each carrot, celery and leek
100 g/3½ oz chopped Savoy cabbage
100 g/3½ oz cold butter

Sauté the shallots in the hot butter until translucent; cool. Mix the ricotta, egg yolks and breadcrumbs in a bowl. Add the sautéed shallots and basil, and season with salt, pepper and nutmeg. Roll out the pasta dough as thinly as possible and cut into 4 cm/ 1½ in squares. Place a little stuffing on each square and shape into tortellini as described on page 179. If possible, leave to dry for 1–2 hours before cooking. Cut the carrot, celery and leek in julienne strips. Blanch the vegetables, including the cabbage, in succession in boiling water; drain and keep warm. Cook the tortellini in boiling salted water until they rise to the surface; remove with a slotted spoon and keep warm. Thicken 100 ml/3½ oz of the cooking liquid with the cold butter and toss the vegetables and tortellini in it. Check the seasoning and transfer to pre-warmed plates.

CIALZONS

In this version of an Italian dish, traditional in Friuli-Venezia Giulia and Trentino-Alto Adige, pasta half-moons are stuffed with a mixture of rye breadcrumbs, spices and chard. The recipe will make 36–40 stuffed pasta shapes.

For the pasta dough:
200 g/7 oz plain flour
2 eggs, salt
For the chard stuffing:
200 g/7 oz Swiss chard leaves
30 g/1 oz dry rye breadcrumbs
2 tablespoons milk, 1 egg
a pinch each of ground cinnamon and cloves
1 tablespoon each chopped fresh thyme and parsley
1 tablespoon ground juniper berries
salt and freshly ground pepper
In addition:
1 egg white, lightly whisked with a fork
100 g/3½ oz butter, melted
freshly pared Parmesan

1 tablespoon finely chopped fresh parsley

Sift the flour on to a work surface, form a well in the middle and add the eggs and a little salt. Mix the ingredients together, starting from the middle and working out, and knead to a smooth, pliable dough. Wrap in cling film and put aside to rest. To make the stuffing, blanch the chard leaves until they begin to wilt, then drain and refresh in cold water. Press out excess water. Finely chop the chard and put in a bowl. Soak the breadcrumbs in the milk, squeeze out excess milk and add to the chard with all the other stuffing ingredients. Mix thoroughly. Roll out the pasta dough until paper thin and cut out discs about 7 cm/2¾ in in diameter, preferably using a fluted cutter. Place 1 teaspoon of the filling in the centre of each disc, brush the edges with egg white and fold over to form half-moons, pressing the edges firmly together to seal. Cook the pasta in boiling salted water until *al dente* (5–7 minutes). Drain and arrange immediately on pre-warmed plates. Drizzle with the melted butter and sprinkle with Parmesan shavings and parsley.

PANSOTI WITH WALNUT SAUCE

Pansoti (also spelled pansotti), which means 'chubby', is a dish from Liguria. The pasta triangles are stuffed with herbs and cheese and served with a walnut sauce. This recipe will make about 80 pasta shapes.

350 g/12 oz fresh pasta dough no. 3 (see page 40)
For the herb stuffing:
125 g/4½ oz mixed fresh herb leaves
125 g/4½ oz fresh basil leaves
60 g/2 oz fresh borage leaves (or use another herb)
1 small egg, 1 garlic clove, finely chopped
60 g/2 oz ricotta cheese
25 g/scant 1 oz Parmesan cheese, freshly grated
salt and freshly ground pepper
For the walnut sauce:
40 g/1½ oz white breadcrumbs
1 tablespoon water, 125 g/4½ oz walnut pieces
3 tablespoons olive oil, 4 tablespoons cream, salt
To serve:
125 g/4½ oz Parmesan cheese, freshly grated

To make the stuffing, briefly blanch all the herb leaves, refresh in cold water and dry with paper towels. Finely chop the herbs and purée with the other ingredients in a food processor. Roll out the pasta dough thinly and cut out 5 cm/2 in squares. Put 1 teaspoon of the stuffing on each square, brush the edges with water and fold over into triangles, pressing the edges together firmly to seal. To make the sauce, moisten the breadcrumbs with the water. Continue as shown in the picture sequence. Cook the pansoti in boiling salted water for about 10 minutes, then drain and serve with the sauce and Parmesan.

Making the walnut sauce:

Using a pestle and mortar, pound the walnuts to a paste, then grind them in a blender or food processor with the breadcrumbs.

Mix in the oil and cream alternately, then season with salt. Stir until the sauce has a smooth consistency.

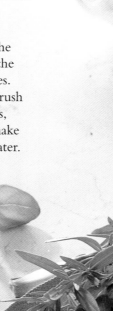

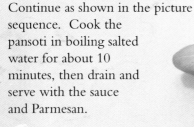

Delicious meat stuffings

The shape of the pasta does not matter too much here – what it contains is the important thing

TORTELLI
WITH OXTAIL STUFFING

Making *pasta ripiena*, or stuffed pasta, takes a lot of time. For this recipe, you'll have to allow even more time, to cook the meat for the stuffing. But your labours will be rewarded with a truly wonderful dish, ideal either as a starter or a main dish. The following recipe is sufficient for 8 servings.

1 quantity of fresh pasta dough no. 3 (page 40)
egg white lightly whisked with a fork
For the stuffing:
1 oxtail, weighing about 1.5 kg/3⅓ lb
1 teaspoon salt, freshly ground pepper
4 tablespoons vegetable oil
1 garlic clove, unpeeled but bruised
100 g/3½ oz carrots, diced
100 g/3½ oz celery, thinly sliced
100 g/3½ oz leeks, thinly sliced
30 g/1 oz diced Hamburg parsley (optional)
5 juniper berries, 1 bay leaf
5 fresh sage leaves, 2 tablespoons tomato purée
500 ml/18 fl oz red wine (Merlot)
1 tablespoon plain flour
1 tablespoon chopped fresh herbs: parsley, lovage or celery leaves

Locate the joints in the oxtail by pressing with your thumbs, then cut across into sections (or ask your butcher to do this).

Season the oxtail. Heat the oil in a roasting tin and brown the oxtail. Add the garlic and all the prepared vegetables.

Cook for about 10 minutes, stirring well. Add the juniper berries, bay leaf, sage and tomato purée and pour in the red wine.

Take out the pieces of oxtail, remove as much of the meat from the bones as possible and chop it finely.

Strain the sauce, pressing on the vegetables and seasonings with a ladle so that some of the vegetables are forced through into the sauce.

Distribute the meat stuffing, evenly spaced, on one sheet of dough. Brush a little egg white on the dough round each portion of stuffing.

Lay the second sheet of dough over the top. Cut out tortelli using a fluted 6 cm/2¼ in round cutter.

1 egg yolk
To finish:
500 g/1lb 2 oz fresh chanterelles, 40 g/1½ oz butter
salt, 2 tablespoons chopped fresh parsley

Prepare the oxtail as shown in the first three steps of the picture sequence. Cover the roasting tin and braise in the oven at 180°C/350°F/gas 4 for about 2 hours; stir occasionally. After 1 hour, dust the meat with the flour. Continue as shown in the next two steps of the picture sequence. Mix the meat with the chopped herbs and egg yolk; add a few spoonfuls of the sauce to moisten the stuffing. Allow the stuffing to cool. Roll out the dough in two thin sheets. Stuff and cut the tortelli as shown in the last two steps of the picture sequence. Allow the pasta to dry a little. In the meantime, clean the chanterelles very carefully; if they are large, cut them in smaller pieces. Boil the sauce to reduce it a little. Cook the tortelli in boiling salted water until they rise to the surface; lift out with a slotted spoon and arrange in pre-warmed dishes. Heat the butter in a large pan, add the chanterelles and season with salt and chopped parsley. Sauté for a few minutes over high heat. Mix with the sauce and pour over the tortelli.

AGNOLOTTI
WITH RABBIT STUFFING

'Agnolotti' is the term for ravioli in Piedmont, and they can be either round or square. There is a particular type of square agnolotti described as '*dal plin*', which means 'with a pleat'. These may contain various stuffings, although they are usually made with meat.

1 quantity of fresh pasta dough no. 3 (see page 40)
For the stuffing:
300 g/10½ oz boned rabbit meat from the leg
200 g/7oz lean boned pork
3–4 tablespoons vegetable oil, 1 garlic clove, finely chopped
2 tablespoons chopped shallots
85 g/3 oz each diced carrot and celery
1 teaspoon chopped fresh thyme
some chopped fresh rosemary
1 teaspoon salt, freshly ground pepper
about 500 ml/18 fl oz veal stock, 500 g/1 lb 2 oz spinach
85 g/3 oz Parmesan cheese, freshly grated, 2 eggs
To finish:
a handful of fresh sage leaves, 60 g/2 oz butter

Carefully trim the rabbit and pork and cut into even-sized pieces. Heat the oil in a suitably sized pan and quickly brown the meat. Add the garlic, shallots, carrot, celery and herbs and season lightly with salt and

pepper. Fry over a fairly high heat for about 15 minutes, stirring so that the ingredients brown evenly. Pour on half the veal stock and simmer until the meat is cooked (about 1 hour). Drain the meat in a sieve set in a bowl; reserve the liquid. Leave the meat to cool, then put through a mincer or chop in a food processor. Wash the spinach thoroughly, remove the stalks and blanch briefly in boiling salted water. Drain, press dry and finely chop. Add to the meat together with the Parmesan and eggs and stir to form a thick paste. In the meantime, mix the reserved liquid with the rest of the veal stock and boil to reduce until only 2–3 tablespoons remain. Mix this into the stuffing and check the seasoning. Roll out the pasta dough as thinly as possible and make the agnolotti as shown in the picture sequence. A 'pleat' can be pinched or pressed into each square. Leave to dry for at least 2–3 hours, then cook in boiling salted water until they rise to the surface (about 3 minutes). Remove with a slotted spoon and arrange on pre-warmed plates.

A delicious variation is to serve the agnolotti with jellied meat juices. And during the truffle season in Piedmont, agnolotti are topped with paper-thin slivers of white truffle. They also taste superb served with nothing more than butter.

Preparing agnolotti:

Mark out rectangles, 4 x 6 cm/1½ x 2¼ in, on the thin sheet of dough. Put a small ball of stuffing on half of each rectangle.

Cut out the rectangles using a fluted pastry wheel. Brush the edges of each rectangle with water to moisten.

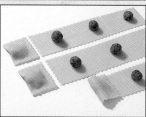

Fold the dough over to enclose the stuffing and press the edges together firmly to seal.

Agnolotti are splendid served with sage butter. Simply toss the sage leaves in hot melted butter and pour over the pasta.

RAVIOLINI WITH MEAT STUFFING

The lightly spiced stuffing here is made from beef and pork, plus generous quantities of spinach and mushrooms. It can be used to stuff many other shapes of pasta – from cannelloni to tortellini – as well as the small ravioli called raviolini. It is worth making a little more of the stuffing than required (the following recipe is sufficient for 8 servings), since the remainder can be frozen.

1 quantity of fresh pasta dough no. 3 (see page 40)
For the meat stuffing:
1 garlic clove, 4 tablespoons vegetable oil
85 g/3 oz finely chopped onion, 100 g/3½ oz diced celery
40 g/1½ oz diced carrot
200 g/7 oz each boned pork and beef, freshly minced
1 teaspoon salt, ¼ teaspoon freshly ground pepper
2 teaspoons paprika, 2 teaspoons tomato purée
200 g/7 oz spinach, washed
500 ml/18 fl oz beef stock (see page 82)
150 g/5½ oz mushrooms, diced
2 tablespoons chopped fresh parsley, 2 egg yolks
To serve:
tomato sauce (see page 70)
freshly pared Parmesan cheese, 50 g/1¾ oz butter, melted

Peel and finely chop the garlic. Heat the oil and sauté the onion and garlic until translucent, then add the celery and carrot and sauté for a few more minutes. Add the minced meats to the vegetables and brown over high heat, stirring to break up any lumps. Season with the salt, pepper and paprika and stir in the tomato purée. Coarsely chop the spinach and add to the meat mixture. Remove from the heat immediately and leave to cool. Over a low heat, boil the stock until reduced to 4–5 tablespoons; stir into the stuffing. Work the stuffing, in batches, in a food processor to make it a little smoother but not enough to turn it into a paste. Add the mushrooms, parsley and egg yolks and mix well. Roll out the pasta dough in two sheets and lay one over a well-floured raviolini mould; trim off excess dough. Spoon the stuffing into a piping bag fitted with a plain tube and pipe a small quantity in each hollow (or you can spoon in the stuffing). Lay the second sheet of dough on top and roll lightly with a rolling pin to seal and cut out the raviolini. Tap the raviolini from the mould. Cook in boiling salted water until they rise to the surface; remove with a slotted spoon and arrange on pre-warmed plates. Spoon a little tomato sauce over each serving, sprinkle with Parmesan shavings and drizzle on the melted butter.

The meat stuffing should be worked in a food processor until finely chopped but not puréed. Use the pulse button so the stuffing remains quite coarse in texture.

TURKISH PASTA TRIANGLES WITH BEEF STUFFING

'*Manti*' is the Turkish name for these small triangles of stuffed pasta.

1 quantity of fresh cornmeal pasta dough (see page 43)
For the beef stuffing:
1 garlic clove, 5 tablespoons olive oil
60 g/2 oz finely chopped onion
85 g/3 oz finely chopped spring onions
50 g/1¾ oz diced carrot
40 g/1½ oz diced Hamburg parsley (optional)
300 g/10½ oz boned beef, freshly minced
1 fresh chilli, 1 tablespoon chopped fresh parsley
1 tablespoon chopped fresh mint
½ tablespoon salt, freshly ground pepper
For the sauce:
2 garlic cloves, 200 ml/7 fl oz plain yogurt
½ teaspoon salt
To finish:
85 g/3 oz butter, 1 tablespoon paprika

Allow the cornmeal pasta dough to rest for at least 1 hour. Peel and finely chop the garlic. Heat half of the oil in a suitably sized pan and sauté the onion and garlic until translucent. Add the spring onions, carrot and Hamburg parsley (if using) and cook until the vegetables are soft. Heat the remaining oil in a second pan and brown the meat over high heat, stirring to break up lumps. Add the sautéed vegetables. Cut the chilli in half lengthways, remove the core and seeds and finely chop. Add to the meat mixture with the parsley and mint and season with salt and pepper. Mix everything together thoroughly and leave to cool. Roll out the pasta dough as thinly as possible. Cut out 3 cm/1¼ in squares. (To prevent the dough from drying out, keep the squares covered with a slightly damp cloth.) Place a small ball of stuffing on each square, fold the squares over into triangles and press the edges together firmly to seal. If necessary, dampen the edges slightly with water so that they stick together. To make the sauce, peel and finely chop the garlic; mix with the yogurt and season to taste with salt. Cook the pasta parcels in boiling salted water until they rise to the surface. Remove with a slotted spoon and arrange on 4 pre-warmed plates. Spoon the yogurt sauce over the pasta. Melt the butter with the paprika until it foams and pour over the top.

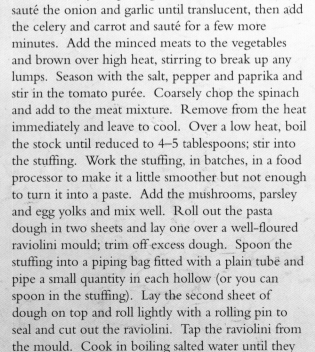

MAULTASCHEN

This is a southern German version of ravioli. The recipe will make about 24 squares.

For the dough:
300 g/10½ oz plain flour, preferably type 00
3 eggs, 1 teaspoon salt, 1 tablespoon oil
1 egg white, lightly whisked with a fork
For the stuffing:
2 stale bread rolls (85 g/3 oz), crumbled
100 ml/3½ fl oz lukewarm milk
85 g/3 oz streaky bacon
40 g/1½ oz butter, 60 g/2 oz chopped onion
60 g/2 oz chopped spring onions
200 g/7 oz bratwurst, removed from casing
200 g/7 oz spinach, 2 eggs
½ teaspoon salt, freshly ground white pepper
1 tablespoon dried marjoram
1 tablespoon finely chopped fresh parsley
To finish:
1 litre/1¾ pints meat stock
50 g/1¾ oz butter, 100 g/3½ oz chopped onion
1 tablespoon chopped fresh chives

Sift the flour on to a work surface and make a well in the middle. Break the eggs into the hollow and add the salt and oil. Mix the ingredients together with a fork, then knead into a pliable dough. Shape into a ball, cover with a cloth and leave to rest for 15 minutes. Soak the bread in the milk and squeeze dry. Cut the bacon into small squares. Heat the butter and sauté the onion and spring onions until translucent; add the sausage and cook, stirring. Continue as shown in the picture sequence left. Roll out the pasta dough thinly on a floured work surface. Using a ruler and pastry wheel, cut out rectangles about 6 x 12 cm/2½ x 5 in. Continue as shown in the picture sequence below. Heat the butter and lightly brown the onion. Arrange the cooked pasta squares on plates and pour a little of the stock over them. Garnish with the browned onion and chives.

For the stuffing, blanch the spinach, refresh in cold water, squeeze dry and finely chop. Combine the spinach, soaked bread, sautéed onions, bacon and the remaining stuffing ingredients and mix well together.

Put a small spoonful of stuffing on one half of each pasta rectangle. Brush the edges with egg white, then fold the rectangles over into squares and press to seal.

Bring the stock to the boil in a large pan, add the stuffed pasta and cook until they rise to the surface.

SCHLUTZKRAPFEN

This speciality from the southern Tyrol, with its delicate spinach stuffing, is very similar to ravioli. The dough contains rye flour, which gives these pasta parcels from Italy's northernmost province a robust flavour. The recipe will make about 45.

For the dough:
150 g/5½ oz plain flour
100 g/3½ oz rye flour
½ teaspoon salt
1 egg, 1–2 tablespoons olive oil
about 5 tablespoons water
1 egg white, lightly whisked with a fork
For the spinach stuffing:
375 g/13 oz spinach
1 tablespoon chopped fresh parsley
1½ teaspoons chopped fresh lovage or celery leaves
15 g/½ oz butter
2 tablespoons finely chopped onion
4 teaspoons plain flour, 125 ml/4 fl oz hot milk
salt and freshly ground pepper
freshly grated nutmeg
3 tablespoons freshly grated Parmesan cheese
To serve:
50 g/1¾ oz Parmesan cheese, freshly grated
50 g/1¾ oz butter, melted

Mix together the two kinds of flour and pour on to a work surface. Form a well in the middle and add the salt, egg, oil and 4 tablespoons of the water. Mix the ingredients together with a fork, working from the middle outward, and knead into a pliable dough. Add more water if necessary. Wrap in cling film and leave to rest. Blanch the spinach in boiling salted water until it wilts. Refresh in cold water, squeeze dry and finely chop. Mix with the herbs. Heat the butter in a saucepan and sauté the onion until translucent. Sprinkle on the flour, stir well and cook for 1 minute. Stir in the milk, bring to the boil and simmer gently until thickened. Stir in the spinach mixture, salt, pepper, nutmeg and, finally, the Parmesan. Put to one side. Roll out the pasta dough very thinly and cut out discs 8 cm/3 in in diameter. Place ½ tablespoon of stuffing in the middle of each disc, brush the edge with egg white and fold over into a half-moon shape. Press the edges together with a fork to seal. (The rolling out and stuffing must be done as fast as possible, because the rye flour in the dough makes it dry out quickly.) Cook the pasta in boiling salted water for about 10 minutes; remove with a slotted spoon and arrange on plates. Sprinkle with the cheese and pour the melted butter over the top.

Polish pierogi

Pierogi, Polish stuffed pasta, have their origins in ancient Slav cuisine

The name of these stuffed pasta shapes has its roots in '*pir*', meaning banquet or feast, but where they may once have been a delicacy, pierogi have become an everyday dish. They can be made with a wide range of substantial stuffings, depending on individual taste and the season of the year. The recipes here will make about 30 pierogi.

PASTA DOUGH FOR PIEROGI

300 g/10½ oz plain flour, preferably type 00
1 egg, ½ teaspoon salt, 125 ml/4 fl oz water
In addition:
1 egg white, lightly whisked with a fork

Make the pasta dough as directed on page 41. While it is resting, prepare the stuffing (see recipes on this and the facing page). Roll out the dough thinly and cut out discs 7 cm/2¾ in in diameter. Brush the edges with egg white. Put about ½ tablespoon of stuffing in the middle of each disc, fold over into a half-moon shape and press the edges together firmly to seal. Cook in batches in boiling salted water. When the pierogi have risen to the surface, cook for 5 minutes longer, then remove with a slotted spoon.

MUSHROOM PIEROGI WITH FOIE GRAS

For the mushroom stuffing:
½ tablespoon oil, 1 onion, sliced
100 g/3½ oz mushrooms, diced
salt and freshly ground pepper
freshly grated nutmeg, 1 egg
To finish:
250 g/9 oz foie gras, thinly sliced
20 g/scant ¾ oz butter
salt and freshly ground pepper
2 tablespoons finely chopped shallots
2 tablespoons veal stock, fresh flat-leaf parsley

Heat the oil and sauté the onion until translucent. Add the mushrooms and cook for 10 minutes. Season with salt, pepper and nutmeg. Remove from the heat and stir in the egg. Allow to cool. Stuff the pierogi and cook as directed. Meanwhile, brown the foie gras in the butter. Season with salt and pepper and remove from the pan. Sauté the shallots in the pan until translucent. Add the stock and stir to form a sauce. Arrange the pierogi on plates with the foie gras, pour the sauce over and garnish with parsley.

PIEROGI WITH SAUERKRAUT AND BACON

For the sauerkraut stuffing:
300 g/10½ oz sauerkraut
1 onion
2 tablespoons oil
salt and freshly ground pepper
To finish:
15 g/½ oz butter
85 g/3 oz finely chopped bacon
50 g/1¾ oz finely chopped onion
1 tablespoon chopped fresh parsley

Cook the sauerkraut in a little water for 15–20 minutes; leave to cool slightly, then squeeze dry and finely chop. Transfer to a bowl. Cut the onion into thin slices and brown lightly in the oil. Mix with the sauerkraut and season to taste. Allow to cool. Stuff the pierogi and cook them as directed. Heat the butter until it foams and sauté the bacon briefly. Add the onion and cook until it has browned slightly. Stir in the parsley. Arrange the pierogi on plates and pour the bacon and onion mixture over them.

MEAT PIEROGI WITH TOMATOES

For the meat stuffing:
1 small stale bread roll, crumbled, 1 tablespoon water
1 onion, 1 tablespoon oil
150 g/5½ oz mixed minced meats: beef, pork, veal
1 tablespoon stock
salt and freshly ground pepper
To finish:
30 g/1 oz butter
2 shallots, finely chopped
3 tomatoes, peeled, deseeded and roughly chopped
1 tablespoon shredded fresh basil to garnish

Moisten the bread with the water. Finely chop the onion. Heat the oil and sauté the onion until translucent. Add the minced meats and fry, stirring to break up lumps. Add the moistened bread and stock and stir until the liquid has evaporated. Season with salt and pepper and leave to cool. Stuff the pierogi and cook as directed. Heat the butter and sauté the shallots until translucent. Add the tomatoes and cook briefly. Arrange the pierogi on plates, pour the tomato mixture over and garnish with basil.

Sauerkraut and meat are typical stuffings for pierogi. There are also sweet stuffings in Polish cooking, for example blueberries mixed with sugar and white breadcrumbs.

Sophisticated stuffings

Definitely not everyday recipes: unusual stuffings for pasta

TORTELLINI WITH SEAFOOD AND TWO PEPPER SAUCES

Green pasta stuffed with fish and prawns and served with red and yellow pepper sauces is a combination as original as it is delicious. If you prefer a meat stuffing, use that for the raviolini on page 188.

1 quantity of fresh green pasta dough (see page 46)
For the stuffing:
300 g/10½ oz sole or turbot fillet
100 ml/3½ fl oz cream
100 g/3½ oz prawns, finely chopped
salt and freshly ground pepper
1 tablespoon chopped fresh dill
For the pepper sauces:
450 g/1 lb each yellow and red peppers
40 g/1½ oz butter, 2 shallots, diced
1 garlic clove, chopped, salt and freshly ground pepper
2 sprigs of fresh thyme, 2 bay leaves
5 tablespoons Sauternes, 300 ml/½ pint veal stock
To serve:
85 g/3 oz pecorino cheese, freshly grated

Cut the fish into cubes and purée in a blender or food processor, then pass through a sieve. Mix to a smooth paste with the cream. Stir in the finely chopped prawns, season and add the dill. Cover and refrigerate. Make the red and yellow pepper sauces separately, using half of the ingredients for each one. Remove the core and seeds from the peppers and dice them. Heat the butter and sauté the shallots and garlic until soft. Add the diced peppers, season with salt and pepper and add the thyme and bay leaf. Pour on the wine and stock and simmer until the peppers are soft and the liquid has almost all evaporated. Pound with a potato masher and pass through a sieve (or work in a mouli-légumes). Roll out the pasta dough thinly and cut out 4 cm/1½ in squares with a pastry wheel. Place a ball of filling the size of a hazelnut in the middle of each square and shape the tortellini as shown on page 179. Cook the tortellini in boiling salted water until they rise to the surface. In the meantime, heat the pepper sauces. Remove the tortellini with a slotted spoon and arrange on plates. Spoon over the red and yellow pepper sauces and sprinkle with pecorino.

PUMPKIN RAVIOLI

This stuffing derives its interesting flavour from the contrast between the pumpkin, glacé fruits and amaretti biscuits on the one hand and the cheese and seasonings on the other. This combination of tastes is extremely popular in Italy and is well worth trying. A glass of *vin santo* from Tuscany is the perfect accompaniment.

1 quantity of fresh pasta dough no. 3 (see page 40)
1 egg white, lightly whisked with a fork
For the stuffing:
1 pumpkin, weighing about 700g/1½ lb
3 amaretti biscuits
100 g/3½ oz glacé fruits in syrup, drained and finely chopped
65 g/2¼ oz Parmesan cheese, freshly grated
salt and freshly ground pepper
freshly grated nutmeg
To finish:
100 g/3½ oz butter
a handful of fresh sage leaves
100 g/3½ oz Parmesan cheese, freshly grated

Bake the pumpkin, whole, in the oven at 200°C/400°F/gas 6 for about 50 minutes; cool. Break the amaretti into small pieces – the best way is to put them in a plastic bag and crush them with a rolling pin. Cut the pumpkin in half, remove the seeds and scoop out the flesh; finely chop it. Put into a bowl with the glacé fruit, the amaretti and the Parmesan and mix well. Season with salt, pepper and nutmeg. Roll out the pasta dough thinly and cut out discs about 5 cm/2 in in diameter, preferably using a fluted cutter. Put a small ball of stuffing on half of the discs, brush the edges with egg white and cover with the remaining discs. Press the edges together firmly to seal. Cook the ravioli in boiling salted water until they rise to the surface. In the meantime, heat the butter until it browns slightly, then add the sage leaves. Remove the ravioli with a slotted spoon, arrange on plates, pour the sage butter over and sprinkle with Parmesan.

Spring rolls

These Chinese appetizers are simple to make

CRISPY SPRING ROLLS

Spring rolls have their origins in southern Chinese cooking, but many other Asian countries, from Vietnam to the Philippines, have their own variations. Spring roll wrappers can be found in Chinese supermarkets. You could also use round rice paper wrappers.

For the stuffing:
3 tablespoons oil
200 g/7 oz firm tofu, cut into 2 cm/¾ in strips
1 or 2 garlic cloves, cut into thin strips
1 tablespoon fermented black beans, crushed
2 teaspoons water
450 g/1 lb canned bamboo shoots, cut into thin strips
300 g/10½ oz white radish (mooli), cut into thin strips
300 g/10½ oz boiled fresh belly pork, with its cooking liquid
½ teaspoon caster sugar, 1 teaspoon dark soya sauce
300 g/10½ oz prawns, peeled and deveined
salt and freshly ground pepper
300 g/10½ oz beansprouts
3 tablespoons chopped fresh coriander
For the egg rolls:
40 spring roll wrappers, 21.5 cm/8½ in square
1 tablespoon flour, mixed with 1½ teaspoons water
oil for frying

For the chilli and garlic sauce:
4 garlic cloves
2 fresh red chillies
1 teaspoon caster sugar, 2 teaspoons rice vinegar
1 teaspoon salt

Heat 2 tablespoons of oil in a wok and brown the tofu lightly over very high heat, stirring constantly. Put to one side. Pour the remaining oil into the wok and brown the garlic lightly over low heat. Add the fermented black beans and stir-fry until lightly browned, then mix in the water. Add the bamboo shoots and radish and stir-fry for 2 minutes. Stir in a little of the pork cooking liquid, the sugar, soya sauce, prawns and pork, cut into strips. Stir-fry until everything is cooked. Season with salt and pepper. Put the tofu back into the wok and simmer gently until the liquid has almost all evaporated. Leave the stuffing to cool, then use to make the spring rolls as shown in the picture sequence right. Before rolling up the wrappers, sprinkle the beansprouts and coriander evenly over the stuffing. Seal the ends with the flour and water paste. Heat oil in the wok until it is almost smoking and fry the spring rolls until golden brown all over. Serve with the chilli and garlic sauce or sweet soya sauce. To make the chilli and garlic sauce, pound the garlic and chillies to a paste in a pestle and mortar, then mix in the sugar, rice vinegar and salt.

LUMPIA

These are the Filipino version of spring rolls. Only half the size of the Chinese variety, they can be steamed as well as deep-fried.

For the stuffing:
1 fresh red chilli, 2 garlic cloves
4 tablespoons groundnut oil
200 g/7 oz cooked pork, finely chopped
200 g/7 oz cooked chicken breast, finely chopped

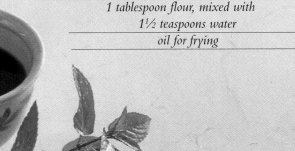

Making spring rolls:

Stir-fry the ingredients for the stuffing, adding them in the order specified so that they cook quickly and evenly.

Vegetables in the stuffing should remain a little crunchy. Remove the stuffing from the wok and leave to cool.

Lay out the spring roll wrappers on a work surface and put about 1 heaping tablespoon of the stuffing in the middle of each one.

Fold the bottom edge of the wrapper over the stuffing. Brush all the edges with egg white, or use a flour and water paste to seal.

Fold the sides in and then roll up neatly. Press all the edges firmly to seal.

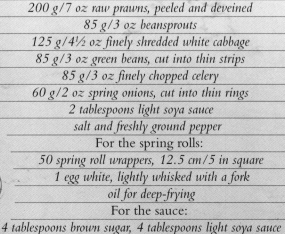

200 g/7 oz raw prawns, peeled and deveined
85 g/3 oz beansprouts
125 g/4½ oz finely shredded white cabbage
85 g/3 oz green beans, cut into thin strips
85 g/3 oz finely chopped celery
60 g/2 oz spring onions, cut into thin rings
2 tablespoons light soya sauce
salt and freshly ground pepper
For the spring rolls:
50 spring roll wrappers, 12.5 cm/5 in square
1 egg white, lightly whisked with a fork
oil for deep-frying
For the sauce:
4 tablespoons brown sugar, 4 tablespoons light soya sauce
250 ml/9 fl oz clear chicken stock (see page 86)
2 tablespoons cornflour, 4 tablespoons cold water
1 garlic clove, salt
4 teaspoons lime juice

Cut the chilli in half, remove the seeds and finely chop. Peel and finely chop the garlic. Heat the oil in a wok and fry the garlic briefly. Add the pork, chicken and prawns – in that order – and stir-fry for about 2 minutes. Add the beansprouts, cabbage, beans, celery, spring onions and chilli and stir-fry for 3 minutes – the vegetables should remain crunchy. Add the soya sauce, season and drain off any excess liquid. Leave the stuffing to cool. Put 1 tablespoon of stuffing on each wrapper, brush the edges with egg white and roll up as shown in the picture sequence. Heat a deep pan of oil to 180°C/350°F and fry the lumpia until golden and crisp (about 4 minutes). Drain on paper towels and serve hot, with the sauce for dipping. To make the sauce, combine the sugar, soya sauce and stock in a pan and bring to the boil. Mix the cornflour with the cold water and add to the sauce; simmer gently, stirring, until the sauce thickens. Finely chop the garlic and add to the sauce with a little salt and the lime juice.

Baked pasta dishes

Baked pasta dishes are very popular, both as a separate course, the *primo*, as in Italy, and as one-dish meals needing only salad and, perhaps, bread as accompaniments. Whether you are using fresh or dried pasta, it must be cooked before going into the oven (unless you are using pasta that requires no pre-cooking), as must all the other components of the dish, since the baking serves only to heat everything through or just crisps the surface. This crisping can also be achieved simply by placing the dish under the grill.

Dishes such as noodles baked with ham and cream sauce or macaroni and cheese are common all over Europe and North America. However, the real classics come from Italy, with pride of place going to lasagne in all its variations. Cannelloni and other stuffed pasta are also often browned in the oven or under the grill. Cheese always plays an important role here, whether it is the mild-flavoured mozzarella or the stronger-tasting Parmesan, or other cheeses that melt easily.

Pasta by itself would turn brittle in the heat of the oven, so it needs to be in a liquid, such as a tomato sauce or a little cream, often mixed with cheese. The béchamel sauce in lasagne serves this purpose. When cooking pasta for a baked dish, it is important that the pasta be almost but not quite *al dente*, since it always absorbs a little sauce during the baking, which of course softens it a little. This is why it is preferable not to use very thin pasta for baked dishes.

One unusual speciality from the Po Valley is pasta '*in sarcofago*' – a stuffed pasta, such as tortellini, packed into a sort of pastry case. At the Restaurant Fini in Modena, shortcrust pastry is used for the case, although it could also be made with puff pastry. The pastry case is cut open at the table, so that guests can enjoy the wonderful aroma of mushrooms and herbs that rises from the filling.

With vegetables or ham

Whether made with vegetables or with meat, baked pasta dishes with an egg and cream sauce always taste splendid

PASTA AND VEGETABLES AU GRATIN

This is just one example of the many dishes that a creative cook can produce from a combination of pasta and vegetables. Other good examples are cauliflower or broccoli with tomatoes, or fennel and aubergine seasoned with anchovies and topped with blue cheese. The quantities given here will produce 4–6 servings.

300 g/10½ oz elicoidali or rigatoni
butter for greasing the baking dish
50 g/1¾ oz butter, melted
For the vegetables:
250 g/9 oz aubergine, 200 g/7 oz courgettes
100 g/3½ oz celery, 1 garlic clove
300 g/10½ oz ripe tomatoes
4 tablespoons olive oil, 60 g/2 oz finely chopped onion
1 tablespoon chopped fresh thyme
½ tablespoon salt, freshly ground black pepper
125 ml/4 fl oz dry red wine
For the cheese sauce:
100 g/3½ oz pecorino romano cheese, freshly grated
200 ml/7 fl oz cream, 3 egg yolks
1 tablespoon chopped mixed fresh herbs: parsley, lovage or celery leaves, savory, rosemary
salt and freshly ground pepper
freshly grated nutmeg

Remove the stalk end from the aubergine and cut into 1 cm/⅜ in cubes. Slice the courgettes and celery thinly. Peel and finely chop the garlic. Blanch the tomatoes, peel them, cut in half, remove the seeds and dice. Heat the oil in a large pan and sauté the onion and garlic until translucent. Add the aubergine, courgettes and celery and fry over high heat for 4–5 minutes, stirring. Add the tomatoes and thyme, season with salt and pepper and pour in the red wine. Cook, uncovered, over high heat until the vegetables are soft and the red wine has reduced by half. Cook the pasta in boiling salted water until almost *al dente*, drain and mix with the vegetables. Transfer the mixture to a buttered baking dish. To make the sauce, whisk the pecorino with the cream and egg yolks, add the chopped herbs and season with salt, pepper and nutmeg. Pour the sauce over the pasta and vegetables. Bake in the oven at 200°C/400°F/gas 6 for 20–25 minutes, moistening the top occasionally with the melted butter. For a particularly crisp topping, mix equal quantities of fine white breadcrumbs and freshly grated Parmesan cheese and sprinkle over the top of the dish half-way through the baking time.

HAM AND PASTA BAKE AUSTRIAN-STYLE

This dish uses home-made pasta squares (quadrucci). The quantities given here will make enough for 4–6 servings.

For the pasta dough:
300 g/10½ oz plain flour, preferably type 00
3 eggs, 1 teaspoon salt, 1 tablespoon vegetable oil
For the ham:
50 g/1¾ oz prosciutto, 200 g/7 oz cooked ham
85 g/3 oz finely chopped onion, 30 g/1 oz butter
For the sauce:
3 eggs, 125 ml/4 fl oz soured cream, 125 ml/4 fl oz milk
1 teaspoon salt, freshly ground pepper
In addition:
butter for greasing the baking dish
60 g/2 oz butter, melted
1 tablespoon chopped fresh chives

Make the pasta dough as directed on page 41 and leave to rest, then roll out and cut quadrucci (see page 54). Cut the prosciutto and ham into small cubes. Sauté the onion in the butter until translucent. Cook the pasta squares in boiling salted water until almost *al dente*, drain and rinse briefly with cold water so that they do not stick together. Continue as shown in the picture sequence. Bake in the middle of the oven at 200°C/400°F/gas 6 for 30–40 minutes until the top is crisp and golden brown. Brush occasionally with the melted butter so that the top does not dry out. Sprinkle with chopped chives before serving.

The Austrians like this dish to have a good, hearty flavour, which is why both prosciutto and cooked ham are used. For an even richer flavour, cook the pasta in ham or chicken stock.

Preparing the ham and pasta bake:

Put the cooked pasta squares in a bowl, add the prosciutto, ham and sautéed onion and mix together.

Butter a baking dish and pour in the pasta and ham mixture. Smooth the surface.

Whisk together the eggs, soured cream and milk and season. Pour this mixture evenly over the pasta.

Macaroni bakes

These are some of the most popular pasta dishes outside Italy

WITH AUBERGINE AND RABBIT

Macaroni and other tubular pasta, such as the thinner bucatini or the fatter ziti, could have been created especially for baked dishes. They lend themselves readily to layering and the finished dish is easily cut for serving. The following recipe is similar to the Greek dish *pastitsio*, although it uses rabbit instead of lamb, and the pasta is cooked in veal stock. The quantities given are sufficient for 6–8 servings.

For the aubergine:
1 aubergine, weighing 300–400 g/10½ –14 oz
1 garlic clove
½ teaspoon salt, freshly ground pepper
125 ml/4 fl oz vegetable oil
For the macaroni:
300 g/10½ oz long macaroni
1.5 litres/2¾ pints veal stock
For the rabbit stuffing:
2 rabbit haunches, weighing about 600 g/1 lb 5 oz
½ teaspoon salt, freshly ground pepper
1 fresh chilli
500 g/1 lb 2oz ripe tomatoes
2 tablespoons vegetable oil
150 g/5½ oz smoked streaky bacon, finely chopped
60 g/2 oz each finely chopped onion and leek
40 g/1½ oz finely chopped carrot
2 tablespoons chopped fresh herbs: thyme, parsley, lovage or celery leaves
For the cheese sauce:
20 g/scant ¾ oz butter, 20 g/scant ¾ oz plain flour
250 ml/9 fl oz milk
salt and freshly ground pepper
50 g/1¾ oz Gruyère cheese, grated
In addition:
butter to grease the baking dish

Cut the aubergine in 5 mm/¼ in slices. Peel and finely chop the garlic. Marinate the sliced aubergine as shown in step one of the picture sequence. Cook the macaroni in the boiling veal stock until almost *al dente*; drain, reserving the stock. Cover the macaroni and put to one side. Bone the rabbit haunches, discarding skin and sinews. Dice the rabbit, put in a bowl and season with salt and pepper. Cut the chilli in half, remove the seeds and finely chop; add to the meat. Blanch the tomatoes, peel them, cut into half, remove the seeds and dice. Heat the oil in a suitably

Preparing the macaroni bake:
Layer the sliced aubergine in a shallow dish, seasoning each layer with garlic, salt and pepper. Pour the oil over, cover and leave to marinate.

Cover the bottom of a buttered baking dish with a layer of macaroni and spoon half of the meat stuffing on top.

Make another layer of macaroni on top of the meat stuffing and arrange the aubergine slices on top, overlapping them slightly.

Cover the aubergine with another layer of macaroni, then spoon on the rest of the meat stuffing.

Add a final layer of pasta on top of the meat. Pour the cheese sauce over the surface and spread out evenly.

Depending on the size of the portions, *baked pasta dishes can be served either as a first course or as a filling main dish. A crisp salad is an excellent accompaniment.*

sized pan and sauté the bacon, onion, leek and carrot over high heat. Add the rabbit and brown for a few minutes, stirring constantly. Stir in the tomatoes and simmer for 5–10 minutes. Pour in the reserved veal stock, add the chopped herbs and cook slowly, uncovered, until the liquid has almost all evaporated. To make the sauce, melt the butter in a small pan, sprinkle on the flour and cook, stirring, for 1–2 minutes; do not brown. Pour in the milk and mix to a smooth consistency, then season and cook gently for about 20 minutes, stirring from time to time. Add the cheese and stir until melted. Butter a 2.5 litre/4½ pint baking dish and layer the prepared ingredients in it as shown in the picture sequence. Bake in the oven at 200°C/400°F/gas 6 for 30–40 minutes.

With beef – a popular variation. Cook 250 g/9 oz long macaroni until almost *al dente*, drain and cool. Heat 2 tablespoons oil in a large pan and brown 150 g/5½ oz sliced fresh mushrooms; remove the mushrooms from the pan. Brown 85 g/3 oz chopped smoked streaky bacon in the same pan. Pour off any excess fat, then add 120 g/4 oz chopped onion and 2 finely chopped garlic cloves and fry until soft. Add 250 g/9 oz minced beef and fry over high heat for 2–3 minutes, stirring to break up lumps. Season with 1 teaspoon salt, some pepper, 1 tablespoon paprika and 1½ teaspoons chopped fresh marjoram.

Add 2 tablespoons tomato purée and 400 g/14 oz diced tomatoes and simmer for 5 minutes. Pour in 125 ml/4 fl oz each robust red wine and meat stock and simmer for a further 15 minutes. Drain the meat mixture, reserving the liquid. Add ½ teaspoon sugar to the liquid and boil to reduce by about half. Make a layer of macaroni in a buttered baking dish. Arrange the meat and tomato mixture and the sliced mushrooms on top and cover with the remaining macaroni. Pour the reduced cooking liquid over the top and sprinkle with 100 g/3½ oz grated Emmental cheese. Bake in the oven at 200°C/425°F/gas 7 for 15–20 minutes.

Stuffed and baked

Large pasta shapes are ideal for stuffing and baking

STUFFED PASTA ON A BED OF PEPPERS

Mezze maniche rigate, a short thick tubular pasta, is perfect for stuffing. Here a delicious combination of venison and peppers is used.

300 g/10½ oz mezze maniche rigate or similar pasta
For the stuffing:
400 g/14 oz boned shoulder of venison
200 g/7 oz unsmoked streaky bacon
1 teaspoon salt, freshly ground pepper
2 juniper berries, crushed
a pinch of ground allspice, 1 teaspoon paprika
grated zest of ½ orange
200 ml/7 fl oz cream
For the peppers:
3 tablespoons oil
85 g/3 oz finely chopped onion
1 red, 1 green and 1 yellow bell pepper, deseeded and diced
½ garlic clove, finely chopped, ½ teaspoon salt
freshly ground pepper
In addition:
100 g/3½ oz gorgonzola cheese, diced
180 ml/6 fl oz cream, 2 egg yolks
2 tablespoons chopped mixed fresh herbs: thyme, parsley, rosemary
salt and freshly ground pepper
40 g/1½ oz Parmesan cheese, freshly grated

Cook the pasta in boiling salted water until almost *al dente*, drain and rinse with cold water. To make the stuffing, trim the venison and cut into cubes. Cut the bacon into cubes. Sprinkle with all the seasonings, cover and leave to marinate for 1–2 hours. Mince the meat with some of the cream, in batches, in a food processor. Mix in the rest of the cream. Press the stuffing through a fine-mesh sieve, then put it into a piping bag fitted with a small round tube. Use to stuff the pasta. To prepare the peppers, heat the oil in a pan and sauté the onion until translucent. Add the peppers and garlic, season with salt and pepper and cook over moderate heat for 5–6 minutes. Layer the prepared ingredients in the baking dish as shown in the picture sequence. Bake in the oven at 200°C/400°F/gas 6 for 40 minutes. After 20 minutes, sprinkle with the grated Parmesan. Serve hot.

Filling the baking dish:

Cover the bottom of the dish with the pepper mixture. Lay the stuffed pasta on top.

Scatter the diced gorgonzola over the pasta. Mix the cream with the egg yolks, herbs and seasoning and pour over the top.

PIPE RIGATE
WITH VEAL STUFFING

The alternative name for this shape of pasta is lumaconi or lumache (snails). Baked in a creamy sauce, the pasta is deliciously moist and the cheese topping turns beautifully brown.

20 pipe rigate
For the stuffing:
200 g/7 oz ripe tomatoes
3 tablespoons vegetable oil
30 g/1 oz finely chopped shallots
60 g/2 oz each finely chopped spring onions and celery
2 tablespoons chopped mixed fresh herbs: parsley, oregano, basil, thyme
salt and freshly ground pepper
300 g/10½ oz boned veal
In addition:
butter for greasing the dish, 120 ml/4 fl oz cream
40 g/1½ oz Parmesan cheese, freshly grated
30 g/1 oz butter, cut into small pieces
a knob of butter, fresh sage leaves

Blanch the tomatoes, peel them, cut in half, remove the seeds and chop. Heat the oil and sauté the shallots and spring onions until translucent. Add the celery and fry briefly. Add the tomatoes and herbs, season with salt and pepper and cook for 5 minutes. Remove from the heat and leave to cool. In the meantime, cut the veal into cubes. Mince the cooled vegetables with the veal, in batches, in a food processor. Cook the pasta in boiling salted water until almost *al dente*, drain and rinse with cold water. Put the stuffing in a piping bag fitted with a small round tube and use to stuff the pasta. Place the stuffed pasta in a buttered baking dish. Season the cream with salt and pepper and pour over the stuffed pasta, ensuring that it is distributed evenly. Sprinkle with the grated Parmesan. Bake in the oven at 190°C/375°F/gas 5 for about 15 minutes. Dot with the pieces of butter and bake for a further 5 minutes. In the meantime, melt the knob of butter in a small pan and toss the sage leaves in it. Pour over the baked pasta and serve immediately.

KRAUTKRAPFEN

In this traditional dish from Bavaria, the pasta rolls look like pieces of strudel standing upright. The dish can be cooked on the hob or in the oven.

For the pasta dough:
200 g/7 oz plain flour, preferably type 00, 2 eggs
1 teaspoon oil, salt, 1 tablespoon water
For the sauerkraut stuffing:
200 g/7 oz onions
40 g/1½ oz clarified butter
150 g/5½ oz finely chopped bacon
750 g/1 lb 10 oz sauerkraut, rinsed
½ teaspoon salt, freshly ground pepper
a pinch of sugar, 6 juniper berries
2 bay leaves, 150 ml/¼ pint white wine (Riesling)
In addition:
½ egg white, lightly whisked with a fork
150 g/5½ oz butter
1–2 tablespoons chopped fresh chives

Make the pasta dough as directed on page 41. For the stuffing, peel and slice the onions. Heat the clarified butter in a pan and cook the bacon. Add the sliced onions and sauté until translucent. Add the sauerkraut and mix well. Season with salt, pepper and sugar. Add the juniper berries and bay leaves,

The sauerkraut for Krautkrapfen must be well drained. Put it in a sieve and press with a wooden spoon until all the liquid has been squeezed out.

Place the sauerkraut stuffing on the rolled-out dough and distribute evenly with a fork, working from the centre outwards.

Brush the edge of one long side of the sheet of dough with egg white so that the edges stick well when the sheet is rolled up.

Starting from the opposite long side, carefully roll up the sheet of dough tightly and press the edges firmly together.

Holding the roll of dough loosely between the fingers, cut with a sharp knife into 3 cm/1¼ in pieces.

pour in the wine and simmer for 15 minutes, stirring occasionally. Cool, then remove the bay leaves and juniper berries. Roll out the pasta dough thinly into a sheet 45 x 60 cm/18 x 24 in. Continue as shown in the picture sequence. Arrange the pieces of pasta upright in a buttered pan. Do not pack the pan too tightly. Melt the butter and pour half of it over the pasta. Bake in the oven at 200°C/400°F/gas 6 for 20 minutes. Pour on the rest of the butter and bake for a further 20 minutes. Sprinkle with the chopped chives and serve.

With ham and cheese Replace the streaky bacon with 250 g/9 oz of chopped ham, preferably real Bavarian smoked ham or Westphalian ham; add the ham to the softened onions and brown lightly. Shortly before the end of the cooking time, sprinkle the pasta rolls with 100 g/3½ oz grated Emmental cheese and continue to cook until the cheese has melted.

PASTA ROLLS WITH A PORK AND SPINACH STUFFING

This is a recipe from Emilia Romagna. The quantities given will make 24 pasta rolls.

1 quantity of fresh pasta dough no. 3 (see page 40)
For the stuffing:
85 g/3 oz finely chopped onion
2 garlic cloves, finely chopped, 60 g/2 oz butter
350 g/12 oz lean minced pork
150 g/5½ oz pig's liver, finely chopped
400 g/14 oz fresh spinach, washed
150 g/5½ oz mushrooms, roughly chopped
salt and freshly ground pepper
In addition:
1 egg white, whisked lightly with a fork
40 g/1½ oz butter, 2 tablespoons chopped spring onions
2 tablespoons each finely chopped carrot and celery
100 g/3½ oz melted butter, 2 tablespoons breadcrumbs
2 tablespoons freshly grated Parmesan cheese

For the stuffing, soften the onion and garlic in the butter. Add the pork and fry until it changes colour, stirring to break up lumps. Add the liver, spinach and mushrooms and fry briefly to wilt the spinach. Season and set aside. Roll out the pasta dough thinly and cut out 4 sheets, each 15 x 20 cm/6 x 8 in. Cook in boiling salted water for 2 minutes, then remove with a slotted spatula, lay on a damp tea towel and pat dry. Spread the stuffing on the sheets of pasta, leaving the edge of one long side clear; brush this with egg white. Roll up each sheet from the other long side and press the edges firmly to seal. Heat the butter and briefly sauté the spring onions, carrot and celery. Spread over the bottom of a baking dish. Cut each pasta roll across into 6 pieces and arrange upright in the dish. Pour half of the melted butter over the rolls and bake in the oven at 200°C/400°F/gas 6 for 15 minutes. Sprinkle with the breadcrumbs and Parmesan, drizzle with the remaining butter and bake for a further 10 minutes.

Cannelloni

Pasta tubes with endless possibilities

Cannelloni can be filled with a huge variety of
stuffings. The recipe here calls for a meat stuffing,
in fact the one given for raviolini on page 188.
However, cannelloni can also be stuffed with
vegetables, cheese, poultry and seafood. They can be
covered with various sauces, such as a béchamel, or
just with cheese and then baked or browned under
the grill. Making cannelloni from scratch is a long
process, but you can save time by using dried
cannelloni (8 tubes are required for this recipe).

CANNELLONI WITH MEAT STUFFING

This might be regarded as a basic recipe for the
creative cook, as it can be varied in every respect.
For example, the tomato sauce, which keeps the
cannelloni moist, can be replaced by a delicate
vegetable and tomato *brunoise*.

1 quantity of fresh pasta dough no. 3 (see page 40)
1 quantity of meat stuffing (see the recipe for raviolini on page 188)
125 ml/4 fl oz cream
50 g/1¾ oz Parmesan cheese, freshly grated
50 g/1¾ oz butter, cut into small pieces
For the tomato sauce:
50 g/1¾ oz butter, 1 tablespoon finely chopped onion
300 g/10½ oz ripe plum tomatoes, peeled and diced
20 fresh basil leaves, ½ teaspoon salt, freshly ground pepper

First make the sauce: heat the butter and soften the
onion. Add the tomatoes and cook gently until
thick – they should not disintegrate completely. Add
the basil and season with salt and pepper. Pour the
tomato sauce into a baking dish. Roll out the dough
thinly and cut out rectangles 10 x 15 cm/3 x 5 in.
Cook for 2 minutes in boiling water, then remove
with a fish slice. Continue as shown in the picture
sequence. Dot with the small pieces of butter and
bake in the oven at 200°C/400°F/gas 6 for 20
minutes or until lightly browned on top.

Preparing cannelloni:

*Lay the rectangles of dough on
a damp cloth. Spoon some of
the stuffing along a short side
of each rectangle and roll it up.*

*Arrange the cannelloni in the
baking dish on top of the
tomato sauce. The dish
should be big enough to hold
the cannelloni in one layer.*

*Mix the cream with
the Parmesan and
spoon evenly
over the
cannelloni.*

CANNELLONI WITH SEAFOOD STUFFING

½ quantity of fresh green pasta dough (see page 46)
For the stuffing:
400 g/14 oz sea trout (salmon trout) fillets, well chilled
100 ml/3½ fl oz cream, well chilled
salt and freshly ground pepper
8 scampi or raw king or tiger prawns
For the béchamel sauce:
25 g/scant 1 oz butter, 30 g/1 oz plain flour
500 ml/18 fl oz milk, ½ teaspoon salt
freshly ground pepper
a pinch of freshly grated nutmeg
1 egg yolk, 100 ml/3½ fl oz cream
In addition:
3 tablespoons freshly grated Parmesan cheese

Increase the quantity of spinach pulp when making the dough to give it a particularly vivid green colour. Cut the fish fillets into cubes and purée, in batches, in a food processor. Transfer to a bowl and refrigerate as soon as each batch is puréed. Press the purée through a sieve, stir in the cream, season and refrigerate again. Peel and devein the scampi or prawns and refrigerate. To make the béchamel sauce, melt the butter, add the flour and cook, stirring, for 1–2 minutes; do not brown. Pour in the milk, stirring to remove lumps. Season with salt, pepper and nutmeg and cook for 20 minutes, stirring frequently. Whisk the egg yolk and cream with 2 tablespoons of the hot sauce. Remove the sauce from the heat, thicken with the egg-yolk mixture and strain into a clean pan. Keep warm over low heat. Roll out the pasta dough thinly and cut 8 rectangles of 10 x 15 cm/ 2¾ x 3¼ in. Cook in boiling salted water for 2 minutes, then remove with a fish slice, spread out on a damp tea towel and blot dry. Put some of the fish purée on each rectangle, leaving a border clear on all sides. Lay a scampi or prawn in the middle of each rectangle and roll up, pressing the end firmly to seal. Lay the rolls in a buttered baking dish. Pour the béchamel sauce over and sprinkle with cheese. Bake in the oven at 200°C/400°F/gas 6 for about 9 minutes, then place under a hot grill and quickly brown the top.

LASAGNE NEAPOLITAN-STYLE

In this vegetarian version, two kinds of mild cheese make the dish pleasantly light. The quantities given below are sufficient for 8–10 portions.

1 quantity of fresh pasta dough no. 3 (see page 40)
For the tomato sauce:
1 kg/2¼ lb ripe plum tomatoes
or 2 (400 g/14 oz each) cans whole tomatoes
2 garlic cloves, 4 tablespoons olive oil
salt, freshly ground black pepper
For the ricotta stuffing:
500 g/1 lb 2 oz ricotta cheese
40 g/1½ oz Parmesan cheese, freshly grated
½ teaspoon salt, freshly ground white pepper
a pinch of freshly grated nutmeg
In addition:
20 g/scant ¾ oz fresh basil leaves
200 g/7 oz mozzarella cheese

Roll out the pasta dough thinly and cut sheets from it to fit the chosen baking dish. For the tomato sauce, wash and quarter the fresh tomatoes or drain the canned ones. Peel and finely chop the garlic. Heat the oil in a heavy pan and sauté the garlic until it colours slightly. Add the tomatoes, season and stir. Cover the pan and simmer for 30 minutes. Press the sauce through a sieve or mouli-légumes and set aside. Combine the ingredients for the ricotta stuffing in a bowl and mix well. Cook the sheets of dough, one or two at a time, in boiling salted water for 2 minutes. Remove with a fish slice, lay out flat on damp cloths and cover with another damp cloth. Arrange two of the pasta sheets in a buttered baking dish so that they overlap each other and overhang the long sides of the dish by 2 cm/¾ in. Pour one-quarter of the tomato sauce over the pasta and scatter one-quarter of the basil leaves on top. Cover with another sheet of pasta, laid lengthways, and spread with a third of the ricotta stuffing. Put another sheet of pasta on top and cover with a third of the sliced mozzarella. Repeat these layers twice. Cover the last layer of mozzarella with a sheet of pasta and fold the overhanging pasta over the top. Add the remaining tomato sauce and basil and bake in the oven at 220°C/425°F/gas 7 for about 20 minutes.

LASAGNE VERDI BOLOGNESE-STYLE

One of the classic recipes from Bologna, the pasta stronghold. Cooks in this area are not only especially skilled at making exquisite pasta, they also produce the best meat sauces. It is precisely this combination that is required for a good lasagne. The quantities listed here are sufficient for 8–10 servings.

400 g/14 oz fresh green pasta dough (see page 46)
For the bolognese sauce:
3 tablespoons olive oil
250 g/9 oz each freshly minced beef and lean pork
60 g/2 oz finely chopped onion
60 g/2 oz each finely diced carrot and celery
3 tablespoons tomato purée
salt and freshly ground black pepper
500 ml/18 fl oz meat stock
1 tablespoon finely chopped fresh parsley
For the béchamel sauce:
25 g/scant 1 oz butter
30 g/1 oz plain flour, 500 ml/18 fl oz milk
salt and freshly ground white pepper
a pinch of freshly grated nutmeg
In addition:
butter to grease the dish
85 g/3 oz Parmesan cheese, freshly grated

Roll the pasta dough out thinly and cut squares that are slightly smaller than the width of the chosen baking dish. Here a 28 x 16 cm/ 11 x 6¼ in dish was used, so the pasta was cut into 15 cm/6 in squares. For the bolognese sauce, heat the oil in a heavy pan and fry the meat over fairly high heat until browned, stirring to break up lumps. Add the onion, carrot and celery and stir in the tomato purée. Fry briefly with the meat. Season with salt and pepper, pour in the stock and add the parsley. Simmer for 30 minutes. To make the béchamel sauce, melt the butter, stir in the flour and cook for 1–2 minutes without browning. Pour on the milk,

Cover the pasta layer with half of the béchamel sauce. Repeat the layers of pasta, bolognese sauce, pasta and béchamel sauce.

Sprinkle the last layer of béchamel sauce with the Parmesan. Bake in the oven at 220°C/425°F/gas 7 for 20 minutes

Preparing the lasagne:

Cook the pasta squares, one at a time, in boiling salted water for 2 minutes. Remove with a slotted spoon and lay out flat on a cloth to drain.

Butter the baking dish. Arrange two pasta squares in the dish to cover the bottom, overlapping them slightly in the centre.

Spoon in half of the bolognese sauce and spread it out evenly to cover the pasta.

Arrange another two pasta squares on top, overlapping them slightly in the centre as before.

stirring to remove any lumps, and bring to the boil. Season with salt, pepper and nutmeg and simmer over low heat for 20 minutes, stirring frequently. Strain the sauce. Continue as shown in the picture sequence above.

Sweet pasta dishes

Pasta for dessert? Why not? Stuffed pasta in particular opens up a wide range of possibilities. Ricotta cheese, which is neutral in taste, can be seasoned with salt or with sugar, as can unripened soft cheeses such as Quark and fromage frais, and all are ideal for stuffing pasta. A sauce flavoured with vanilla or orange would be delicious as a partner. Other sweet stuffings could be based on cake or breadcrumbs or crushed biscuits. Soft fruit is not such a good choice for stuffing pasta – the juice from raspberries or strawberries, for example, would turn the pasta mushy in seconds.

Pasta doughs containing cocoa powder look appetizing and taste great. The same idea can be applied to make what might be called 'chocolate pasta'. Even a standard egg pasta dough can be used for sweet dishes, as long as the accompanying sauce is carefully chosen. Vanilla, cinnamon, poppy seeds and finely grated lemon or orange zest are particularly good flavourings. A somewhat curious but certainly original dish is sweet lasagne, where the pasta sheets are layered with apples, raisins and crème anglais. This looks most attractive when baked in small individual moulds. And at the other end of the spectrum is a delicious treat for children – pasta simply tossed in butter and sprinkled with cinnamon and sugar.

Deep-fried pasta is excellent served as a sweet dish. In China there are several recipes that use honey as a sweetener. Less familiar are the deep-fried pasta recipes from Italy, which have a long history. For these, the dough, flavoured with a little vermouth, is cut into broad strips, sometimes plaited and then deep-fried. When cooked, the pasta shapes are sprinkled with icing sugar. They make a wonderfully crunchy treat, for which a glass of *vin santo* is the perfect accompaniment.

Poppy seeds *are a popular flavouring for desserts throughout central and eastern Europe.*

BUCATINI WITH POPPY SEEDS, CREAM AND PLUM JAM

Any shape of pasta can be used for this dish, including tagliatelle or spaghetti. However, chunky shapes such as bucatini or elbow macaroni go particularly well with this combination of flavours.

300 g/10½ oz bucatini
70 g/2½ oz butter
60 g/2 oz ground poppy seeds
To serve:
200 ml/7 fl oz double cream, 40 g/1½ oz plum jam
1 tablespoon lemon zest cut into thin shreds
a few fresh lemon balm or mint leaves

Cook the pasta in lightly salted boiling water until *al dente*. Drain thoroughly. Heat the butter in a pan until it begins to foam, add the poppy seeds and stir well; keep warm. Whip the cream until thick. Add the pasta to the butter, stir to coat evenly and transfer to 4 plates. Arrange a portion of whipped cream and plum jam on each plate. Garnish with the lemon zest and herb leaves and serve immediately.

POTATO NOODLES WITH POPPY-SEED BUTTER

The potato dough does not necessarily have to be shaped into noodles. It can also be used to make small dumplings or be cut in strips.

500–660 g/1 lb 2 oz–1 lb 5 oz baking potatoes
150 g/5½ oz plain flour
1 egg, salt and freshly ground pepper
70 g/2½ oz butter, 85 g/3 oz ground poppy seeds
To finish:
30 g/1 oz icing sugar

Bake the potatoes as directed on page 223 and put them through a potato ricer or mouli-légumes while warm. Add the flour, egg and seasoning and mix to a smooth dough. With your palms, roll into noodles about 4 cm/1½ in long with tapering ends. Cook in lightly salted boiling water for about 6 minutes. Melt the butter and add the ground poppy seeds. Remove the noodles from the water with a slotted spoon and drain. Arrange on 4 plates, pour the butter over and sprinkle with sifted icing sugar.

CHOCOLATE PASTA

Children are not the only ones who will love this pasta with its wonderful chocolate flavour.

For the chocolate pasta dough:
250 g/9 oz plain flour, preferably type 00
100 g/3½ oz cocoa powder
30 g/1 oz icing sugar, 4 eggs
1 teaspoon vanilla essence

Sift the flour and cocoa powder on to a work surface. Add the icing sugar, eggs and vanilla and knead to a smooth dough. Wrap in cling film and leave to rest before cutting out the desired pasta shape.

CHOCOLATE TRENETTE WITH CRÈME ANGLAISE

1 quantity of chocolate pasta dough (see above)
For the crème anglaise:
3 egg yolks, 50 g/1¾ oz sugar
250 ml/9 fl oz milk, ¼ vanilla pod
To garnish:
30 g/1 oz chopped pistachio nuts

Roll out the pasta dough thinly and cut out trenette, which are slightly narrower than tagliatelle (see pages 52 and 53). Beat the egg yolks with the sugar until pale and creamy. Pour the milk into a pan, add the vanilla pod, split open lengthways, and heat until scalding hot. Gradually pour the hot milk into the egg yolk mixture, stirring constantly, then pour the mixture back into the pan. Cook over low heat, stirring, until the custard sauce thickens enough to coat a wooden spoon. Remove the vanilla pod. Cook the trenette in lightly salted boiling water until *al dente*, drain and arrange in deep plates. Pour the crème anglaise over and sprinkle with the chopped pistachios.

CHOCOLATE NOODLES WITH HAZELNUT PRALINE AND CREAM SAUCE

1 quantity of chocolate pasta dough (see left)
For the sauce:
75 g/2¾ oz sugar
75 g/2¾ oz roughly chopped hazelnuts
125 ml/4 fl oz double cream

Roll out the pasta dough thinly and cut the thinnest possible noodles (capelli d'angelo). To make the hazelnut praline, melt the sugar in a heavy pan and cook until the sugar syrup turns light brown. Add the hazelnuts, stir in quickly and remove immediately from the heat. Pour the hot mixture on to an oiled marble slab, roll out into a sheet using an oiled rolling pin and leave to cool. When set, crush coarsely with a paperweight or meat bat. Whip the cream until thick and stir in two-thirds of the hazelnut praline. Cook the noodles in lightly salted boiling water until *al dente*, drain and arrange in deep plates. Pour the sauce over them and garnish with the remaining hazelnut praline.

Sweet pasta dishes baked in the oven

Baked in puddings, pasta is beautifully tender and tastes wonderful

BAKED NOODLE PUDDING WITH CHESTNUTS

Peeled chestnuts are available in cans and also vacuum-packed and are very convenient to use, but fresh chestnuts have a much better flavour.

500 g/1 lb 2 oz fresh chestnuts, 300 g/10½ oz tagliatelle
50 g/1¾ oz butter, 150 g/5½ oz icing sugar
3 egg yolks, 1 teaspoon vanilla essence
4 tablespoons cream, 2 egg whites, 50 g/1¾ oz caster sugar
In addition:
30 g/1 oz butter for greasing the baking dish
icing sugar for sprinkling

Cherry compote, spiced with cloves and cinnamon, makes a splendid accompaniment for the noodle pudding with chestnuts. Stoned fresh cherries, or well-drained canned ones, can also be mixed into the pudding before baking.

Using a small sharp knife, cut a cross in the top of each chestnut. Arrange them in a shallow baking tin and bake in the oven at 220°C/425°F/gas 7 until the shells split open and can be peeled off with a knife. Peeling is most easily done while the chestnuts are still warm, so remove them from the oven in batches. Peel off the bitter inner skin, too. Roughly chop the peeled chestnuts.

Cook the tagliatelle in boiling salted water until *al dente*, drain and rinse briefly in cold running water and then drain again well. Continue as shown in the picture sequence. Bake the pudding in the oven at 220°C/425°F/gas 7 for 20 minutes or until the top is browned. Sprinkle with icing sugar.

Making the baked noodle pudding:

Brown the chopped chestnuts in the butter; gradually sprinkle on the icing sugar and continue to cook until the chestnuts are caramelized.

Mix the chestnuts with the cooked noodles. Whisk the egg yolks with the vanilla until foamy and whisk in the cream. Add to the chestnut mixture.

Beat the egg whites with the sugar until stiff, then fold into the noodle mixture. Transfer to a buttered baking dish.

VIENNESE NOODLE PUDDING WITH HAZELNUTS

250 g/9 oz fresh pasta dough no. 4 (see page 40)
85 g/3 oz butter, 85 g/3 oz icing sugar
4 eggs, separated
85 g/3 oz ground toasted hazelnuts
20 g/scant ¾ oz white breadcrumbs
½ teaspoon ground cinnamon
grated zest of ½ lemon
butter and fine breadcrumbs for the baking dish
icing sugar to sprinkle

Roll out the pasta dough thinly and cut out trenette, which are slightly narrower than tagliatelle (see pages 52 and 53). Cook in boiling salted water until *al dente*, drain and rinse briefly in cold water to prevent them sticking together. Beat the butter with half of the icing sugar and the egg yolks until the mixture is thick and pale. Beat the egg whites with the remaining icing sugar until stiff and fold into the egg yolk mixture. Mix the hazelnuts with the breadcrumbs, cinnamon and lemon zest. Add to the egg mixture with the noodles and fold everything together gently. Pour into a baking dish that has been buttered and coated with breadcrumbs. Smooth the surface. Bake in the oven at 200°C/400°F/gas 6 for 25–30 minutes or until set and lightly browned. Sprinkle with icing sugar and serve with stewed fruit and whipped cream.

BAKED NOODLE PUDDING WITH CRANBERRIES

(not illustrated)

250 g/9 oz fresh pasta dough no. 4 (see page 40)
60 g/2 oz butter, 85 g/3 oz icing sugar
4 eggs, separated, 3 tablespoons amaretto liqueur
100 g/3½ oz ground toasted almonds
20 g/scant ¾ oz white breadcrumbs
butter and fine breadcrumbs for the baking dish
200 g/7 oz stewed cranberries, icing sugar

Roll out the pasta dough thinly and cut out tagliatelle or trenette (see pages 52 and 53). Cook in boiling salted water until *al dente*, drain and set aside. Prepare the egg mixture as in the preceding recipe, add the amaretto and fold in the noodles, almonds and breadcrumbs. Butter a baking dish and coat with breadcrumbs. Pour in half of the pudding mixture and smooth the surface. Arrange the stewed cranberries in small piles on top and cover with the remaining pudding mixture. Bake in the oven at 200°C/400°F/gas 6 for 30–35 minutes or until the top is lightly browned. Sprinkle with icing sugar.

QUARK DUMPLINGS WITH CRANBERRIES AND SABAYON

For these dumplings the Quark should be as dry as possible, so drain it in a fine-mesh sieve if necessary. You can also use fromage frais or curd cheese.

For the dumplings:
150 g/5½ oz Quark
3 stale white bread rolls, crusts removed
20 g/scant ¾ oz caster sugar, ½ teaspoon salt
60 g/2 oz butter, melted, 4 tablespoons soured cream
2 eggs, 50 g/1¾ oz plain flour
1 tablespoon white breadcrumbs
For the cranberry compote:
250 ml/9 fl oz water, 140 g/5 oz sugar
2 cm/¾ in cinnamon stick, 2 cloves
juice of 1 orange, 400 g/14 oz cranberries
For the buttered crumbs:
100 g/3½ oz butter
40 g/1½ oz white breadcrumbs
For the sabayon:
3 egg yolks, 100 g/3½ oz caster sugar
125 ml/4 fl oz dry white wine

To finish:
icing sugar

Mix together all the ingredients for the dumplings and work into a smooth dough. Leave to rest for 30 minutes. Shape the dough into 12 round dumplings and place in a pan of boiling salted water. Remove from the heat and leave to stand until the dumplings are cooked (about 10 minutes). To make the cranberry compote, combine the water, sugar, cinnamon and cloves in a saucepan and bring to the boil, stirring to dissolve the sugar. Boil for 3–4 minutes, then strain and return to the pan. Add the orange juice and cranberries and cook until the cranberries begin to pop. Melt the butter in another pan, add the breadcrumbs and fry until golden, stirring occasionally. To make the sabayon, whisk the egg yolks with the sugar in a heatproof bowl until frothy, then set in a *bain-marie* (or use a double boiler). Pour in the wine and whisk until the mixture thickens. Remove the dumplings from the water with a slotted spoon and arrange on plates with the compote and the sabayon. Sprinkle with the buttered crumbs and a little icing sugar.

SEMOLINA DUMPLINGS WITH FIGS AND RED WINE SAUCE

2 ripe figs
For the dumplings:
50 g/1¾ oz stale white bread, crusts removed
2 tablespoons lukewarm milk
50 g/1¾ oz butter, 1 egg
85 g/3 oz semolina
salt, freshly grated nutmeg
For the sauce:
250 ml/9 fl oz red wine, 20 g/scant ¾ oz sugar
a pinch of ground cinnamon
juice of ½ orange
1 teaspoon pared orange zest cut into fine shreds
1 teaspoon cornflour
In addition:
125 ml/4 fl oz double cream
fine shreds of orange zest

Moisten the crumbled bread with the milk. Beat the butter in a bowl, add the egg and beat until creamy. Add the semolina and the softened bread and season with salt and nutmeg. Mix thoroughly. Scoop out spoonfuls and shape into oval dumplings (quenelles). Put in a pan of boiling salted water, remove from the heat and leave to stand until cooked through (about 15 minutes). To make the sauce, combine the red wine, sugar, cinnamon and orange juice in a pan, bring to the boil and reduce to a third of the original volume. Add the shreds of orange zest. Mix the cornflour with a little cold water and use to thicken the sauce. Peel the figs, slice and add to the sauce, letting them soften slightly. Whip the cream until stiff. Drain the dumplings and arrange on plates with the figs in their sauce and whipped cream. Garnish with orange zest and serve immediately.

Semolina dumplings in soup: Beat 60 g/2 oz butter until pale and creamy. Lightly beat 1 egg. Measure 120 g/4 oz semolina. Add the egg and semolina to the butter in 2 or 3 batches and mix to a smooth paste. Season with salt and nutmeg and leave to rest for 30 minutes. Scoop out small spoonfuls, shape into oval dumplings and place in a pan of boiling-hot broth. Leave to stand until cooked through. Ladle into soup cups and serve.

Dumplings and gnocchi

Dumplings may well have originated as a form of food for those who ate with their fingers, a habit that persisted, even in Europe, until well into the 17th century. According to old recipes, dumplings were seldom meatless but contained 'minced meat' of all kinds, which could then be consumed without any cutlery or carving skills being required. Evidence for this goes back as far as the time of Apicius, whose collection of recipes appeared in the time of the Roman emperor Tiberius. This includes a number of recipes for dumplings containing the meat of hare and other animals. Further evidence is to be found in medieval paintings depicting devout ladies and gentlemen consuming all manner of food shaped into small balls – which surely must have been dumplings.

The characteristic that dumplings share with pasta is that eggs are used to bind the dough together; the flour is of secondary importance. The skill in making dumplings lies mainly in producing a dough or paste with a firm yet light consistency. The potato, which became a popular food in the second half of the 18th century, was welcomed because it could be used to make feather-light dumplings with a good texture.

Dumplings without meat – the way we usually prepare them nowadays – may have begun in times of famine, as a way of making the most of scraps of bread, but today's dumplings can be gourmet fare. Semmelknödel and Serviettenknödel, from Germany, are two kinds of bread dumplings served as a side-dish. In Austria a wide range of dumplings are made, both sweet and savoury. Quark or apricots are popular stuffings for sweet dumplings and smaller dumplings known as Nockerln are added to broths, just as elegant quenelles are served in consommé in France. In Italy, the small dumplings called gnocchi may be made with flour, potatoes, semolina, polenta or ricotta cheese and are usually served as a first course. There are also sweet gnocchi and tiny ones for soup. Small dumplings of all kinds, sometimes steamed, sometimes deep-fried, are also a basic part of everyday Asian cooking.

Gnocchi can be made from the potato dough described on these pages. The dough is rolled by hand into long, thin ropes and then cut into small, even-sized pieces. These are pressed against a grater to imprint a lattice-work pattern on them.

Home-made potato doughs

Gnocchi di patate and potato dumplings

Gnocchi have been part of Italian cooking for almost as long as pasta: one has only to think of malloreddus, the small Sardinian gnocchi made from flour and water, or those made from semolina or polenta. And in Verona, it remains the custom even today to distribute enormous quantities of gnocchi on the last Friday of carnival to passers-by in front of the Basilica of San Zeno.

In earlier centuries, gnocchi were made solely of flour and water, for it was not until the beginning of the last century that the Austrians, who had long been familiar with such starchy foods in the form of potato noodles, introduced potatoes into Italy. Cooks in virtually all parts of the Austro-Hungarian Empire made a cheap dough, with a lot of potatoes and just a little flour, that could be used in a variety of different ways: to make flat biscuits, long noodles or small dumplings similar to Italian gnocchi.

Whether the potato dough is shaped into gnocchi, dumplings or noodles, it must be freshly made and prepared as quickly as possible, because otherwise it becomes too soft and sticky to work with. And potato gnocchi and noodles boiled in water must be served immediately after they are cooked if their texture and flavour are to be at their best.

The quality of the potatoes is also of vital importance. Only really floury varieties are suitable and to ensure that they remain as dry and floury as possible, they should be neither steamed nor boiled but baked in the oven. Wrapping them in foil makes them easier to peel afterwards, but it produces moisture, so before they are put through the potato ricer they should be dried thoroughly. Alternatively, they can simply be baked in their jackets, cut open and the flesh scooped out.

Basic potato dough: Bake 600–700 g/1¼–1½ lb of floury potatoes. Peel, or scoop out the flesh with a spoon; there should be about 500 g/1 lb 2 oz of cooked potato. Put the potatoes through a ricer or mouli-légumes. Mix 200 g/7 oz plain flour with 100 g/3½ oz freshly grated Parmesan cheese and season with salt, freshly ground pepper and freshly grated nutmeg. Add the potatoes and 2 eggs. Mix to a smooth dough. If making sweet dumplings, you can omit the Parmesan. Potato dumplings combine splendidly with brown butter (*beurre noisette*), tomato sauce, bolognese sauce and, above all, mushroom and game stews.

1 *Wrap each scrubbed potato in foil, or put directly on to the oven shelf. Bake in the oven at 200°C/400°F/ gas 6 for about 1 hour. If wrapped in foil, peel the baked potatoes; otherwise, cut them in half and scoop out the flesh. Pour the flour on to a work surface, form a well in the middle and add the Parmesan, salt and other seasonings. Press the peeled potatoes through a ricer or mouli-légumes, distributing them evenly over the flour.*

2 *Add the eggs to the well and heap flour and potatoes from the outside over the top. Working from the centre outwards, mix the ingredients together with your fingers. Working as quickly as possible, knead to a smooth dough by pressing and squeezing with both hands. Do not work the dough for longer than is necessary. Leave it to rest briefly, then shape into two long rolls 3–4 cm/ 1–1½ in in diameter. Sprinkle with flour.*

3 *For noodles: using a sharp knife, cut each roll of dough into pieces about 2 cm/¾ in wide. The pressure of cutting partially shapes the fat noodles. Roll each one on the work surface so that it tapers at both ends. Dust with flour to prevent the noodles sticking. Cook them in boiling salted water until they rise to the surface. Remove with a slotted spoon. Arrange on plates and finish with brown butter, freshly grated Parmesan and chopped fresh herbs.*

Gnocchi with pumpkin and mushrooms

Two exquisite gnocchi recipes — a Tuscan dish with a mushroom sauce and a Piedmontese dish with pumpkin

PUMPKIN GNOCCHI WITH SPINACH

For the gnocchi:
1 pumpkin, weighing about 750 g/1 lb 10 oz
1 egg
50 g/1¾ oz plain flour
50 g/1¾ oz Parmesan cheese, freshly grated
salt and freshly ground pepper
For the spinach sauce:
200 g/7 oz spinach
30 g/1 oz finely chopped onion
20 g/scant ¾ oz butter
4 tablespoons white wine
100 ml/3½ fl oz meat stock
1 tablespoon cream
salt and freshly ground pepper
freshly grated nutmeg
To finish:
50 g/1¾ oz Parmesan cheese, freshly grated
85 g/3 oz butter, melted and lightly browned (beurre noisette)

The sauces are interchangeable — tomato sauce also goes well with pumpkin gnocchi, just as spinach sauce does with potato gnocchi.

Cooking the pumpkin:

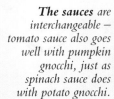

Place the pumpkin on a baking sheet and bake in the oven until a sharp knife can be inserted easily (about 1½ hours).

Leave to cool a little, then cut the pumpkin in half and remove the seeds and fibres from the centre.

Scoop out the flesh with a large spoon. You will need 250 g/9 oz of pumpkin flesh for the gnocchi.

Preheat the oven to 200°C/400°F/gas 6 and bake the pumpkin, whole, as shown in the picture sequence. Purée the pumpkin flesh in a food processor. Work the pumpkin purée with the egg, flour, Parmesan, salt and pepper to a smooth dough. Shape it into gnocchi as directed on page 222. Trim and wash the spinach. Soften the finely chopped onion in half of the butter, add the spinach and cook until wilted. Purée it. Combine the white wine and meat stock in a pan, bring to the boil and reduce a little. Add the spinach purée and bring back to the boil. Add the remaining butter and the cream and season with salt, pepper and nutmeg. Mix thoroughly and keep warm. Cook the gnocchi in boiling salted water for 5 minutes; remove with a slotted spoon and arrange on plates with the spinach sauce. Sprinkle with the Parmesan and drizzle the brown butter over.

POTATO GNOCCHI WITH TOMATO AND MUSHROOM SAUCE

A Tuscan recipe for autumn, when fresh wild mushrooms are plentiful.

For the gnocchi:
600–700 g/1¼–1½ lb floury potatoes
50 g/1¾ oz ricotta cheese, 1 egg yolk
85 g/3 oz Parmesan cheese, freshly grated
2 tablespoons plain flour
salt and freshly ground pepper
freshly grated nutmeg
For the tomato and mushroom sauce:
300 g/10½ oz ripe tomatoes, 2 shallots
1 garlic clove, 4 tablespoons olive oil
salt and freshly ground pepper
300 g/10½ oz fresh ceps, 1 tablespoon butter
1 tablespoon chopped fresh parsley

Bake the potatoes as directed on page 223. While still hot, peel them, or scoop out the flesh and put through a ricer or mouli-légumes into a bowl. You need 500 g/1 lb 2 oz of potato. Cool a little, then add the ricotta, egg yolk, Parmesan, flour, salt, pepper and nutmeg and work to a smooth dough. Shape into gnocchi (see page 222). Blanch the tomatoes, peel them, remove the seeds and dice. Peel and finely chop the shallots and garlic. Heat the oil in a pan and sauté the shallots and garlic until translucent. Add the tomatoes, season and simmer gently for 15 minutes. In the meantime, clean and slice the ceps. Heat the butter in a pan and sauté the ceps; sprinkle with the chopped parsley and season with salt and pepper. Add the tomato sauce to the ceps and stir to mix. Add the gnocchi to a pan of boiling salted water, reduce the heat and simmer until cooked through (about 3 minutes). Remove with a slotted spoon, arrange on plates and pour the sauce over.

Semolina and polenta gnocchi

These can be rolled into oval shapes or cut from a block with a pastry cutter

POLENTA GNOCCHI WITH BACON AND GORGONZOLA

100 g/3½ oz streaky bacon, cut into small cubes
For the polenta:
1.25 litres/2 pints water, 1 teaspoon salt
350 g/12 oz polenta
In addition:
butter for greasing the baking dish
180 g/6 oz gorgonzola cheese
50 g/1¾ oz Parmesan cheese, freshly grated
150 ml/¼ pint cream, 50 g/1¾ oz butter, melted
1 heaping tablespoon fresh basil cut in strips

Cook the bacon in a frying pan without additional fat. Drain on paper towels. Bring the water and salt for the polenta to the boil in a large pan. Pour in the polenta in a thin stream, stirring constantly and ensuring that the water is boiling all the time; this will prevent lumps from forming. Keep stirring, in

Making polenta gnocchi:

Stir the bacon into the polenta, mixing thoroughly.

Using a wet spoon, scoop out portions of the polenta and bacon mixture and shape into smooth ovals in your wet hands.

Arrange the gnocchi in a buttered baking dish, slightly overlapping and leaning against each other at an angle.

Cut the gorgonzola into cubes and scatter evenly over the gnocchi.

Sprinkle with the Parmesan, then spoon on the cream, covering all the gnocchi evenly. Drizzle with a little of the melted butter.

the same direction as much as possible. When the mixture begins to thicken into a smooth mass, the task becomes more arduous, since it will take about 20 minutes for the polenta to cook. It is done when the polenta comes away from the side of the pan. Then continue as shown in the picture sequence.

Put the baking dish in the oven at 200°C/400°F/ gas 6 and bake for 25–30 minutes, basting the gnocchi frequently with melted butter. Garnish with basil and serve hot.

GNOCCHI ALLA ROMANA

For the polenta:
500 ml/18 fl oz water, ½ teaspoon salt
150 g/5½ oz polenta (coarsely ground yellow cornmeal)
For the herb butter:
100 g/3½ oz butter, 1 garlic clove, finely chopped
2 tablespoons chopped fresh herbs: parsley, oregano, rosemary
In addition:
40 g/1½ oz Parmesan cheese, freshly grated

Prepare the polenta as in the recipe opposite. Pour on to a moistened baking sheet, smooth it out into a sheet about 1 cm/⅜ in thick and leave to cool.

When the polenta has set, continue as shown in the picture sequence. To make the herb butter, melt the butter in a pan, soften the garlic and stir in the herbs. Place the gnocchi in the oven at 220°C/425°F/gas 7 and bake for 11 minutes. Brown under the grill.

Preparing gnocchi alla romana:

Using a 6.5 cm/2½ in round pastry cutter, cut out ovals from the polenta.

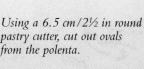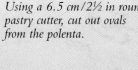

Layer the ovals in a buttered baking dish so that they overlap like roof tiles. Sprinkle with the Parmesan.

Spoon the herb butter evenly over the gnocchi, ensuring that all of them are moistened.

Gnocchi alla romana are traditionally made with semolina, which can be substituted for the polenta. The quantities given here are sufficient for 4 portions as a starter or for 2 portions as a main dish.

Chef Karl Eschelböck
*is a perfectionist –
baking his own bread
for feather-light
dumplings.*

Serviettenknödel – a classic German dish

These light dumplings usually accompany pot roasts. They need plenty of sauce

Although most often served as a side-dish, Serviettenknödel can be enjoyed on their own, freshly sliced and moistened with a little brown butter (*beurre noisette*) and, perhaps, with some grated cheese sprinkled on top. They really come into their own, though, when accompanying meat dishes with plenty of sauce or gravy and simpler dishes such as ceps, chanterelles or other mushrooms in cream sauce. The name comes from the way the dumpling is cooked: wrapped in a cloth (*serviette*). The elongated shape of the Serviettenknödel ensures that it cooks evenly and makes it easy to cut into slices of equal thickness for serving. There are many variations to the basic dumpling dough, such as adding chopped fresh herbs, or a vegetable *brunoise* or sautéed finely chopped mushrooms, or finely diced smoked ham.

SERVIETTENKNÖDEL WITH HERBS

The quantities given here are sufficient for 8 portions.

8 slightly stale white bread rolls
1 onion, 120 g/4 oz butter
4 tablespoons finely chopped fresh parsley
1 tablespoon finely chopped fresh basil
6 eggs, separated
1 teaspoon salt, a pinch of grated nutmeg
250 ml/9 fl oz cold milk
In addition:
1 damp cloth or napkin, about 80 cm/32 in square
string or twine

Remove the crusts from the rolls and cut them into small cubes. Peel and finely chop the onion and soften in 20 g/scant ¾ oz of butter. Mix in the herbs. Beat the remaining butter with the egg yolks

Making Serviettenknödel:

Put the cubes of bread in a large bowl and pour on the cold milk. Leave to soak until the bread is soft.

Add the onion and herb mixture and the egg yolk and butter mixture and mix well together.

Whisk the egg whites until stiff. Fold into the bread mixture a few spoonfuls at a time.

With a spoon or wet hands, shape the mixture into an elongated sausage shape on the cloth. The dumpling should be of even thickness.

Roll up the dumpling in the cloth – loosely because it expands on cooking. Tie the cloth at both ends with string or twine.

Immerse in boiling salted water and partially cover the pan. Cook for 45 minutes, turning over half-way through.

until pale and creamy and season with salt and nutmeg. Continue as shown in the picture sequence. When cooked, remove the dumpling from the cloth and slice for serving.

SERVIETTENKNÖDEL

This is a particularly light dumpling, perfect as a side-dish with pot roasts and meat stews. The quantities given are sufficient for 4 portions.

Roasts with gravy *are perfect partners for this light bread dumpling.*

250 g/9 oz sliced white bread, crusts removed
50 g/1¾ oz butter, 30 g/1 oz finely chopped onion
160 ml/5½ fl oz cold milk, 2 eggs, 2 egg yolks
salt and freshly ground pepper
freshly grated nutmeg

Cut the bread in small, even-sized cubes and place in a bowl. Melt the butter in a pan and soften the onion. Mix the onion with the bread and pour on the milk. Mix the eggs and egg yolks together and season with salt, pepper and nutmeg. Pour over the bread mixture and mix to a paste. Leave to rest for at least 15 minutes. Shape the paste into an elongated dumpling. Put a large sheet of damp greaseproof paper on a large piece of foil and place the dumpling on top. Fold the paper and foil around the dumpling to make a neat parcel and seal well. The parcel should not be wrapped too tightly, since the dumpling will expand slightly during the cooking process. Immerse the dumpling in a pan of boiling water and simmer for 25–30 minutes.

A neat presentation *is assured if your dumpling is of even thickness.*

With cheese – hearty and delicious

Dumplings enriched with strong-flavoured cheese are very popular

CHEESE DUMPLINGS

Tyrolean Graukäse
has a very strong flavour when mature. If you cannot find Graukäse, you can use Emmental instead.

These tasty dumplings, called Kasnocken, come from the southern Tyrol, where they are made with local cheeses such as Graukäse or Bergkäse. Emmental can also be used. The quantities listed here will make about 16 dumplings.

250 g/9 oz stale white bread rolls
200 ml/7 fl oz lukewarm milk, 1 small onion
250 g/9 oz Bergkäse or Emmental cheese
a small knob of butter, 15 g/½ oz plain flour
2 eggs, 1 egg yolk
2 tablespoons chopped fresh herbs: parsley, chives
salt and freshly ground white pepper
a pinch of freshly grated nutmeg
To serve:
85 g/3 oz butter
85 g/1¾ oz Parmesan cheese, freshly grated

Thinly slice the bread rolls, place in a small bowl, pour the milk over and soak until soft. Peel and finely chop the onion. Cut the cheese into small cubes. Melt the butter in a small pan and sauté the onion until soft and golden. Mix with the bread and milk mixture and add the cheese, flour, eggs and egg yolk. Mix thoroughly. Add the herbs and season with salt, pepper and nutmeg. Moisten your hands with water. Take a tablespoon of the dough and mould into an egg-shaped dumpling. When all the dumplings have been shaped, put them in a pan of boiling salted water, reduce the heat and simmer gently until cooked through (12–15 minutes). Remove carefully with a slotted spoon and drain on paper towels or a cloth. Heat the butter in a pan until it foams and begins to turn brown. Arrange the dumplings on pre-warmed plates, sprinkle with Parmesan and drizzle the melted butter over.

BUCKWHEAT DUMPLINGS WITH CHEESE

These delicious dumplings are hearty enough to be served as a main course, with vegetables. The Tyrolean cheese Graukäse is the traditional one to use, but you can substitute Emmental. If coarsely ground buckwheat flour is not available, then use a food processor to grind the buckwheat yourself.

100 g/3½ oz stale white bread rolls
85 g/3 oz stale rye bread
150 ml/¼ pint lukewarm milk
1 garlic clove, finely chopped
60 g/2 oz finely chopped onion
50 g/1¾ oz leek, cut into strips
20 g/scant ¾ oz butter
2 tablespoons chopped fresh herbs: parsley, chives, lovage or celery leaves
½ teaspoon salt, a pinch of freshly grated nutmeg
freshly ground white pepper, 2 eggs
60 g/2 oz buckwheat flour
180 g/6 oz mature Graukäse or Emmental
To serve:
85–100 g/3–3½ oz butter

Thinly slice the bread, put into a bowl, pour the milk over and soak for at least 15 minutes. Sauté the garlic, onion and leek in the hot butter until translucent; mix with the soaked bread. Add the herbs, seasonings, eggs and flour and mix to a light paste. Leave to rest for 15 minutes. Cut the cheese into small cubes and knead into the paste. Shape into 12 small round dumplings. Put the dumplings in a pan of boiling salted water, reduce the heat immediately and simmer gently until the dumplings are cooked through (about 12 minutes). Remove from the water with a slotted spoon, drain and arrange on plates. Pour plenty of foaming brown butter over, or serve with freshly cooked vegetables.

Buckwheat *has triangular seeds, which are ground to make buckwheat flour. Buckwheat groats are the hulled, crushed kernels and when roasted are called kasha.*

Bread dumplings

Made with ham or fresh mushrooms, these are much too good to be a mere side-dish

BREAD DUMPLINGS WITH FRESH CEPS

A treat for the autumn mushroom season. To make the most of their wonderful flavour, the dumplings must be served straight from the pan. The quantities given below will make about 12 dumplings.

200 g/7 oz stale white bread, crusts removed
4 tablespoons cream
100 ml/3½ fl oz milk
50 g/1¾ oz butter, melted
3 eggs
½ teaspoon salt
freshly ground pepper
freshly grated nutmeg
400 g/14 oz fresh ceps
20 g/scant ¾ oz finely chopped shallots
1 garlic clove, finely chopped
50 g/1¾ oz butter
1 tablespoon chopped fresh parsley
1 teaspoon chopped fresh oregano
40 g/1½ oz flour

Cut the bread into very small cubes and place in a bowl. Pour the cream, milk and melted butter over,

add the eggs and season with salt, pepper and nutmeg. Clean the ceps and cut into small cubes. Continue as shown in the picture sequence.

Preparing dumplings with ceps:

Soften the shallots and garlic in the hot butter. Add the ceps and sauté briefly, then sprinkle the herbs over.

Let the cep mixture cool before adding it to the bread and milk mixture. Add the flour and mix together to make malleable dough.

Divide the dough into 12 pieces and shape each into a round dumpling, moistening your hands to prevent sticking.

Put the dumplings in boiling salted water, reduce the heat and cook until they float to the surface (about 12 minutes).

Foaming melted butter *is the best sauce, together with freshly grated Parmesan. With a crisp green salad, dumplings with ceps make a splendid first course as well as a main dish.*

The quality of the ham *is particularly important for this recipe. Westphalian or Bavarian smoked ham would be ideal.*

DUMPLINGS WITH HAM

Serve these with salad or with a vegetable such as asparagus for a light meal.

240 g/8½ oz stale white bread, crusts removed
160 ml/5½ fl oz lukewarm milk
½ teaspoon salt
freshly ground white pepper
freshly grated nutmeg
2 eggs
3 egg yolks
120 g/4 oz butter
30 g/1 oz finely chopped onion
100 g/3½ oz mushrooms, diced
400 g/14 oz lean cooked ham, diced
30 g/1 oz plain flour

Cut the white bread into small, even-sized cubes, put into a bowl and pour the milk over. Season with salt, pepper and nutmeg. Mix the eggs and egg yolks together, pour over the bread and leave to soak. Melt half of the butter in a suitably sized pan and soften the onion, making sure it does not brown. Add the mushrooms and sauté briefly; leave to cool. Add the mushroom mixture, ham and flour to the bread mixture and mix to a soft paste. Moisten your hands with water. Divide the paste into small pieces, about 60 g/2 oz each, and shape each piece into a round dumpling. Place in a pan of boiling salted water, reduce the heat immediately and simmer the dumplings until cooked through (about 12 minutes). Remove the dumplings with a slotted spoon and arrange on plates. Melt the remaining butter and drizzle over the dumplings.

A delicious variation can be made by adding some extra mushrooms. Clean 200 g/7 oz of any flavourful mushrooms and finely chop. Melt 20 g/scant ¾ oz of butter in a pan and soften 1 tablespoon finely chopped shallots. Add the mushrooms and sauté for a few minutes. Season with salt and pepper. After forming the dumplings, open them slightly and stuff the sautéed mushrooms into the centre. Reshape the dumplings and cook as directed above.

Subject index

Recipes and culinary techniques